Nongovernmental Organizations in International Society
Struggles over Recognition

Volker Heins

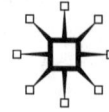

NONGOVERNMENTAL ORGANIZATIONS IN INTERNATIONAL SOCIETY
Copyright © Volker Heins, 2008.
All rights reserved. No part of this book may be used or reproduced in any manner whatsoever without written permission except in the case of brief quotations embodied in critical articles or reviews.

First published in 2008 by
PALGRAVE MACMILLAN™
175 Fifth Avenue, New York, N.Y. 10010 and
Houndmills, Basingstoke, Hampshire, England RG21 6XS.
Companies and representatives throughout the world.

PALGRAVE MACMILLAN is the global academic imprint of the Palgrave Macmillan division of St. Martin's Press, LLC and of Palgrave Macmillan Ltd. Macmillan® is a registered trademark in the United States, United Kingdom and other countries. Palgrave is a registered trademark in the European Union and other countries.

ISBN-13: 978-0-230-60036-2
ISBN-10: 0-230-60036-0

Library of Congress Cataloging-in-Publication Data

Heins, Volker, 1957–
  Nongovernmental organizations in international society : struggles over recognition / Volker Heins.
    p. cm.
  Includes bibliographical references and index.
  ISBN 0-230-60036-0
  1. Non-governmental organizations. I. Title

JZ4841.H437 2008
361.7'7—dc22   2007039393

A catalogue record of the book is available from the British Library.

Design by Scribe Inc.

First edition: April 2008

10 9 8 7 6 5 4 3 2 1

Printed in the United States of America.

Contents

List of Tables		v
Acknowledgments		vii
List of Abbreviations		ix
1	Introduction: Nailing Down a Moving Target	1
2	What Is Distinctive about NGOs?	15
3	Why Did NGOs Emerge and Prosper?	43
4	What Are NGOs Actually Doing?	65
5	Where Do NGOs Seek Involvement?	113
6	How Do NGOs Succeed (or Fail)?	139
7	Conclusion: Paradoxes of Organized Goodness	159
Notes		167
Selected Bibliography		195
Index		205

Tables

2.1	The ideal type of an NGO	26
2.2	Types of harm and their moral fallout	30
2.3	Theories about NGOs	37
3.1	Conditions for the rise of NGOs	62
4.1	NGOs and their moral geographies	87
4.2	Cases of cosmopolitan harm prevention: The NGO perspective	102
5.1	Generating issues for NGOs: A menu	117
5.2	Types of victims and ways of relating to perpetrators	129

Acknowledgments

The chapters of this book came out of many discussions and seminars as well as earlier texts written in German across the last years. For inspiration, encouragement, and critical comments, I thank Michael Barnett, Elizabeth Bloodgood, David Chandler, Ariel Colonomos, Biswajit Dhar, Michael Flitner, Nobuki Fujimoto, Michael Goldman, Mark Hill, Andreas Langenohl, Claus Leggewie, Sarah Kenyon Lischer, Catherine Lu, Rachel Schurman and Susan Sell. Ingrid Tamm carefully read the entire manuscript and offered many valuable suggestions on ways to improve both the structure and the substance of the book.

I am particularly grateful to Axel Honneth and my home institution, the Institute of Social Research in Frankfurt, which over many years has offered me a profoundly inspiring environment. Thanks also to Michael Ignatieff and the Carr Center for Human Rights Policy at Harvard University, where I was a fellow in the 2003/04 academic year, and to my colleagues at the Centre for Human Rights and Legal Pluralism at McGill University, especially to René Provost, Colleen Sheppard, and Nandini Ramanujam. I am indebted to the Volkswagen Foundation, which has generously supported much of my research. Finally, I wish to thank Toby Wahl and Emily Hue at Palgrave Macmillan for their guidance and thoroughness.

Abbreviations

ACF	*Action Contre la Faim* (Action Against Hunger)
CAN	Climate Action Network
CASI	Campaign Against Sanctions on Iraq
CBD	Convention on Biological Diversity
CGLQ	*Coalition gaie et lesbienne du Québec* (Gay and Lesbian Coalition of Quebec)
CRS	Catholic Relief Services
CSE	Centre for Science and Environment
ECOSOC	United Nations Economic and Social Council
EED	Protestant Church Development Service, Germany
EPIC	Electronic Privacy Information Center
ETC	Action Group on Erosion, Technology and Concentration
FAO	Food and Agriculture Organization
FoE	Friends of the Earth
G77	Group of 77; intergovernmental organization of seventy-seven developing countries (without China)
G8	Group of 8; international forum for the governments of Canada, France, Germany, Italy, Japan, Russia, the UK, and the United States
GEF	Global Environment Facility
GMOs	genetically modified organisms
HPI	Happy Planet Index
HRW	Human Rights Watch

IBP	International Biological Program
ICBL	International Campaign to Ban Landmines
ICC	International Criminal Court
ICRC	International Committee of the Red Cross
IMF	International Monetary Fund
IPRs	intellectual property rights
IRRI	International Rice Research Institute
ISAF	International Security Assistance Force
IUCN	The World Conservation Union
LRA	Lord's Resistance Army, Uganda
MDM	*Médecins du Monde* (Doctors of the World)
MSF	*Médecins Sans Frontières* (Doctors Without Borders)
NATO	North Atlantic Treaty Organization
OECD	Organization for Economic Cooperation and Development
PAN	Pesticide Action Network
PETA	People for Ethical Treatment of Animals
PHR	Physicians for Human Rights
QUANGO	quasi-autonomous nongovernmental organization
RAFI	Rural Advancement Foundation International
RAN	Rainforest Action Network
RFSTE	Research Foundation for Science, Technology and Ecology
TAC	Treatment Action Campaign
TRIPS	trade-related aspects of intellectual property rights
TWN	Third World Network
UIA	Union of International Associations
UNCED	United Nations Conference on Environment and Development
UNCHE	United Nations Conference on the Human Environment
UNDP	United Nations Development Program
UNEP	United Nations Environment Program

UNESCO	United Nations Educational, Scientific and Cultural Organization
UNFCCC	United Nations Framework Convention on Climate Change
UNICEF	United Nations Children's Fund
UNPAN	United Nations Online Network in Public Administration and Finance
UNSD	United Nations Statistics Division
USAID	U.S. Agency for International Development
WCED	World Commission on Environment and Development
WFM	World Federalist Movement
WHO	World Health Organization
WRI	World Resources Institute
WTO	World Trade Organization
WWF	World Wide Fund for Nature

CHAPTER 1

INTRODUCTION
NAILING DOWN A MOVING TARGET

This book provides a critical introduction to the study of international nongovernmental organizations (NGOs). "Critical" means that while I am convinced that many NGOs are forces for good in international society, I also believe it is important not to take their self-images at face value and to remain skeptical about their claims of being morally superior to governments, corporations, and ordinary citizens. The second meaning of "critical" is that there are limitations to the power of NGOs that are often ignored by social scientists sympathetic to the moral causes advanced by these groups. With this in mind, I make three arguments.

First, I argue that it is wrong to interpret the prominence and impact of globally active NGOs as symptoms of the much-touted "end of sovereignty" or the rise of a post-Westphalian world order. NGOs are forces within international society that, far from undermining sovereign statehood, often contribute to its resilience.

Second, to the extent that NGOs are symptomatic for a fundamental change, they signal the shift away from a politics based on national and class interests to a politics based on moral values and emotions. NGOs epitomize the rise of an "other-regarding" ethic that is increasingly taking hold in Western societies, often cutting across the divide between governmental and nongovernmental forces. The Western world has institutionalized solid patterns of self-criticism, and NGOs are a prominent facet of this pattern. I will show that the critical social theory of "recognition" provides an important tool for analyzing, comparing, and contrasting NGOs.

Third, NGOs are independent political and moral actors, but they are not independent in the sense that they flourish in a distinct sphere beyond the reach of mundane forces such as governments, international organizations, donor agencies, and corporations. Quite the reverse, NGOs are social analogues to "benign parasites" that seek to "infect" and thereby change the behavior of their hosts without harming them. They are independent in that they choose their own programs and targets; but they need other, more powerful agents to support, take up, and implement these programs.

Empirically speaking, NGOs have proliferated in number, grown in visibility, and gained in standing in many domestic and international arenas over the course of the last decades. They have staged public protests, lobbied for international treaties, monitored the behavior of states and firms, and participated in the "global governance" of an increasing number of policy areas. In some cases, they have directly aided official national delegations in drafting policy positions on issues from climate change to whaling to nonproliferation. Often in conjunction with international organizations, NGOs are redefining and defending the rights of refugees, children, indigenous peoples, small farmers, migrant workers, consumers, minorities, journalists, homosexuals, women, prisoners, future generations, and endangered animals. Politicians and business leaders are careful not to antagonize the new actors who enjoy high levels of public trust. Consultancies specialize in the detection of emerging reputational threats to specific business activities, financial institutions, and investment sectors. At the same time, many international NGOs active in areas such as the environment, human rights, or global poverty are emulating the entrepreneurial spirit of multinational corporations. They carefully manage their public image. Their professional structures are increasingly businesslike. In the offices of some of the bigger NGOs, visitors can see large world maps, like in corporate boardrooms, with little colored flags indicating hotspots of activity. Yet it is not easy to tell what NGOs do or what they are.

People working for these organizations do many different things that do not seem to have an obvious common denominator. NGOs participate in public and private regulatory bodies that oversee food, labor, or environmental standards. Physicians for Human Rights (PHR) searches mass graves from the Balkans to Sri Lanka to collect evidence of war crimes. Greenpeace alerts developing-country governments to the dangers of unlabeled genetically modified seeds sneaking into the food chain. The French group Action Against Hunger/*Action Contre la Faim* (ACF) runs nutritional surveillance programs in southern Sudan and elsewhere. Doctors Without Borders/*Médecins Sans Frontières* (MSF) and the South African Treatment Action Campaign (TAC) have helped to bring down prices for antiretroviral AIDS drugs. Women's rights groups submit third-party *amicus curiae* briefs to international criminal tribunals that provide facts on crimes and often have a direct influence on the jurisprudence of these tribunals. Animal rights groups such as the Best Friends Network put pressure on the mayors of Bucharest and other East European cities to stop the killing of stray dogs. The Canadian-founded antiwhaling organization Sea Shepherd has even engaged in direct-action tactics by chasing and ramming Japanese whaling vessels in the southern Pacific. Through the effective *mise en scène* of all these activities, NGOs have become constant and familiar fixtures of the political landscape. Media clichés that depict NGOs as present-day incarnations of small David fighting the warrior champion Goliath have further enhanced the reputation of these organizations. NGOs are everywhere, and it is nice to be associated with them. Some people even wish to metamorphose into an NGO, like former President Bill Clinton who said one day, "Shortly after I left Office, I was shaving and I looked in the mirror and I thought, my God, *I have become an NGO*."[1]

Against this backdrop, this book looks behind the hype that was created around these new actors. Particularly in the 1990s, many serious observers indulged in describing the world in sometimes openly millenarian terms. State sovereignty was declared dead, democracy had vanquished its enemies for good, and the world had become "borderless."[2] Depending on the perspective, NGOs and the social movements surrounding them were likened to swarming locusts descending on the summit meetings of the powerful,[3] standard-bearers of a "transnational associational revolution,"[4] emerging "new global potentates,"[5] or—in the words of former Canadian foreign minister Lloyd Axworthy—the "world's new superpower."[6] It is time, I believe, to pour some cold water on these wild hopes (or apocalyptic fears) and come to more sober conclusions about the real significance of NGOs in the current international order. Along with other nonstate actors such as multinational corporations and criminal networks, NGOs are playing a continuing, possibly even growing, role as intermediaries between states, international organizations, firms, and highly heterogeneous publics. But they are neither going to replace the nation-state nor threaten in any way the international order based on sovereign statehood.

To gain a detached, systematic understanding of what NGOs are, this book dispels the sense of familiarity and obviousness surrounding these organizations by conceptualizing them in a rigorous way. Max Weber already noted that "what is 'taken for granted,' because it is intuitively obvious, tends to be 'thought' about least."[7] Of course, the literature on NGOs has produced a wealth of insights about the roles and the significance of these new actors in establishing or challenging new modes of governing. However, scholars have not given systematic attention to what NGOs *are* and to explain what NGOs *do* in light of what they are.

My analysis is grounded in the fact that NGOs are *post-traditional civil associations*. They represent a distinctive social form that has organizational characteristics and behavioral proclivities different from states, firms, political parties, trade unions, or nonpolitical voluntary associations. What is "post-traditional"? Three aspects are to be noted. First, post-traditionality means that NGOs are not well captured by a classical definition of what is "political." Weber, for example, defined "politics" as "the striving for a share of power, or the attempt to influence the distribution of power, whether this is *between* states or between human groups *within* a state."[8] The second part of Weber's definition underscores the relevance of nonstate forces in politics. But NGOs are nonstate forces that are *not* confined to the imaginary space of an enclosing state. Human groups can seek alliances with sympathetic groups *outside* their own state in order to influence the behavior of both states and other human groups. This is the first meaning of being post-traditional.

Furthermore, it would be inaccurate to say that post-traditional associations are in fact striving for a share of power; although we can say that they strive to *influence* the distribution of power. Unlike political parties, NGOs do not desire to occupy political offices or run countries. They are close to states and international organizations without being either a part of them or their living antithesis. Avoiding such binaries, we can say that post-traditional associations are nesting in the interstices of power in order to modify the way in which power is *exercised*. This is the second meaning of the term.

A third meaning of post-traditionality is that international NGOs tend to be universalistic and other-regarding in orientation. They do not want to further the cause of their members, nor that of any particular nation or social class; and they break with older beliefs that for a particular class or nation, self-interested action coincides with the needs of humanity as a whole.[9] Post-traditionality here does not mean that we are dealing with a very recent phenomenon. The current organizational form of NGOs may have been unknown until a few decades ago, but the ideal of universal and impartial benevolence and the confidence that we can live up to this ideal have been essential to the moral culture of modernity since its beginning.[10]

Two Dominant Accounts

Post-traditional civil associations change the parameters of solidarity and the methodology of political action. In doing so, they escape the alternative between narrowly state-centered or society-centered theories that have been most prominent in the literature to explain the rise and the behavior of NGOs in world politics. The first theory (or family of theories) is built around the concept of "global civil society" and depicts NGOs as harbingers or vanguards of a postnational public sphere. NGOs are seen as the rosy side of globalization. The assumption is that global modernization processes produce harmful, but unintended consequences that boomerang on the societies driving those processes to the effect that citizens around the world combine their strengths to grapple with those consequences. As modernization is rebounding on itself, NGOs sensitize societies to the task of actively coping with the social and environmental "externalities" of successful modernization such as global warming, poverty, and civil strife.[11]

Pointing to the steep rise of the number of transnational associations, theorists of global civil society treat their object both as an evolving historical reality and as political project based on the global projection of the normative values associated with the old liberal idea of civil society. Accordingly, NGOs are one group of actors among others within global civil society that is seen as restoring liberal and social democratic values against the rule of increasingly anonymous and unaccountable forms of global governance. Political scientist Mary Kaldor describes the new situation as follows:

> This is what has changed. . . . Whether we are talking about isolated dissidents in repressive regimes, landless labourers in Central America or Asia, global campaigns against land mines or third world debt, or even religious fundamentalists and fanatic nationalists, what has changed are the opportunities for linking up with other like-minded groups in different parts of the world, and for addressing demands not just to the state but to global institutions and other states. . . . In other words, a new form of politics, which we call civil society, is both an outcome and an agent of global interconnectedness.[12]

Kaldor and other theorists of global civil society are taking seriously the idea that groups of citizens are vying for political influence by cultivating connections among people from *different* states. Ultimately, their account of the new reality is based on a political ontology that gives moral as well as empirical primacy to presumably cosmopolitan nonstate actors over nation-states. My arguments against this view are both theoretical and empirical. First of all, I contend that "global civil society" relies on *overstretching* the meaning of the historical concept of civil society. This meaning has been extended so as to include both actors and circumstances very different from those that allowed the active citizenry in liberal nation-states to flourish; at the same time, these differences are obscured. One of the aims of this book is to show how overstretching the classic liberal notion of civil society miscasts the reality of what is specific about transnational NGOs and their behavior. The problem with using the concept of "global civil society" lies precisely in the unfortunate binary models and metaphors of political opposition that it drags out. It is problematic, for example, to compare the realm in which transnational activists operate to a self-sustaining biosphere threatened by invasive species.[13] Instead of being distinct from and opposed to the political organization of global power, global civil society is in many ways imbricated in the exercise of this power.

Describing the behavior of NGOs along a binary model makes us blind to the remarkable *ironies* of the kind of civic activism promoted by the new organizations. I want to mention three such ironies. First, NGOs *call for more democracy* without being themselves democratically organized. They have been commended for their role in making international organizations more accountable and advancing the "globalization of deliberation."[14] In reality, however, they often depend on and partake in the bureaucratic nature of international organizations. As bureaucracies, these international organizations, including the United Nations, suffer from well-known control deficits that bring them into conflict with basic requirements of liberal democracy.[15]

Second, NGOs want to *constrain big business* and the rule of the market in pursuit of human rights or pro-environmental goals, but at the same time they are mimicking corporate behaviors. Their organizational makeup often bears a strong family resemblance to corporations: NGOs typically do not allow their members to elect their leadership, and they are even less accountable to their members and sympathizers than publicly listed companies, in which at least the shareholders have a say.[16] Like their corporate rivals, they often excel in globalizing their moral appeal, operational reach, and sources of income. NGOs are not only entrepreneurial in the sense that they create and advertise new norms.[17] Raising funds from a variety of sources, assessing and hiring dedicated personnel, and marketing a specific "product" require entrepreneurial skills in quite a literal sense. In brief, NGOs are the political analogues to startup companies (or their more established successors).

Third, NGOs are *run by activist staffers* and volunteers; but the downside of this activism of highly motivated groups is a widespread decrease in political involvement of the majority of citizens in democratic societies who prefer to be spectators rather than participants, in spite of the fact that they are increasingly resourceful and knowledgeable about politics.[18]

NGOs are using this trend and are often perfectly happy with various kinds of "armchair activism," such as donating money online, placing ethical banners on Web sites, or adopting a "cruelty-free" lifestyle.[19]

In view of all these facts, NGOs appear to be truly odd beasts: democracy promoters who eschew popular control, business critics who mimic business structures, and activists who thrive best where politics is seen as a spectator sport. I contend throughout this book that for the analysis of this seemingly paradoxical mix of characteristics, we need a language that goes beyond the classical vocabulary of civil society.

A second dominant account that is often used to make sense of the NGO phenomenon is organized around the fashionable concept of "Empire." Like their liberal "global civil society" rivals, theorists of Empire believe that the period of sovereign nation-states is over and that we live in an age of global problems, unsettled subjectivities, mobile citizens and noncitizens, and that the social sciences have been unable to come to grips with the new reality. Yet, while global civil society accounts see NGOs as independent forces for good, anti-Empire writers profess much less favorable views. Michael Hardt and Antonio Negri, in particular, have heaped scorn on the new voluntary associations, which they see as agents of "moral intervention" in the service of an emerging new global power structure:

> We are referring here principally to the global, regional, and local organizations that are dedicated to relief work and the protection of human rights, such as Amnesty International, Oxfam, and Médecins sans Frontières. Such humanitarian NGOs are in effect (even if this runs counter to the intentions of the participants) some of the most powerful pacific weapons of the new world order—the charitable campaigns and the mendicant orders of Empire.... Within this logical framework it is not strange but rather all too natural that in their attempts to respond to privation, these NGOs are led to denounce publicly the sinners (or rather the Enemy in properly inquisitional terms); nor is it strange that they leave to the "secular wing" the task of actually addressing the problems. In this way, moral intervention has become a frontline force of imperial intervention.[20]

For all its air of radicalism, the authors offer a thesis that is, in fact, shared by many conservative or mainstream commentators. Harvard historian Niall Ferguson, for example, has outlined the contours of an emerging American empire that rules "mainly through firms and NGOs."[21] Following 9/11 and the invasion of Afghanistan, former U.S. Secretary of State Colin Powell praised humanitarian nongovernmental organizations for their role as a "force multiplier" for the U.S. government.[22] Hardt and

Negri would reject the positive value judgments implicit in these comments, but they claim—without any empirical evidence—that NGOs are indeed instruments of some kind of imperial foreign policy.[23]

Relief workers and humanitarian activists are said to have their own "intentions," although they are "in effect" unknowingly subservient to the scheme of an ominous new Empire. Falling victim to a common functionalist fallacy, the authors do not identify a mechanism linking the benefits supposedly reaped by the Empire from moral interventions to the emergence and perpetuation of the norms motivating those interventions. Why should a capitalist system of domination, one might ask, inspire people to save the habitats of orangutans or denounce child sex tourism, and how exactly does the system benefit from such activities? The inability to answer such questions is also common among less extravagant Marxist academics who have attempted to make sense of NGOs from a neo-Gramscian perspective. They also criticize the state-centrism of many social inquiries and maintain that the separation between state and society, mandatory and voluntary activities, is not real, but illusory. Here again, NGOs are seen as little more than tailors of the emperor's new clothes.[24]

An Alternative Conceptualization

The paradigmatic assumptions summarized under the headings of "global civil society" and "Empire" are reproduced in much academic and journalistic writing today. The alternative conceptualization I am proposing is based on the combination of two master concepts featured in the title of the book: "international society" and "struggles over recognition."

The notion that states form a distinct international "society" is central to a loose group of mostly (but not exclusively) British writers on international political theory and history who have come to accept the label "English School" for themselves.[25] The most prominent theoretical expression is Hedley Bull's *The Anarchical Society* (first published in 1977), in which the author stresses that states can and do act in line with shared norms instead of fighting to increase their own power by all means and at the expense of everybody else.[26] Writings associated with the English School of international relations offer a toolkit of concepts and methods that capture both the trend toward global institutions and governance *and* the persistence of sovereign statehood and power politics.

English School theorists share the conviction that states are collective persons whose behavior vis-à-vis each other is regulated by shared norms and ideas in a way that resembles the normative regulation of the behavior of natural persons within states. However, English School writers have warned against the application of standards of judgment based on domestic experience to the discussion of world affairs. The use of the "domestic analogy" is mostly misleading, because the international society of states is a society *sui generis* with its own, nondomestic-type rules and institutions.[27] In spite of frictions between the "pluralist" and "solidarist" camps within the English School, there is a broad consensus that state sovereignty is a civilizational achievement worth defending; at the same time, individual persons have been famously characterized as the ultimate units of an emerging world society that is "more fundamental and primordial than international society" and "morally prior to it."[28]

More recently, Andrew Linklater and Hidemi Suganami have compiled a history of international agreements aimed at constraining the power of states to harm their own and other citizens. In this context, they emphasize the importance of human agency in creating and enforcing new norms without jeopardizing the international order.[29] It is here that the English School of international relations exhibits its potential for contributing to the analysis of NGO activism. At the most general level, NGOs participate in the ongoing process of defining the normative context that shapes internationally held understandings of what constitutes appropriate state behavior and where to draw the line between permissible or unavoidable harm, on the one hand, and unjustifiable violations of rights, on the other hand. The international order is formally anarchical in the sense that it is characterized by the absence of any overarching political authority, but at the same time states follow rules that are accepted by other states as well. NGOs try to change these rules in accordance with ideals of justice that are in turn hotly contested among states and citizens. Navigating the tension between defending international principles of legitimacy that constrain the power of states, and principles that entitle both states and citizens to use their power even to the point of interfering in the "internal affairs" of other states, NGOs often behave in ways that defy easy categorization.

NGOs are neither mere instruments of states, nor do they reside in a separate sphere untouched by the interplay of states. In many ways, they have begun to influence key institutions of international society by monitoring the conduct of wars, lobbying for trade rules, insisting on limits to state sovereignty, and reporting human rights violations. Moreover, they are expected and claim to be able to foster a cosmopolitan culture. As Bull notes, "The future of international society is likely to be determined, among other things, by the preservation and extension of a cosmopolitan culture, embracing both common ideas and common values, and rooted in societies in general as well as their elites."[30] Such a cosmopolitan culture would be different from a Western culture inflated to global proportions and would have to "absorb non-Western elements"[31] in order to be truly universal. Again, this is something many NGOs clearly claim to do, and I will try to give some hints as to whether this claim is justified.

Concepts borrowed from the English School—or international society theory—have shaped much of my overall argument about the place of NGOs in world affairs. Yet in order to widen and sharpen my focus, I have also drawn on recent developments in critical social theory associated with the Frankfurt School. The main feature shared by the otherwise completely heterogeneous traditions of the English School and the Frankfurt School is the common break from a functionalist approach, which typically explains social actions by pointing to the beneficial consequences of those actions for some dominant structure or systemic equilibrium. Instead, both theories stress human agency and communicative performance as well as the openness of struggles between groups and states.[32] It is also worth recalling that younger representatives of the English School have themselves attempted to mark out areas of convergence between their own tradition and certain ideas of critical theory.[33] My attempt to amalgamate English School with Frankfurt School concepts is deliberately eclectic but, as I hope to demonstrate, adequate to the task of conceptualizing NGOs in international society. The need to complement international relations theory with elements of a more sociologically oriented critical theory arises as soon as we are no longer only interested in the sources of state conduct or in conflicts over state power. I will show that recent debates over the concept of "recognition" help us to illuminate aspects of NGO behavior that are missed by authors who, for example, reduce NGOs to advocates or conduits for the redistribution of material resources to the global poor.[34]

In critical theory, "mutual recognition" does not refer to the diplomatic practice of granting certain rights and duties to territorial entities bearing the marks of statehood. Rather, the term is used in a very different sense to denote positive responses to the basic rights and needs of individuals and groups as well as sources of conflicts in modern societies that result from not responding adequately to those rights and needs. Accordingly, I will argue that NGOs should be conceived of as actors involved in struggles over recognition against basic forms of abuse that include the willful neglect of needs of others, the denial of human rights, and the denigration of ways of life.[35] What observable NGO activities—protesting, lobbying, advising, collecting information, or filing complaints—have in common is their shared opposition to elementary forms of abuse, disrespect and misrecognition.

Of course, placing the analysis of NGOs in the wider context of a phenomenology of forms of abuse is only a first step that leaves a host of other questions unanswered. First of all, what counts as an abuse is culturally and institutionally *mediated*. Some people are seriously concerned about children in poor countries who are being forced to work or for baby seals chased by fur hunters, while others may acquiesce to such practices for a variety of reasons. Post-traditional associations help to trigger strong public responses to perceived violations of standards of recognition; they also attempt to shape habits of response by telling indifferent people why they *ought* to feel angry or ashamed when confronted with harm done to others. NGOs do not simply publicize undesirable facts in the hope to stir public protests and policy initiatives. More importantly, they display and attempt to generalize normative expectations in the light of which a given state of the world appears deficient or unbearable, thereby calling for heightened attention and action.

This Book

Do NGOs live up to their own ideals? How can we best describe the strategic interaction between NGOs and donor states or international organizations? When do NGOs succeed, and do we have reasons to take the "goodness" of NGOs for granted? Are NGOs contributing to an emerging cosmopolitan culture that eases the tension between different value systems in international society? How has the rise of non-Western states and NGOs changed the picture? These are the questions I will try to answer in the following, loosely organized chapters. Readers will find that I am drawing on examples, findings, and theories from a large variety of sources that also include my own research. The early origins of the book can be traced back to a comparative research project on environmental and anti-globalization NGOs in western Europe, the United States, and India, which I began in 1998.[36] Later I have refined my analysis by combining concepts from sociology and social philosophy ("struggle for recognition") as well as from political science ("international society"). I wish to add that I am biased in favor of many of the values professed by modern NGOs such as freedom and diversity. However, like all human institutions, we should not judge NGOs, or post-traditional associations, by transcendent moral standards or by their good intentions, but by their behavior and the consequences of that behavior which, as we will see, are not automatically beneficial to everybody.

Chapter 2 defines the concept of a nongovernmental organization. NGOs are post-traditional and other-regarding civil associations that act on behalf of distant strangers, including future generations and nonhuman species. I argue that NGOs must be seen as acting vicariously for individuals and groups who are misrecognized in the sense that they do not enjoy the rights they should be granted, the social esteem they deserve, or the love and care they need. Drawing on both English School and recent Frankfurt School sources, NGOs can also be described within the framework of broader movements for the prevention of harm to others and for the civil repair of the consequences of harmful acts and conditions.

Chapter 3 describes some of the normative and empirical controversies on the reasons of the numerical growth and increased legitimacy of NGOs in international society. I discuss both bottom-up explanations, which focus on societal and cultural factors, and top-down explanations, which point to international organizations and changing norms as the main facilitators of the growth of NGOs. Instead of simply taking sides between the proponents of these approaches, I offer an explanation that, in the Weberian spirit, distinguishes between ultimate, intermediate, and proximate preconditions for the rise of NGOs.

Chapter 4 begins by showing how NGOs can be understood in the light of the nineteenth-century antislavery movement, which is in many ways the paradigm of an alternative tradition of nonrevolutionary modern social movements. Abolitionism is relevant because of its distinctly other-regarding ethical outlook, its strong concept of common humanity, and its opposition not only against the denial of rights but also against other forms of withholding recognition of fellow humans. The abolitionists were active both in communicative and in rule-making institutions. All this is true for present-day NGOs as well.

As communicators, NGOs divide the social world into good and evil, without essentializing evil. The traditional opposition between friends and foes is replaced by the post-traditional opposition between victims and perpetrators. I illustrate this shift drawing on examples from environmental activism in the United States, Europe, and India. Next, I discuss NGOs as rule makers. The new organizations are actively involved in the struggle for cosmopolitan harm conventions that protect individuals as such, regardless of their belonging to a state. I examine several cases of treaties and policies to show how NGOs advocate different kinds of harm-preventing rules. I conclude this chapter by arguing that NGOs tend to strengthen states instead of weakening them. Here we are confronted with a seeming paradox: NGOs are struggling to tame the sovereigns in the name of norms of mutual recognition. Yet, in their search to find agents who can remedy bad situations, NGOs often call upon states to assume new obligations, even if these states are not responsible for the creation of the situation.

In chapter 5, I take a close look at the spatial contexts of NGO activities. The question of *where* NGOs become active requires different answers depending on whether we talk about thematic *areas*, geographical *scales*, or physical *places* that can be located on maps and globes. The first of these contexts is spatial only in a metaphorical sense. NGOs have mandates covering certain issue "areas," and sometimes they redefine their mandates to cover more areas. I propose a model that gives us an idea about the limits to what NGOs can take on as a theme. It is interesting to see that while there are only three sources of harm and injustice identified by NGOs—states, war, and industry—there is an ever-growing list both of victims of injustices and methods of victimization.

The next section of chapter 5 is devoted to the reasons and resources mobilized by NGOs to shift geographical scales by going "local" or "global" as they see fit. Here I explore the rhetoric and spatial strategies of NGOs as well as the peculiar moral meaning of global summits for NGOs. The remainder of the chapter is devoted to humanitarian organizations, which, by their very nature, are "local" or "multilocal" agents specialized in particular face-to-face interactions in difficult places.

Chapter 6 introduces a number of distinctions that shed light on the often neglected question of whether NGOs are "successful." I start out by distinguishing simple successes from strategic successes, such as the cosmopolitan harm conventions I introduce in chapter 4. Second, I argue that apart from ultimate impact, there are two lesser forms of success worth considering: NGOs influence both the knowledge and the preferences of the public and of decision makers.

What are the limits of the success of NGOs? I believe that some limits are structural. In order to be successful, NGOs need to shoehorn complex problems into issues organized around identifiable victims and perpetrators, which sometimes proves impossible. The issue of the diffusion of small arms and light weapons is a case in point. Another crucial limit both to the success of NGO campaigns and to the very rise of issues is the *shameability* of targeted perpetrators or their accomplices. NGOs are successful when they can ruin the reputation of politicians or a brand, but they have no chance to succeed in situations in which perpetrators can not be shamed, because there is no overlap between their and their critics' standards of judgment, or simply because the perpetrators are fanatics or criminals.

I wrap up chapter 6 by asking whether success is always *desirable*. At first sight, this question seems pointless since NGOs are forces for good, and everybody wants the good guys to prevail. Yet, as Weber has demonstrated, there are two ways of being good, depending on whether we define moral goodness in terms of good "convictions" or of the "consequences" flowing from actions inspired by those convictions. A closer looks reveals that NGOs have tried hard to escape the dilemmas of modern politics, but to no avail.

In the concluding chapter 7, I draw together the threads by suggesting a number of paradoxes bedeviling post-traditional associations by turning their strengths into weaknesses, or the other way around. NGOs are good researchers, but victims of wishful thinking. They put themselves in the shoes of distant strangers, but their empathy is often laced with misanthropy. They speak on behalf of others without being able to represent them. Their conspicuous goodness sometimes plays into the hands of the most mundane strategic interests. Finally, NGOs mobilize moral feelings, but they also expropriate the moral outrage of the wider public by confining the arena of struggles over recognition to media campaigns, professional lobbying, and the efficient delivery of human services. There is no doubt they are bulwarks against public cynicism and the excesses of governments and corporations. But if they want to realize their better intentions, they will always have to tap into the power of forces bigger than themselves.

CHAPTER 2

WHAT IS DISTINCTIVE ABOUT NGOS?

POST-TRADITIONAL CIVIL ASSOCIATIONS

Before delving deeper into specific aspects of NGOs in international society, it is important to define what is meant by a "nongovernmental organization." First of all, we need to distinguish labels from concepts. The term "NGO" is mostly used as a label, and different observers use this label in different ways. Some tend to classify any well-intentioned civic association as an NGO, while others prefer a more restrictive usage of the term. But most observers avoid any serious definitional labor. Similar to observers, participants in public life also use the label with all kinds of political, polemical, or fundraising purposes in mind. The NGO label testifies to the symbolic power of international organizations to classify social worlds, fix meanings, and create new categories of actors.[1] Most important here are the United Nations (UN) and its Economic and Social Council (ECOSOC). When the UN Charter was drafted in 1945, civic associations attending the San Francisco conference lobbied successfully to obtain Article 71, which provides for "consultative arrangements" with ECOSOC. NGO participation rights in the UN were first codified by ECOSOC Resolution 288 X(B) of February 27, 1950, and after that revised a few times.[2] It is fair to say that in many ways the UN system did not simply discover NGOs, but actively created them as a distinct category of international actors. Prior to the UN, there were no NGOs, but other, less strictly delineated groups such as "international private organizations" or "trans-national associations."[3]

An important part in this creation is played by the process of quasi-diplomatic accreditation, which is granted on a case-by-case basis by a nineteen-member standing committee of ECOSOC called the Committee on

Non-Governmental Organizations. In addition, NGOs other than those with a consultative status granted by the committee have increasingly been invited to participate in international conferences convened by the UN. In these cases, both the determination of eligibility and the final accreditation are in the hands of the member states. Here more than anywhere else we can see the artificial and manufactured character of the NGO status. If we look, for example, at the list of NGOs that were ad hoc accredited to the 2001 World Conference against Racism in Durban, South Africa, we realize that an extremely heterogeneous spectrum of private organizations struggled to be internationally recognized and seen through UN eyes as NGOs. They were eager to obtain a temporary status and a form of legitimacy above and beyond the legitimacy they have at home. Widely differing organizations that otherwise preferred to describe themselves as alliances, foundations, centers, networks, societies, or leagues mutated into NGOs for a few days, often just by filling out and submitting forms available as PDF downloads.[4] NGOs are, as Raymond Bryant observes, constantly preoccupied with enhancing their moral "reputation";[5] but before that they have to struggle to be recognized at all as an NGO.

In short, the term "NGO" betrays its origin as a classificatory device in international organizations that was created by governments to include and raise the status of entities other than governments. Of course, from an analytic point of view, it is unsatisfactory to define NGOs simply by invoking the prefix "non" to hint by antithesis at something otherwise undefinable. The "non" might give comfort to those eager to avoid the taint of "governmental" politics, but it does not tell us anything about what nongovernmental organizations have in common apart from not being part of any government. The term refers to real-world organizations, but also to authoritative statements made about these organizations and acts on the parts of committees granting a (temporary or permanent) status to a specific organization. This messy situation has led many authors to avoid the term altogether and replace it with expressions such as "civil society organizations" or "advocacy networks."[6] But these concepts are misleading as well. The first is rather self-ennobling and idealistic and takes for granted that NGOs are indeed the new face of "civil society," something that in my mind has yet to be demonstrated. The term "advocacy networks," on the other hand, is unhelpful because it glosses over important nonadvocacy functions of NGOs, such as the provision of human services. An exclusive focus on advocacy would leave out the entire sector of humanitarian action, which is defined by the tensions between service and advocacy functions (as I will show in chapter 5). For this reason, and for want of any better alternative, I suggest sticking to the old-fashioned expression "NGOs" and turning it from a strategically used label attached to a wide range of organizations into a proper *ideal type* that sheds light on what is specific about a new organizational form characterizing the present age.

A Working Definition

How do NGOs differ from bureaucracies, firms, social movements, or professional associations? If "nongovernmental organization" is to be grasped as a distinct concept—not merely a sample of exemplars dependent on the classifier's whim—the concept requires sharp boundaries. Such boundaries are provided by defining NGOs as an ideal type. An ideal type of a phenomenon is not the result of a generalization or averaging of a set of facts. An ideal type of "bureaucracy," for example, deliberately accentuates certain aspects of bureaucracies in light of what is considered significant within a society. As such, it may well differ a great deal from average bureaucracies at a given time in a given region. The purpose of the construction of an ideal type is twofold: to serve against unchecked intrusion of subjective values into the research process, and to establish a measuring stick to ascertain similarities as well as deviations in concrete cases. It is important to note that, as mental constructs, ideal types always entail an element of arbitrariness and imaginative surplus.[7]

With this clarification in mind, I propose to define NGOs in a first step as voluntary associations. Voluntary associations are groups "formed through agreement, whose statutes have valid authority only for members who have joined out of personal choice."[8] It is obvious that this definition is too broad to be of immediate use. Trade unions, political parties, golf clubs, and criminal rackets also fall under this rubric. A better term has been suggested by Jeffrey Alexander: civil associations. Voluntary associations have a distinctly civil quality if they are oriented to groups outside of themselves and to the public at large. Civil associations attempt to influence how the public thinks and feels about particular policy issues, many of which have been brought up only by these associations.[9] Yet for our purposes, this definition is still too broad, since we are interested in groups whose outward orientation goes beyond the boundaries of their own country and its institutions. Therefore, I define NGOs as a *subset* of civil associations that is characterized by three main features.

First, NGOs are not part of conventional struggles for power within a state or between states. The formal independence from governments and political parties is accentuated by a certain *aloofness* from politics. To illustrate the meaning of aloofness, I give a few examples. The founders of

Doctors Without Borders (MSF) were considered to be passionate political activists; yet, at the same time, they exhibited an "almost playful"[10] attitude toward conventional politics and did not care about whether they would be seen as left wing or right wing. After 9/11, officials at Amnesty International felt that they could not speak out in favor of democracy because in an age of global terrorism, "democracy" had become a battle cry.[11] The first generation of Greenpeace activists told the public that the fault lines of the Cold War were simply irrelevant in light of "bigger" problems; and they confidently advertised their own new form of politics as "unpolitics."[12] Similarly, human rights groups across the world have been described as pursuing a "politics of being non-political."[13]

Remaining aloof from conventional politics has also meant an almost exclusive focus on a small set of narrowly defined problems and issues and no comments on the rest. Again, MSF offers good examples for this economy of attention. "We have no specific view about air strikes,"[14] declared the president of MSF-France during the NATO intervention in Kosovo in 1999. Next, aloofness from politics means to dodge what Michael Walzer has called the "problem of dirty hands."[15] This problem arises in situations in which political leaders have to violate their moral principles for a weightier moral end, for example, by negotiating with terrorists in order to free hostages, or by imposing sanctions on a tyrannical and dangerous regime that will also hurt ordinary people. NGOs ignore the paradox that doing the wrong thing can turn out to be the right thing to do. They can thus appear more morally pure than those forced to compromise principles by the constraints they find themselves in. Finally, aloofness from politics facilitates the accommodation of divergent ideological orientations. Post-traditional civil associations often commend themselves for maintaining and respecting diversity and heterogeneity, either as an end in itself or as a condition for being better able to connect within wider networks of changing partners, themes, and circumstances.[16]

Second, NGOs activities are, to a large extent, driven by the interest in the well-being, not of the associated members, but of nonmembers who sometimes might not even be aware of the existence of the association. NGOs not only display a strong orientation to issues and groups outside of themselves; they act vicariously for distant and disadvantaged others, by lobbying on their behalf, by introducing their perspectives in various fora, and by eliciting sympathy for their plight. In Britain, for instance, both NGOs and the government are fiercely committed to combat global warming, because others are likely to suffer from its consequences, whereas Britain might actually *gain* from warmer temperatures (which will bring higher crops yields, etc.).[17]

For this to be possible at all, the civil society from which NGOs emerge must have undergone important cultural changes. The "others" toward which the work of NGOs is directed must have been transformed from outsiders to be feared and kept at bay into people in need of being rescued, liberated, empowered, and respected.[18] In contemporary society, this shift applies not only to distant strangers, but also to iconic animals such as whales and dolphins, which, for many, have moved from natural resources to be killed and exploited to partners in interspecies relationships. NGOs must be defined in terms of moral purposes—unlike the state, which can only be defined in terms of the means employed to reach whatever its purposes are at a given moment.[19]

Third, NGOs activities are not confined to a given territory. International NGOs are by definition *nonterritorial* political actors who choose their sites of engagement, who seek out sources of information and income on a transnational scale, and who make contact with people regardless of their national background. In organizational terms, nonterritoriality either means that NGOs seek to establish federations composed of various national branches united under one umbrella organization, or it means the establishment of centralized organizations that create national affiliates in the image of the "mother organization."

These aspects—aloofness from conventional politics, the prevalence of other-regarding orientations, and nonterritoriality—can be merged into a single working definition: *NGOs are voluntary associations that neither struggle for a share of governmental power nor have a mandate from the government or the state for their existence and activities. They stand up and speak out not for themselves, but for others who are symbolically represented as innocent, oppressed, deprived, neglected, underrepresented, dispossessed, disdained, excluded, disenfranchised, and forgotten. The activity on behalf of others is closely intertwined with systematically cultivating alliances across international borders and is, at least to a large extent, inspired by universalistic ideals.*

This definition delineates an ideal type that is not directly extracted from reality but is rather superimposed on observable facts to better understand what is historically distinctive about this organizational form and where to draw the line between this form and others. By including "universalistic ideals," the definition contains a minimal normative component that does not flow from my personal preferences but corresponds to values that define, at least to a large extent, the shared self-understanding around which contemporary modern culture itself is organized. Without such a minimal normative component, certain Islamic voluntary relief agencies that establish a "hierarchy of victims"[20] by excluding non-Muslims from the benefits of their humanitarian work would be in the same category as egalitarian groups. A term such as "anti-human rights NGOs"[21] would not sound oxymoronic. However, I am convinced that we would do a poor job as political scientists by treating things that are utterly different as if they were alike.[22]

A key advantage of my definition is that it does not only focus on the difference between governments and nongovernmental forces, but also on differences within the extended family of nonstate actors. Noteworthy are, in particular, the striking dissimilarities between political parties and NGOs. Political parties are also associations based on voluntary membership, but unlike NGOs, they were created to gain a share of power in modern states. Weber established a connection between the interest of political parties in gaining governmental power and their territorial mode of operation. They "can exist only *within* a group body (*Verband*), in order to influence its policy or gain control of it."[23] Furthermore, the difference between political parties and post-traditional associations is not that the former are struggling exclusively for material benefits while the latter have moral ideals. In fact, modern parties and their leaders were often committed to ambitious ideals. However, every political party was typically considered a vehicle of attaining material and ideal advantages "for its members"[24] and their social milieus. In sharp contrast, the definition given above insists on the prevalence of *other*-regarding interests as a hallmark of contemporary NGOs. To use the language of eighteenth-century political theory, we can say that the aloofness from conventional politics and nonterritoriality of a typical post-traditional civil association define its "particular structure," whereas "the human passions that set it in motion"[25] are about putting the well-being of others on center stage.

STRUCTURE AND PASSION

It is important to understand the distinctiveness of this passion. Most progressive historical movements and their political parties were about the self-emancipation of an oppressed class, nation, gender, or race. The Other was represented as an enemy to be feared and resisted by an imagined Self. It would not have occurred to the theorists of those movements that there is something morally reprehensible in pursuing a self-regarding politics. To be sure, the rhetoric of self-emancipation always appealed to solidarity as a force to overcome individual selfishness. But solidarity was invoked only to further the ulterior cause of strengthening collective selfhood. Similarly, spokespersons of national liberation movements from the American Revolution onwards took it for granted that their struggle was for the attainment of self-government as opposed to the government by others. Intellectuals sympathizing with such movements provided moral and historical arguments against the moralistic plea to overcome or disown one's self in the name of "higher" goods. It is hardly surprising that an essay by Max Horkheimer, in which he justified the historical self-centeredness and collective "egoism" of emancipatory movements, served as a key reference text for the entire Frankfurt School circle in the 1930s.[26]

NGOs and their intellectuals break with this tradition, or maybe I should say, they are thriving on the ruins of that tradition. Should we think of other-regarding orientations as superior to traditional self-regarding interest politics? It seems by no means self-evident that the switch to other-regarding interests is a good thing, if only because in a world of "moral entrepreneurs," it can be advantageous to appear as a victim and to score points in the ongoing media contest for the status of worst victimized. I am not concerned with the general question of whether or to what extent people are or can be honestly other-regarding in their everyday life.[27] The point is rather to explain the motives behind the other-regarding behavior of NGO professionals and their supporters. There are two points to be made here. First, as Joel Feinberg puts it cautiously, people can effectively desire the well-being of others "at least partly as an end in itself,"[28]—a claim that is hardly extravagant, at least not for anybody who has had experiences of personal love or of raising a child. Second, and more importantly, Feinberg convincingly argues that in certain cases, the promotion of a person's own interests and her active promotion of other persons' interests are not only compatible, but mutually implicative. Some other-regarding actions are, in fact, a species *within* the genus of self-interested actions. This is the case when actors have a personal stake in the well-being of others. Apart from lovers, Feinberg cites the example of "public-spirited zealots" who act neither selfishly nor with sublime disregard for their own interests; rather, they feel the plight of others on their very nerve endings, so that their own good *depends* on the success of their efforts to contribute to the good of others.[29]

The general public, on the other hand, is composed of citizens who tend to support NGOs or else a variety of goals aimed at improving and relieving the plight of others in need. Even if citizens genuinely empathize with distant others, they rarely define their own well-being in terms of the well-being of others. Instead, their desire to help is often shallow, episodic, and subject to media-attention cycles and the "selling" of humanitarian crises by NGOs. Since most NGOs are staff driven and lack large membership bases, the distance between the passionate staff at the top of the organizations and the public supporting their policies is much greater than that between traditional political parties and the public, where ordinary members have more opportunities to develop a sense of being actively involved.[30] NGOs maintain a wall between passionate professionals on the one side, and episodic donors and volunteers on the other side, in order to safeguard both their specific prestige and their professionalism. Using Weber's definitions, this allows us to establish a distant family resemblance between post-traditional civil associations and "religious sects," "groups of warriors," or indeed "mendicant orders."[31]

THE SUBJECTS OF NGOS

Largely unhampered by membership pressure, NGO staffers are free to redirect the focus of an organization on a variety of distant and absent nonmembers. The activity on behalf of these "others" is based on a social chain: NGOs are connecting the moral sentiments and beliefs of the *public*, including small and large *donors*, with specific *target groups* who are meant to benefit from the resources generated by those sentiments and beliefs.[32] These supposed beneficiaries are not members of the intervening organization; they typically do not even belong to the same nation, the same social class, and sometimes not even the same biological species. By virtue of institutionally mediated connections, moral impulses extend to different, distant, and unknown others. How can we characterize these unknown others? I propose a tripartite classification.

First, NGOs based in developed countries care for people in need living in *geographically distant* regions. It is in postcolonial countries where fellow humans seem to suffer the most from massive human rights violations, lack of economic opportunities, or the consequences of ill-devised development policies. Sometimes NGOs also focus on the "third world within" their own countries. Japanese human rights activists, for example, advocate the cause of the indigenous Buraku communities who have been treated as outcasts since feudal times. I should add that by "geographical distance" I do not mean any distance that can be measured in miles or kilometers. I am using the term in the psychological sense that strangers in need are constructed as living in places where most donors would never set foot in. Distance is constructed, for example, by using photographs that show rural people living in mud huts or working with simple tools in a field.[33] At the same time, of course, the distant others are represented as being "like us" and morally close.

Second, NGOs often focus on *temporally distant* strangers who will be born as members of future generations, or who have died as victims of forgotten or underreported state crimes. Climate change activism is a good example for organized political efforts on behalf of people whose future suffering in a world ravaged by drought, flooding, and disease is being anticipated today. "Intertemporal equity" is one of the watchwords of these groups. At the end of the spectrum of time-sensitive groups, we can locate organizations that are demanding reparation and redress for the heirs of history's victims, or at least remorse and remembrance.[34] Memory activism is not primarily driven by NGOs, nor is it always other-regarding. However, with the internationalization of truth commissions in war-torn societies, truth seeking about past atrocities has been adopted by major human rights NGOs as a general policy goal.[35] An example of a non-Western NGO fighting cultural amnesia is Memorial in Russia, which has pushed for official truth telling about the victims of Stalinism in the Soviet Union, both Russian and non-Russian. The passion of memory activists consists in forcing a detour through the horrors of the past and to remember and commemorate "everyone"[36] in order to foster a rights-respecting political culture.

A third category of post-traditional civil associations deals with *nonhuman* species and their habitats. Cultural changes and societal shifts that beset the United States and all advanced industrial democracies since the late 1960s and early 1970s have led to a completely altered manner as to how humans in these societies have come to relate to animals and other sentient nonhuman beings. Although the movement against "speciesism" is weaker than movements against racism or sexism, animal activists have had some success in representing animals as unfairly excluded, denigrated, and mistreated creatures. These efforts were traditionally directed toward the endangered megafauna of polar bears, gorillas, elephants, and whales, but have in recent times been expanded to farm animals and pets.

To varying degrees, real-world groups championing causes under these three rubrics meet the criteria laid out in my working definition. Many of them profess a strongly universalistic program in the sense that they seek to identify, prevent, or repair acts of harm or wrong as well as harmful or unjust conditions, regardless of who happens to suffer from these acts and conditions. Thus, human rights groups oppose censorship, torture, and summary executions, regardless of who the victims are. Humanitarian agencies try to rebuild the shattered lives of those affected by war and internal violence, regardless of the victims' social affiliations. Climate change activists want to curb greenhouse gas emissions, even if some regions may somehow benefit from higher temperatures. Animal rights groups do not wish to protect one nonhuman species at the expense of others.

POLITICS OF VICTIMHOOD

My definition entails that NGOs act vicariously on behalf of others, and that these others are "symbolically represented" as victims. An important by-product of the symbolic representation of victims is the self-representation of NGOs as altruistic advocates and rescuers. Victimhood is socially constructed, and so is the public image of those who speak on behalf of victims.

The proposition that others are symbolically represented as victims by NGOs is based on the insight that victimhood—the state of having been wronged and of suffering—is rarely as obvious as in the case of the roadside victim spotted and rescued by the biblical Good Samaritan. Even if we are pretty sure who the victims are in a specific context, we usually have not witnessed massive rights violations ourselves. Investigative NGOs rely on written records, witness accounts, and sometimes physical evidence. Most of the time, it is not the event, but the event's telling that counts. The process of establishing the facts of victimhood plays itself out through language (including pictures), which implies that it is inherently contestable. There are also cases where witnesses agree on the facts but continue to "see" quite different things. Is the killing of seals in Canada a cruel, barbaric ritual or a legitimate, sustainable, and humane practice? Where is the threshold beyond which aggressive interrogation techniques used to obtain intelligence from terrorist suspects slide into torture? These examples illustrate that claims to be a victim or to recognize victimization are a matter of moral and legal controversy. As Judith Shklar notes, "We are often not even sure who the victims are. Are the tormentors who may once have suffered some injustice or deprivation also victims? Are only those whom they torment victims? Are we all victims of our circumstances? Can we all be divided into victims and victimizers at any moment?"[37]

The answer is, of course, that often we cannot. One could even argue that in some cases—the figure of the modern soldier springs to mind—the difference between victim and victimizer collapses completely. Still, in many circumstances, there are clear situational differences between groups that are described by NGOs as differences between victimizers and victims. Like other political forces, NGOs build up symbolic power in order to answer the question, who is the victim? by fixing socially influential meanings and classifications. Sometimes this is done on behalf of distant strangers whose voices could otherwise not be heard (prisoners held incommunicado or women in extremely patriarchal societies) or who are inarticulate (animals). Sometimes NGOs amplify the voices of others who claim to be victims.

It is fair, then, to say that NGOs represent others in the literal sense that they *make* them present although they are not in fact present. But this does not imply that they represent others in the *political* sense of the word, that is, in the same way as governments represent their citizens. Political representation would imply that the actions of NGOs could in some way be ascribed to those on whose behalf they are acting.[38] It is often overlooked that NGOs are not only advocating "good" causes, but are also providing a range of services for their target groups as well as public goods to the public in general. NGOs distribute food in refugee camps, help clean up oil spills when tankers run aground, and build biodiversity inventories and pesticide databases open to everybody. But serving is not representing. Like doctors who cure their patients or postmen who deliver mail for others, they do not "represent" those they "serve."[39]

WHAT MAKES NGOS SPECIAL?

At this point, I wish to draw some boundaries between the ideal NGO, real NGOs, and non-NGOs. Table 2.1 lists the defining features of the ideal typical NGO and compares them with non-NGOs as well as with embryonic or mixed forms that to varying degrees resemble genuine NGOs. The second column starts with groups that deviate from the ideal typical qualities of independence and a minimum of political aloofness to an extent that political scientist Raymond Bryant has called them "mutant NGOs"—impostors who pretend to serve altruistic goals, whereas in reality they are harnessing the prestige of the NGO label to benefit themselves and their elite sponsors.[40] Stephen Jackson has discovered "mushroom NGOs" in Africa that spring up over night as soon as they can pull in some foreign money only to disappear the next day.[41] Another species are government-organized NGOs (Gongos), which are initiated by some state governments to secure an advantage in the representation of human rights violations or environmental damage to the outside world.[42]

Quangos are a third category of hybrid NGOs. Unlike mutants and Gongos, they do not pretend to be something they are not and usually enjoy a great deal of respect. The label "Quango" was coined in the early 1980s as a joking acronym for "quasi-autonomous nongovernmental organizations," which are characterized by the fact that they typically receive public funding and fulfill regulatory or other public functions, while being at the same time largely independent from elected politicians. Like NGOs, Quangos have proliferated in the last decades and are now forming a distinct "layer of governance"[43] between the private and the public sector in many democracies. In international society, and for the purposes of our discussion, the most prominent example of a Quango is the International Committee of the Red Cross (ICRC), which is often

Table 2.1 The ideal type of an NGO

Features of the ideal typical NGO	Embryonic or mixed forms	Non-NGOs
Political independence and aloofness	Mutant NGOs Mushroom NGOs Gongos Quangos	Governments Business companies
Transnational linkages	National public-interest associations	National state-centered organizations
Other-regarding advocacy and non-advocacy work	Human service providers	Self-regarding interest groups Social movements

mistaken for an NGO. However, although the ICRC is the prototype of a privately initiated, ostensibly neutral and other-regarding association formed under the Swiss Civil Code, its key activities—to provide protection and assistance to victims of armed conflict and internal violence—are mandated by all states that have ratified the Geneva Conventions. Therefore the ICRC, unlike NGOs, is recognized as having various legal privileges and an international status of its own.

Next, I take "transnational linkages" as a defining feature of international NGOs without drawing a hard and fast line between "international" NGOs and "internationally oriented" NGOs.[44] Both international federations and "internationally oriented" groups are characterized by transnational patterns of funding and activity, which mark their difference vis-à-vis national public-interest organizations. In reality there are, as always, many gray areas, and some national public-interest organizations may well have the potential to develop into full-fledged international NGOs. Furthermore, I believe we must not overlook nonadvocacy activities such as the provision of human services when investigating the NGO phenomenon. Some critics go as far as describing much of today's activism as a branch of the "global service industries."[45] While service is certainly essential, purely operational groups with no advocacy component whatsoever are "embryonic" NGOs at best.[46] The right-hand column of table 2.1 largely states the obvious by listing governments, corporations, and national political organizations such as political parties as "non-NGOs." I also draw a line between NGOs and social movements, although in reality this line can be fuzzy since both movements and NGOs are incarnations of what Sydney Tarrow has called the "new transnational activism."[47] But they also differ in a number of respects. In particular, social movements do not provide a conduit or interface for otherwise politically disaffected citizens to act "at a distance" by donating a share of their money or time.

Struggles over Recognition

The Statistics Division of the United Nations (UNSD) classifies NGOs by primary area of activity. The classifications range from "education and research" and "social services" to "law, advocacy, and politics" and "philanthropic intermediaries and voluntarism promotion," among others.[48] This system is designed to facilitate global data collection by making it easy for respondents to surveys to classify themselves. However, similar to the United Nations category of "NGOs" that does not tell us what NGOs *are*, this system does not tell us much about what they are *doing*. So, what is it that post-traditional organizations are ultimately struggling for or against?

My preliminary answer to this question is that NGOs are struggling for binding rules that are designed to prevent harm by constraining the power of states and firms, as well as for institutions of civil repair and moral regeneration where harm has already been done. Sometimes these goals are pursued indirectly, for example, when human rights or environmental activists seek to dissuade consumers from buying certain products in order to exert pressure on firms and lawmakers.[49] In any case, there is always some notion of harm that is at the center of the activity. Joel Feinberg has distinguished between the broad meaning of "harm" as any setback to interests and the narrower use that reserves "harm" for the experience of being treated unjustly. Harming in this narrow sense is synonymous to *wronging* somebody.[50] Few would claim, however, that in particular circumstances even the infliction of massive harm—for example, against armed hostage takers—is necessarily wrongful. In light of this important distinction, many of today's interpretive struggles waged by NGOs turn out to be about two questions that are often confused. The first question is whether certain acts, rules, or conditions are in any sense *harmful* or not. For example, are genetically modified crops noxious to anybody, are the rules of the World Trade Organization (WTO) preventing or supporting economic development, does foreign aid have detrimental side effects? The second question is whether identifiable acts of harming—killing seals, burning fossil fuels, or sending combat troops—are always and necessarily *wrongful*? Are there legitimate points of view from which such practices can be justified?

Feinberg skips this second question by *equating* harming with wronging. To inflict harm in the narrow sense of wronging somebody is by definition morally indefensible, because it implies the violation of a person's *rights*.[51] Accordingly, NGOs defend rights, in particular human rights, which are invoked where they cannot yet be enjoyed or exercised as mundane constitutional rights of citizens. These rights include the right to life, the right not to be imprisoned without due process, the right not to be harmed in violation of the legal constraints on warfare, the right against torture and enslavement, rights to resources of subsistence, the right to association, freedom of expression, and freedom from discrimination on grounds of religious belief, race, gender, or sexual preferences.

Preventing harm by defending the rights of strangers is certainly on the minds of many of today's transnational activists, but that is not all the activists do. One of the key advantages of the critical theory of recognition is, as we will see, that it distinguishes between "law-based" and "law-transcending" forms of recognition.[52] This distinction becomes clear when we look at NGOs who attempt to assist poor, overlooked, and dispossessed groups by catering to their *needs*, which in turn may not necessarily be backed by rights. For example, there is no such thing as a right to have parents, yet child sponsorship programs run by international NGOs claim to cater to the needs of orphans by channeling not only money, but also "love" across borders—the love of distant surrogate parents. Thus, apart from invoking the rights of others, NGOs are also drawing attention to the absence of care and the neglect of needs that affect the lives of many people.

Furthermore, we are witnessing struggles over what counts as a valuable contribution to the well-being and reproduction of society. From the perspective of environmental groups, for instance, simply *not* driving a gas-guzzling sports utility vehicle or not using unrecycled paper can be a valuable contribution to the "survival of the planet" and hence an activity to be socially appreciated and rewarded. Other examples concern the reevaluation of the unacknowledged contributions of marginalized groups to the welfare of everybody—struggles that, again, can not be reduced to struggles for rights. Think of third world groups who have publicly emphasized the role of small farmers all over the world in maintaining and developing crop species or medicinal plants that are the "raw material" for more visible and rewarding activities like scientific plant breeding or drug discovery. Attention to underappreciated kinds of labor and qualification has given rise to transnational struggles for compensation and acknowledgment, for example, in the context of the 1992 United Nations Convention on Biological Diversity.[53]

In order to describe the moral fallout of those harmful acts and conditions against which NGOs are struggling, it is useful to draw on the work of Axel Honneth who has introduced a tripartite scheme of forms of recognition and misrecognition. Accordingly, having *rights* is only one, albeit crucial, form of being recognized; two other forms of recognition are *love* (or *care*) and social *esteem* granted for the achievements of individuals and groups in the light of common value orientations. In order to live a good life, individuals need all of these three things: as autonomous subjects, they want rights that give them self-respect; as embodied and needy beings, they require love and care in order to build up elementary forms of self-confidence; and as members of communities, they strive to be esteemed for their contribution to the well-being of the whole. Conversely, doing harm has three faces: the denial of rights, the neglect of physical and spiritual needs, and the denigration of ways of life and kinds of labor.[54]

Insofar as it is synonymous with respect or esteem, the term "recognition" denotes an evaluative behavior that responds to valuable attributes that we can discern in others to the extent that we have been successfully socialized into modern culture. But the term also hints at a cognitive dimension. We can misrecognize a person or situation when we fail to identify particular features correctly. Many groups, in particular those struggling against "forgetting" past atrocities and the circumstances that led to those atrocities, are combining the search for the "truth" with a struggle for the public "acknowledgment" of that truth—that is, the admission that the public has responsibilities, or that it had failed to meet them. In this context, the opposite of acknowledgment is denial.[55]

Honneth's point is that withholding recognition from individuals and groups is not only unjust from the perspective of moral philosophy; such practices also exhibit exceptional causal force in making people rebellious. The theory claims to be critical in the sense of being connected with norms and principles that are already socially valid. These norms and principles make struggles for recognition legitimate and mark their difference from irrational desires for applause, honor, or fame. As a result, struggles for recognition have nothing in common with the constant quarrels described by Hobbes that can be triggered in some men by small gestures such as "a word, a smile, a different opinion, and any other signe of undervalue." [56] Unlike these Hobbesian quarrels, principles of recognition give rise to normative expectations that hold the promise of a better society.

The upshot of this brief digression is that "recognition" is a rich concept that in my view allows us to examine afresh the practices and experiences of contemporary post-traditional associations, in particular their focus on different forms of harm. Campaigns against discrimination on grounds of ethnicity, race, gender, or sexual preference; campaigns against potentially noxious chemicals in foods, clothes, or toys; and campaigns

Table 2.2 Types of harm and their moral fallout

	Simple harm	Structural harm	Accumulative harm
Empirical dimension	Persecution, cruel punishments, unreasonable prohibitions	Severe poverty, underdevelopment	Severe unintended environmental damage
Moral dimension	Denial of rights, loss of self-respect and self-confidence	Neglect of needs, disintegration of solidarity, loss of self-esteem	Neglect of needs, loss of self-confidence

aimed at well-off people in developed countries to become sponsor parents of children in poor countries can all be read as struggles for the application of standards of mutual recognition. Three basic forms of harm can be distinguished, each of which affects those who are suffering from them in specific ways. Table 2.2 gives a rough overview. *Simple* harm is inflicted by easily recognizable acts of denying basic rights to others. *Structural* harm does not consist of a distinct harmful act but describes a condition like poverty and underdevelopment rooted in global inequalities or economic mismanagement. Severe poverty is a state in which the problem is not whether the contribution people make to the well-being of the community goes unacknowledged or not, because they no longer have the means to contribute at all. The third type, *accumulative* harm, has been defined by Feinberg.[57] It consists of actions that are in themselves harmless but can produce harmful consequences beyond a certain threshold. The fumes exhausted from cars constitute a public harm only if a large number of people drive cars. Much environmental damage does not follow the rule "A harms B," because it is the unintended outcome of millions of small actions that individually are neither harmful nor done with malicious intent. Besides, as accumulative harm has a tendency to boomerang back to those responsible for it, A cannot be neatly distinguished from B.

Two Flaws in Recognition Theory

While I consider the critical theory of recognition to be extremely valuable for the analysis of the factors that drive the social conflicts of our time, it is—in its present form—not without shortcomings. Honneth describes the connection between institutional principles of recognition, feelings of being treated without respect and dignity, and social struggles as follows:

What motivates individuals or social groups to call the prevailing social order into question and to engage in practical resistance is the moral conviction that, with respect to their *own* situations or particularities, the recognition principles considered legitimate are incorrectly or inadequately *applied*. It follows from this . . . that a moral experience that can be meaningfully described as one of "disrespect" must be regarded as the motivational basis of *all* social conflicts: subjects and groups see *themselves* as disrespected in certain aspects of their capacities or characteristics.[58]

From the perspective of an analysis of NGO activism, I would point out two flaws in this account. Honneth presupposes the existence of *principles* of recognition that have already assumed robust institutionalized form, and he neglects *other-regarding* modes of political action. The first assumption implies that principles of recognition are treated as if they were ready to be "applied" and as such no longer controversial. Standards of recognition appear to be set in stone. Yet, this is hardly the case as soon as we broaden the scope of social analysis to include global struggles or transnational struggles that reach beyond the parameters of nation-states. From a global perspective, it is implausible to assume that activists always confine themselves to "apply" already valid moral or legal claims. In controversies over issues such as child labor, humanitarian interventions, women's rights, or the place of religion in society, there is rarely an established consensus on what counts as a valid standard of intersubjective recognition. Hence, there is no reason to take a common normative framework for granted. There are rules and conventions in international society, but neither an overarching political authority nor a set of agreed-upon principles of recognition. Global society remains anarchical in more than one way.

This is why the Canadian political philosopher James Tully points out that contemporary struggles, instead of only voicing demands for the adequate application of already institutionalized norms of recognition, often go further by calling these very norms into question. As he puts it, we are dealing with relational and encompassing "struggles 'over' recognition, not simply 'for' recognition."[59] Struggles for changing the scope of norms often affect their content as well. NGOs have to be understood as parts of a broader alliance of forces that attempts to foster global institutional equivalents of domestic principles of recognition in modern liberal-capitalist societies. Domestic principles of recognition are taken as self-evident standards of justice whenever citizens claim their rights, struggle for the adequate rewarding of their work, or seek the love or sympathy of selected others. In international life, we only have weak stand-ins for these principles such as "manifesto rights" and unstable forms of emotional solidarity.[60]

The other shortcoming in Honneth's theory is that it ignores the significance of the *other-regarding* model of political action exemplified by the advocacy work of post-traditional associations. This model carries the implication that it is not just one's *own* experiences that can trigger social conflicts. If it is true that many institutional changes were engendered by sustained collective responses to "feelings of damaged recognition,"[61] we still may ask *whose* feelings are making a difference. A weakness of the theory of recognition in its current stage of development is that it leaves no room for people who act *vicariously* for others without having themselves gone through a history of experiences of disrespect. We know from empirical studies that many professionals who dedicate their lives to working with human rights groups do not recall any formative event that entails their own or their families' suffering.[62] There appears to be no necessary link between experiences of suffering and moral activism. In contemporary society, social conflicts are oftentimes fueled by the concern for others whose struggles are fundamentally different from our own struggles. In some cases, these "others" would not even be able to respond to injustice themselves because they are not born yet, as recent contributions to the debate on climate change and intertemporal equity have illustrated.

In spite of these shortcomings on the part of theorists who have not taken their theories far enough, I believe and will attempt to show that the concept of recognition is extremely useful for understanding transnational activism and NGOs—more useful than concepts derived from the theories of Gramsci, Foucault, or Bourdieu, which have also received their fair share of attention by NGO researchers.[63] Like these theorists, Honneth, too, acknowledges that politics is not exhausted by state actions, implying that social analysis should legitimately concern itself with nonstate actors as well as state actors. The critical theory of recognition opens up a window onto those "nonstate spaces"[64] of public communication in which feelings of injustice and the demands of moral obligations are initially voiced and weighed. Unlike approaches inspired by Foucault or Gramsci, in particular, these nonstate spaces and their inhabitants are not reduced to performing additional governance functions. Nor are they reified as primary engines of moral progress and human betterment, as the global civil society literature pictures them. In fact, there is no underlying logic or rationality that prevents NGOs from failing their supposed beneficiaries or governments and other actors from being morally ahead of their nongovernmental critics.

MISLEADING ANALOGIES

In the remainder of this chapter, I return to the question of why in my mind "global civil society" and "Empire" are poor instruments for understanding what is distinctive about NGOs. First let us look at two interconnected propositions on which the model of global civil society is based. The first proposition holds that the emerging global analogue to historical civil societies is as autonomous, self-regulating, and independent from state institutions as national civil societies have been. Many years ago, Ken Booth coined the metaphor of international society as "an egg-box containing the shells of sovereignty; but alongside it a global community omelette is cooking."[65] John Keane likened global civil society to a "vast, dynamic biosphere" that, like the real biosphere, is vulnerable to and should be protected against "internal and external interference."[66] Mary Kaldor similarly invoked the image of a pristine space of unrestricted deliberation that is "subject to invasion" by alien social forces.[67]

The second proposition suggests that the new global civic sphere is not only *separate* from the world of states, but as a consequence is also *unified* by universally shared moral values like the protection of human rights or the environment. As Martin Shaw has put it, "ideas and values . . . become increasingly commonly held."[68] Most authors within this tradition have also been outspoken about the likely political significance of the emerging global ethic. The commonly held ideas of the new age are believed to prevail over the basics of the state-centered world—the protection of sovereignty and the struggle for power—in the same way as the moral consensus of national civil societies historically constrained the actions of political rulers in democracies.

Regarding the first proposition, there can be no doubt about the impact of a multitude of sometimes obstreperously independent civil society actors in today's liberal democracies—actors that are independent from state agencies in terms of funding sources, agenda setting, and mobilization capacity. NGOs share this independence with a host of other, often "uncivil" actors who are increasingly able to turn their smallness and informality into a weapon against large formal power structures.[69] However, the operational independence of civil associations varies according to the degrees and types of modernization in different world regions. In Western societies, where states have consolidated their autonomy vis-à-vis social groups while being at the same time in touch with them, public interest groups and social movements, too, enjoy a considerable degree of autonomy, not least regarding financial matters. In non-Western regions, NGOs often have to buy their independence from their *own* state by becoming dependent on *other* states that typically funnel public funds through specialized donor agencies or foundations. Robert Rohrschneider and Russell Dalton have observed that the patterns of financial and information flows between environmental NGOs from affluent to less affluent countries follow the same asymmetries that are generally effective in the global system.[70] Even "civil society" itself—ideas and blueprints for civic self-organization—is now being "sold" to presumably less civil societies.[71] These asymmetries lead to a number of pathologies, particularly in those societies where the distinction between social and governmental positions is systematically blurred, to the effect that outsiders (including foreign donors) have a hard time differentiating "genuine" from "mutant" NGOs. In the topsy-turvy world of transnational activism, we can meet state-dependent networks falsely pretending to be independent from the state, but also independent societal organizations seeking to be co-opted by an authoritarian government.[72]

As far as cooperative international action is concerned, NGOs from different backgrounds are wrestling with a level of systematic "organizational insecurity"[73] unknown to voluntary associations in consolidated liberal democracies. Often the expectation nourished by theorists that independent civic organizations cooperate on the basis of shared values and convictions is unrealistic. The dependence on outside funding and on renewable contracts that are performance based and subject to external evaluation procedures leads to enormous institutional pressures. Competition for funds often proves to be working against the noble intentions of many international NGOs. Alexander Cooley and James Ron have observed how in wartime Bosnia in the early 1990s, competition between aid agencies even helped to empower local warlords and military officers seeking to resist international efforts to protect prisoners of war.[74] But even where norms are paramount and external pressures are weak, it is misleading to think of NGO networks as flat and egalitarian. The concept of spontaneously organized civic "networks" underestimates the power exercised by particular "nodes" within those networks to control the flow of information and to make sure that some norms prevail over others.[75] In order to maintain their position within networks, single nodes do not hesitate to call on states for support. For example, in recent years the Japanese branch of the World Wide Fund for Nature (WWF) supported a partial lifting of the international ban on commercial whaling, which prompted the British branch to call on the U.S. government to impose economic sanctions against Japan, following reports of the killing of whales by Japan.[76]

In short, evidence from empirical political science suggests that independence is indeed a quality of many citizen groups in many countries that, however, must not be uncritically turned into a quality of *global* activism. The literature on global civil society tends to even out the historical differences between societies and types of modernity, assigning an ontological status of "independence" to globally connected citizen groups.

As a result, the dynamics of transnational activism, in which different groups play differing roles in multiple arenas, including the state itself, have been obfuscated. In reality, what is depicted as an emerging global civic space is both being traversed by domestic struggles as well as mediated by power relations, some of which are external to NGOs, while others are being felt within NGO networks.

Now let us turn to the second proposition: The global civil society thesis contends that besides the new space of global citizen action, there is also an emerging global ethic animating this space. While this is not completely wrong, the devil is in the detail. There is certainly some convergence of problem definitions and agendas across national and cultural differences. The Climate Action Network (CAN), for example, was founded in 1989 with the purpose of defining a unified position on climate change across national differences, and it largely succeeded in this effort. However, this is not specific for NGOs. Governments, too, often agree on certain policies across national differences. Furthermore, even a showcase example of transnational consensus like CAN reveals internal dividing lines as soon as one takes a closer look. Thus, the founding of CAN was rife with conflicts between European NGOs and their American counterparts, who criticized each other for not being truly global in outlook. A survey of five hundred NGOs commissioned by the Norwegian Ministry of Foreign Affairs has shown that more than 70 percent of mostly small developing-country NGOs who were accredited to United Nations conferences in the 1990s felt sidelined or curtailed in their influence by the major international English-speaking NGOs.[77] From this I conclude that there may indeed be "global" problems; yet, whether they are interpreted and tackled in similar ways across different societies depends on organizations that successfully establish shared "schemes of interpretation"[78] with regard to those problems. It is implausible to take a strong trend toward a convergence among globally active NGOs for granted.

Global civil society theorists tend to view a global ethic as functionally equivalent to the moral consensus in national civil societies in supporting the emerging institutional structures of global governance. Historically, a basic consensus on core values was indeed critical for the viability of civil societies providing the armature of democratic states. Here, it is interesting to recall the example of late nineteenth- and early twentieth-century Germany. This country could in no way be characterized as having a weak or underdeveloped associational life outside the state. Quite to the contrary, civil society was flourishing, without, however, being backed by any consensus about common values worthy of defending.[79] The lack of a moral consensus eased National Socialism's road to power at a time when the citizens in neighboring France were able to curb the extreme right and to stop them from taking over the state. The differences between prefascist Germany and France cannot be explained in terms of different capacities of national civil societies, but are rather due to differing levels of institutionalization of common values and "norms of recognition."

Bearing this historical example in mind, I contend that today's global associational scene is closer to the Germany of the 1920s than to the France of the same time. It has been shown that the emerging global civic space is not populated by like-minded equals "with identical norms and goals as is often implied by the global civil society literature."[80] While aggregated figures on associational life are soaring—as a look at the statistics of the Brussels-based Union of International Associations (UIA) shows—there is also ample evidence about the weakness of institutionalization of common norms and the extent to which divergent associational scenes are digging themselves in, jealously watching their turfs. With regard to the norms and values of liberal democracy, societal modernization, and the limits to state sovereignty, citizen groups from different world regions do not converge on the same worldview, as I will further elaborate in chapters 4 and 5.

Benign Parasitism

The global civil society literature treats NGOs as independent actors that sensitize states and publics to global problems and unintended consequences of globalization that would otherwise go unreported and unchecked. As NGOs and their networks respond to global problems, it is assumed that their agendas tend to converge across national and cultural divides. For critics of Western neoimperialism or "Empire," on the other hand, NGOs are not problem-driven forces for good, but agents of intervention backed by the power of those who define the rules for the capitalist world. Regardless of what activists might think of themselves, they are ultimately implementing imperial designs. Their agendas converge not because of shared understandings about common tasks at hand, but because of powerful donors in the "North" who are funding NGOs in the "South," thereby controlling and streamlining their mandates in accordance with global imperatives (see table 2.3).

English School writers differ from both these accounts by insisting that sovereign statehood is the organizing principle of international society and that this principle shows no signs of being replaced by an alternative way of organizing the public life of humankind. Yet the universal acceptance of sovereignty as an organizing principle does not necessarily imply that governments and nongovernmental actors tend to share similar moral views across economic, political, and civilizational divides. Rather, achieving an intercultural moral consensus on common problems is less likely today, decades after decolonization and the worldwide expansion of international society, than it was at the time when Europe alone formed a society of states—although we may have strong reasons to search much harder than before for such a consensus.[81] Thus, from an international society perspective, it is implausible to believe that objective problems somewhere "out there" can force themselves on the minds of citizen groups all over the world so that their agendas converge; nor is it plausible to assume that the workings of some kind of boundary-busting imperial power can shortcut the process of global consensus building. Although partial convergence is always possible, it is reasonable to accept the plurality of worldviews among both states and nonstate actors as a given.

One question that remains to be answered is what to think about the much-disputed "independence" of NGOs. Are NGOs independent from state power or not? The shortest possible answer to this question is that NGOs are independent in the sense that they do not "have a mandate from the government or the state for their existence and activities," to quote from my working definition above. Yet even without being mandated to perform certain functions, donors, including state agencies, might still be able to turn NGOs into useful tools that make governing easier. At the most fundamental level, NGOs depend on the provision of public goods by governments, from telecommunications to constitutional rights to assembly and free speech. In international organizations, they need the sympathy of friendly governments willing to listen to them,

Table 2.3 Theories about NGOs

	Neo-modernization theories	Neo-Marxist theories	English School theories
Wider context of NGOs	Global Civil Society	Empire	Anarchical Society
NGO relations vis-à-vis states	independent	dependent	'parasitical'
NGO agendas across the world	converging	converging	not converging
Growth dynamics of NGOs	problem-driven	power-driven	organization-driven

to help them get the right to submit statements, or to criticize other governments. This, however, does not imply that NGOs cannot widen their room for maneuver to challenge or embarrass their "own" governments and other powerful actors. Apparently, there are many ways to look at the question of organizational independence, and no easy answer can be given in the abstract.

In order to move forward, I propose to rephrase the question whether NGOs are independent actors or not. The question should be, what do we mean by independence? I believe that at the most general level, it is fair to say that NGOs are independent in the way *parasites* are independent. I hasten to add that I do not use this term in a derogatory sense. "Parasitism" is a useful metaphor that unlocks important insights into the ways in which NGOs relate to states and international organizations. Researchers have already described NGOs as "fragmented sites"[82] and astute "niche players"[83] who evolve in "symbiotic"[84] relationships within larger, themselves always changing networks of power. "Parasitism" makes the meanings of such descriptive terms more precise, although admittedly at the price of inviting new misunderstandings. Being aware of the demagogic connotations of the metaphor and, in general, of the dangers of applying biological images to social phenomena, I suggest to refer to the work of the French philosopher Michael Serres who has, in fact, rehabilitated the figure of the parasite as an indispensable transformative agent in a world of network and complex chains of communication—the profane equivalent to Hermes, god of messengers and travelers, tricksters and orators.[85]

In ancient Greece, a *parasitos* was a temple acolyte who would receive free food in return for religious services such as the sacrifice of corn to the gods (the Greek word literally means "alongside of the corn"). Later on, parasites appeared in Greek and Roman comedies as dinner guests who told jokes and stories in exchange for food. Drawing on these ancient meanings, Serres presents parasites as *active intermediaries in networks* who intercept and transform information in exchange for material, or the other way around. Wherever we have social relations, we find mediators, or intermediaries, trying to transform or disrupt these relations. Applying this to NGOs, my conclusion is that NGOs do not fight the power; rather, they "infect" institutions of power with new messages. International organizations and particularly the United Nations are preferred hosts for NGO strategists, but by no means the only ones. Whoever wields power is screened for his potential to become an ally against the evils of his world—this includes the Washington-based international financial and trade institutions, but also multinational corporations and the armed forces.[86]

Furthermore, as Serres has noted, "parasites" are not a class of actors that can be neatly separated from a corresponding class of "hosts." Being a parasite is a situational property. Parasites may turn into hosts and vice versa, depending on the networks in which they operate. The reason for using the metaphor of parasitism is not to denounce the exploitative behavior of a class of actors as opposed to other, nonexploitative behaviors, but to highlight a distinct mode of survival and growth that is both different from and more common than all-out conflict or predation. NGOs do not seek to *conquer* state power, nor are they *competitors* to the sovereign state, like city-states or city-leagues in the late Middle Ages.[87] A better way to describe them is that they generate influence by being closely attached to other, more powerful actors who are more or less hospitable to them. NGOs are highly niche-sensitive and take the initiative in developing ploys to gain entry to resistant hosts in order to change their behaviors and obtain needed resources such as funds, information, and reputation. As soon as they succeed, legal scholars speak of the expanded "de facto standing" of NGOs within private, governmental, or intergovernmental networks.[88] In many cases, this leads to a situation in which the very distinction between governmental and nongovernmental networks of communication may become opaque.[89]

In nature, the reality of host-parasite interactions often implies the death of the infected host. But we also observe cases where the behavior of hosts is subtly altered and where hosts as well are able to wrestle resources away from their unofficial guests whom they have allowed to slip into their system. Serres, too, distinguishes between "good and bad Hermes,"[90] that is, between open, creative, connective intermediaries and secretive, lethal, disruptive intermediaries. Parasites are not always harmful to their hosts; yet hosts never remain completely unaffected by their parasites.

The parasite metaphor does not dismiss the "ethical" nature of contemporary NGOs, but it supports the observation that NGOs, very much like corporations and other actors, pursue principled beliefs as well as material interests.[91] Yet the more important point of this brief metaphorical exploration is to open our eyes to political and social interactions that cannot be reduced to relationships of dependence versus independence, and in which actors are neither fully autonomous nor simply tools or vehicles of other actors' interests. As benign organizational parasites, NGOs are neither fierce antagonists nor docile allies of the powerful; rather, the metaphor encourages thinking about the possibility of being animated simultaneously by cooperative energies and dissenting forces. In this way, the metaphor draws attention to certain formal characteristics of NGO behavior—characteristics that have been obfuscated by the binary models of "global civil society" and "Empire." NGOs depend on donors, international organizations, and the public, who "feed" and "shelter" them; at the same time, they develop new policy issues and target selected hosts, searching for resources and niches in order not only to implement their own agendas, but also to alter the behavior of those to whom they are attached.

Summary

The aim of this chapter has been to provide a definition of the term "nongovernmental organization" that differs from the strategically motivated classificatory practices of international organizations as well as from self-laudatory characterizations given by NGO spokespersons themselves. First, I have defined NGOs as "post-traditional" and "other-regarding" civil associations, without granting them the privilege of being morally "good" by nature. Second, I have fleshed out my working definition by elaborating on "the others" on whose behalf NGOs are speaking and acting. Drawing on contributions by James Tully and Axel Honneth to a critical theory of recognition, I have argued that NGOs should be seen as acting vicariously for individuals and groups who are perceived (or who perceive themselves) as being denied (1) a minimum of rights-based respect, (2) a measure of esteem for their achievements in furthering the common good, or (3) recognition in the form of "love" or "care." Struggles over recognition are the epochal context that makes post-traditional civil associations meaningful and a distinct feature of our political world.

Seen from a different angle, and using insights from recent English School writings, NGOs can also be described within the framework of broader movements for the prevention of harm to others and for the civil repair of the consequences of harmful acts and conditions. Harming others means treating them unfairly, which in turn is the same as denying them a minimum of recognition in the form of rights, care, and acknowledgment for what they do for others and the community. In this way, I am combining insights and categories from recent Frankfurt School and English School writings.

Against the backdrop of these clarifications, I have taken a second look at "global civil society" and "Empire" as the two master frames for most current writing on NGOs. Global civil society theory rests on basic assumptions: NGOs are increasingly independent from the state system, and their agendas converge across otherwise salient geopolitical divides. My argument has been that both these assumptions are empirically flawed and based on misleading analogies between domestic and international arenas.

Regarding "Empire," I argue that neo-Marxist writers fail to reconcile the appearance of independence of NGOs with the claim that, in the final analysis, they unknowingly serve the needs of an emerging power structure. NGOs do not operate in a distinct sphere outside the power of states. Yet they are still in many ways independent from powerful interests and have occasionally proved that they can thwart these interests; they have changed the course of action of states and firms. Other observations suggest that sometimes they have also been sucked into the orbit of these and other powerful actors. In order to harmonize these divergent truths, I have suggested interpreting NGOs as "benign parasites." This metaphor, which I use in a nonmoralistic sense, takes us beyond instrumentalist and global civil society views, stressing the role NGOs as connectors and transformers of networks and as active interceptors and selective transmitters of information. In light of the parasite metaphor, it appears that global civil society theorists have misread the independence of NGOs, which are not anchored in a universe parallel to and untouched by state power; they also exaggerate the extent to which NGOs become independent forces by virtue of the inherent morality of their norms. Theorists of Empire, on the other hand, underestimate the many ways in which NGOs are exercising discretion in developing new campaign issues, in deciding what messages to pass through which networks, and in selecting partner and host organizations. In subsequent chapters, I will more fully develop the concepts laid out in this chapter.

CHAPTER 3

WHY DID NGOS EMERGE AND PROSPER?

A MORAL SEA CHANGE

There have been many explanations as to why NGOs emerged and began to prosper in international society. Usually, "bottom-up" explanations highlighting sociocultural changes compete with "top-down" accounts focusing on new sources of funding and expanded political access to international organizations. In this chapter, I offer an argument that avoids this alternative by reconstructing a series of conditions for the rise of post-traditional associations. I begin with the most basic and hence often overlooked background conditions, and then move on to discuss some crucial intermediate and proximate conditions that ultimately enabled the distinctive form of modern NGOs.

Effective governmental institutions are a crucial background condition for the rise of nongovernmental organizations. A legal system based on the concept of universal citizenship is logically and historically prior to the rise of active citizen groups. Moreover, only governments of sovereign states can provide what economists refer to as public goods. Public goods are things that, once provided to one group, cannot be denied to other groups (for example, security and personal safety). Under conditions of lawlessness and insecurity, we still observe people forming voluntary associations; but these associations tend to be militias and other tightly knit groups aimed at self-preservation, not morally motivated groups advocating the cause of distant strangers. Next, there must be not only a state, but a *liberal* state. Illiberal states know all kinds of hybrid and mutant NGOs but no legally operating independent organizations. Instead, independent groups go underground. Groups from abroad are banned from entering the country. Nobody would even think of interfering with nuclear tests planned by such a government (unlike Greenpeace against the United States and France).

The social preconditions for the rise of NGOs and their networks involved some level of affordable communication and transportation technologies. Transportation is often underestimated, but crucial. I once interviewed a staffer who aptly described her NGO as a "helicopter organization" for being able to move quickly from one place to another within no time.[1] The widespread willingness to use emerging technologies is also crucial and not always a given. The best technology is worthless in a heavily segmented polity in which collective attitudes bred by a caste order inhibit the circulation of people and ideas. Once the merits of association with strangers and social interflow are appreciated, a minimum of travel infrastructure, long-distance telephone connections, and express mail is needed to build up transnational networks of citizens. In more recent times, the Internet's euphoric boom and advances in teleconferencing have further facilitated transnational organizational efforts.

Other fundamental preconditions were not technical and economic, but moral in nature. No other-regarding activism can emerge in societies in which narrow and fanatical ideologies stifle the growth of warmer human feelings. In his magisterial work on the making of the modern identity, Charles Taylor has, more specifically, reconstructed a fundamental shift from the aristocratic obsession with honor, glory, and fabulous deeds to the "affirmation of ordinary life" brought about by Enlightenment thinkers, Puritan sects, and others.[2] The ethical goal was no longer the detachment from the ordinary life of work, family, and sexuality, but its appreciation and reorganization along ideals accessible to everybody. Corollaries to the affirmation of ordinary life were a distinct concern with the avoidance of unnecessary suffering, the idea that pain is evil, a revaluation of sentiment and happiness, and an "ethic of benevolence."[3] We tend to take the "new model of civility"[4] for granted, which Taylor has traced back to the eighteenth century. Yet it is such a model that must be available in order for a range of forms of moral activism to emerge.

Taylor is aware that it was not the new model of civility that actually shaped the behavior of rulers and ruled in much of the twentieth century. Rather, the impartial ethic of benevolence was muted by a number of other factors that proved to be formidable obstacles to the rise of NGOs. Three ways of dealing with the suffering of others that are not guided by ideals of universal benevolence can be distinguished: wickedness, denial, and secular theodicies. The weakening or removal of these obstacles created a moral climate in which post-traditional civil associations could emerge.

Obstacles to Civility

Writing after World War II, Arthur Koestler pondered how to characterize the average German who supported Hitler. He suggested that one think of him as a *moral chimera* who, like the mythological creature it is named after, was composed of two different species. For him, ordinary Germans were "mimophants" able to combine in one person the "delicate frailness of the mimosa," hypersensitive to any setback to his own interests, with "the thick-skinned robustness of the elephant trampling over the feelings of others. . . . They were capable of shedding genuine tears at the death of their pet canaries; what they did at other times is perhaps better forgotten."[5] Raymond Aron painted a similar grim picture when he recalled groups of citizens in Paris who after 1933 organized events and published manifestos in favor of the persecuted Jews of Germany, only to be told by the "reactionaries and pacifists" among their compatriots that they should "mind their own business."[6] It would be inaccurate to say that these examples are about people who rather look the other way if an injustice does not directly affect them. The two examples are not about moral blinkers but about situations in which large groups *knowingly* accept the manifest suffering of others as long as they benefit from the situation or are at least not harmed themselves.

Such cases of plain wickedness and collective egoism need to be distinguished from more subtle mechanisms of denial that are often unintentional. Where denial is at work, spectators and bystanders sometimes *know* what is happening without being fully *aware* of the moral implications of what they know—to the effect that they do not act in light of their own healthy moral convictions. Some forms of desensitization toward misery and bad news can be unavoidable or even helpful, and we have no obligation to root them out. As Stanley Cohen has pointed out, we better have ways to cope with the sight of "beggars, runaways, homeless people, bag ladies, the slightly deranged, druggies and alcoholics" on our streets or, for that matter, with the knowledge that we are going to die sooner or later. "Spectators" are not necessarily "bystanders" in the pejorative sense of being unresponsive to information that calls for immediate intervention.[7]

A third way of dealing with the misery of others is to superimpose a hidden meaning on the reality of suffering. Traditionally, this is what happened when people had to reconcile the reality of their own misery with their moral orientations and their belief in a benevolent, almighty God. The old term "theodicy" refers to systematic attempts to explain the apparently senseless suffering of ordinary people as having some kind of implicit meaning within the God-given order of things. As they satisfy the search for meaning in life, theodicies are mentally comforting. With a proper theodicy in place, those struck by disasters and diseases are able to make sense of their fate by interpreting it as a punishment for sins or an admonition to repent. Some religious traditions even know the concept of completely unmerited, blameless suffering and go so far as to glorify the suffering of the believers.⁸ Onlookers, too, use theodicies as a sense-making device. For instance, when the Indian state of Bihar was shaken by a powerful earthquake in 1934, Mahatma Gandhi interpreted it as a divine punishment for the sinful refusal to grant the "untouchables" equal status in society.

In modern times, religious modes of "explaining away" the suffering of others were increasingly replaced by "secular theodicies"—or "sociodicies"—that assist modern men in coping with the persistent suffering of distant others who do not yet enjoy the fruits of the modern age.⁹ Only the demise of secular theodicies cleared the path for the rise of new forms of transnational moral activism. I will briefly comment on three secular theodicies, which for some time have occulted the model of civility outlined by Taylor: Marxism, Malthusianism, and modernization theory.

Orthodox Marxists, Malthusians, and modernization theorists acknowledged certain sufferings but also considered them inevitable and meaningful in light of an intelligible cause or purpose. Marxism, in particular, was certainly fueled by moral outrage, but Marx himself, not to mention his numerous followers, was at times remarkably callous about the suffering of others. In what can be seen as a classical exercise in secular theodicy, he famously vindicated the "misery inflicted by the British on Hindostan" in terms of universal progress toward the radiant future of modernity, which has made England "the unconscious tool of history." And in case somebody would still feel bad about this explanation, he added that vis-à-vis history, "our personal feelings" (read: our moral judgments) do not count.¹⁰ The British economist Thomas Malthus took a much more drastic stand when he interpreted famines as necessary checks on excessive population growth that in turn was explained by the unbridled reproduction on the part of a morally feckless underclass. Early liberal modernization theory was hardly better than Marxism and Malthusianism. The historian David Engerman has shown that before World War II, many Western observers studying the early Soviet Union clearly valued the potential fruits of rapid industrialization above its enormous human costs. As a saying went at that time, the USSR was "starving itself great."¹¹

Malthusianism can be seen as a disciplinary narrative that establishes a moral causality between pain and punishment (the sufferers have contributed to their suffering which they therefore deserve). Marxists and liberal modernizers, on the other hand, construct a linkage between current pain and future gain; people have to pay a price if they want to be free eventually. Pain and suffering are seen as a hidden blessing, as just a step on the ladder toward the end-state of modernity to be taken by every social class or nation.

The Demise of Secular Theodices

The ultimate conditions for the emergence of transnational and other-regarding associations include the demise of secular theodicies. As long as a relevant section of the public sincerely believes that innocent people somehow "deserve" to suffer or die because there is a price to be paid for some historical or divine reason, other-regarding activism has no chance. NGOs can flourish only where legitimate belief systems able to lend meaning to massive social suffering have lost their plausibility. I contend that today, in the Western world at least, secular theodicies are dead, and NGOs have emerged against the backdrop of their slow death.[12] Marxism as a political ideology is irrelevant today; modernization as it is professed by the World Bank and other development institutions has been "greened" and softened; and Malthusianism has either been replaced by a much-sanitized version of its misanthropic forerunner, or by heavily funded anti-Malthusian initiatives with titles like *Saving Newborn Lives* (a program funded by the Bill and Melinda Gates Foundation and implemented by Save the Children.)[13] The power of human rights discourses and the growth of morally motivated agencies is not the cause, but the consequence of the evaporation of modern theodicies.

In France, in particular, the spectacular rise of organizations "without borders" since the 1970s can be traced directly to the loosening grip of Marxism and its concomitant secular theodicy on the public mind. Public intellectuals like Bernard Kouchner, the founder of Doctors Without Borders (MSF), rejected traditional ideologies as mental blinkers that made the public blind and indifferent to the world.[14] Similarly, the contestation of what was left of Malthusian accounts of the causes of famines worldwide led to the foundation of new humanitarian agencies such as Action Contre la Faim (ACF), which denounced the various political uses of deliberately "provoked," "denied," or "exposed" famines.[15] In India, the origins of Centre for Science and Environment (CSE), an influential environmental group funded by donors in Sweden, Germany, and the United States, can be traced back to the frustration and anger of young intellectuals over the costs and failures of grandiose schemes of modernization that were seen as glossing over the complexities of the living conditions of people on the ground.[16]

What accounts for the loss of faith in modern theodicies? The short answer is that the project of Western-dominated world mastery based on homogeneous populations and consolidated elites sure of their "universal mission" and "national interest" has come to an end, not the least because the discourses of postcolonialism and, more specifically the memory of the Holocaust, has shaken us into *seeing ourselves through the eyes of others*.[17] A more detailed answer would have to include an important undertow in modern consciousness that was sometimes suppressed without ever being completely muted. Some modern NGOs, in fact, can trace the sources of their primary moral inspiration back to the British and American antislavery crusade in the early nineteenth century, as well as to numerous temperance and civil rights movements that, according to Charles Taylor, "reflect, and have helped to propagate and intensify, the imperatives of universal benevolence and justice."[18] Of course, this does not necessarily imply that the motivational resources needed for actively *inflicting* harm are dwindling. What I do say, however, is that in the eyes of the public, it has become harder to justify and make sense of what appears to be unnecessary and undeserved suffering. In order to cope, spectators can no longer rely on ready-made justifications, but have to resort to largely individual, intrapsychic defense mechanisms. These defense mechanisms, in turn, are directly attacked recurrent "appeals for acknowledgement"[19] of easily avoidable suffering launched by NGOs.

All this sounds like good news. Yet I do not wish to preclude the possibility of a more skeptical appraisal of the demise of secular theodicies. After all, these belief systems were elements of larger forward-looking political projects. What happens to a society that has lost faith in shaping its future in line with a collective project? As the French international relations scholar Zaki Laïdi has convincingly argued, without a compelling and encompassing narrative that lends meaning to political decisions, the projection of power in the international sphere lacks meaning and purpose. This in turn prepares the ground for purely emergency-oriented policies that are no longer embedded in a common vision for the future. Because of the crisis of meaning and lack of perspective, we have become "slaves of emergencies"[20] who focus our energies on stopping the killing of distant others and on ending world poverty or global warming. This might still be the right thing to do, provided that we have the means to do it. Still, Laïdi's reasoning suggests that Western leaders and NGOs are turning a fundamental weakness—the lack of purpose and meaning—into a semblance of virtue. I will take up this point again in chapters 6 and 7 when I discuss some of the inherent limits of the new transnational activism.

Spurring the Growth

The next links in the causal chain are political and cultural. We no longer live in societies organized around an imagined, proud Self, nurtured by uniform education, uniform consumption, and nationalism, pitted against a denigrated Other to be feared and excluded. Instead, the old fear *of* the Other has been overlaid by a widespread fear *for* the Other whose needs have moved to the center of attention.[21] Against the "realist" tradition in international relations theory, political scientist David Chandler has provocatively argued that the times have changed since other-regarding arguments in the foreign policy of Western powers could be dismissed as ideological maneuvers designed to manipulate public opinion. According to him, humanitarian interventions, human rights conditionalities in foreign aid allocation, changes in military ethics, or voluntary attempts to repair the harm caused by predecessor governments point to fundamental shifts in the relation between politics and morality. Morality is no longer a pretext behind which "real" interests can be deciphered—quite the reverse. Governments pretend to pursue a national interest that they can no longer define in a consensual manner:

> Today the key actor in international relations, the nation-state, appears to have lost the capacity or will to pursue its self-interest defined in terms of power. Commentators from a variety of theoretical perspectives argue that the most developed nation-states increasingly see themselves as having moral obligations to international society. The key theoretical framework for understanding the international sphere, that of state interest . . . appears to have lost its explanatory power. Rather than states and national interests shaping the direction of policy it appears that there is a new agenda set by non-state actors.[22]

Even if Chandler may be overstating his case, there can be little doubt that the self-confidence and moral certainty surrounding classical notions of the national interest have disintegrated. Following Chandler, I would count the decline of national interests as one of the great intermediate conditions of the emergence of NGOs as international actors.

What brought about this disintegration of national interests? Part of the answer is that in some policy areas, decision makers simply do not know what kind of action or inaction would be beneficial for their country. Climate change is a case in point. In Britain, global warming might only lead to roses blooming early, but since nobody can rule out harmful or even catastrophic consequences, it is rational to act not only for Britons, but—as former Prime Minister Tony Blair has put it—"for our planet and for the people who live on it."[23]

Digging a little deeper, Chandler points to the Culture Wars of the 1960s as a cause of lasting national disintegration.[24] According to him, those conflicts were largely successful in changing the terms of any future debate about the moral character of the nation in which they took place. Beginning with controversies about which literary texts were being taught in schools and universities, the Culture Wars quickly spread to almost every corner of social and cultural life and propagated an ethos of self-exploration and consciousness raising. In the United States, this trend ultimately undermined the belief of the establishment in America's manifest destiny and, more broadly, the general belief of Western elites in the innate superiority of their specific brand of modernity and development.

Historical studies have shown that the Culture Wars contributed directly to the primordial ooze out of which some of the early post-traditional associations emerged.[25] Beatnik writers such as Jack Kerouac, New Left figures like Herbert Marcuse or Erich Fromm, Gestalt therapists, and the theatrics and attention-getting techniques of the American Yippie movement had a huge influence on the founders of Greenpeace before the organization much later became something like the equivalent of McDonald's in international environmentalism. In challenging the Cold War framework for making sense of the world, early West Coast activists began to denounce the ills of consumerism, "industrial poisoning," the separation of man from nature, and the primacy of the politically defined "citizen" over the life of "man" itself. Older precepts of universal benevolence were radicalized and transformed into what Bob Hunter, one of the founders and presidents of Greenpeace, called an ethic of "brotherly love"[26] that would not only transcend international borders, but also the boundaries between human and nonhumans.

It is interesting to note that the impulse to dismiss politics and "the citizen" in favor of "the human being" stripped of any membership in political communities is a recurrent feature of modern consciousness. Already in the 1950s, Judith Shklar has eloquently described a powerful stream of contemporary thought, which claims that

> there is a very clear conflict between "the man" and "the citizen." All political institutions are only so many means of transforming the former into the latter. All are "intervening abstractions" that prevent us from recognizing each other as individuals. . . . All politics are mere barriers to genuine personal relationships. If there is such a thing as a romantic political theory today, it consists in rejecting all historically possible forms of political life.[27]

I have referred to the West Coast milieu of the founders of Greenpeace, although the founders of Doctors Without Borders in Paris in the late 1960s offer a strikingly similar example of an innovative organizational effort inspired by an essentially romantic political theory. Like their distant American and Canadian cousins, they were describing their project as one "defending the human being outside of the ideologies" and "revaluing the face-to-face relationship with suffering individuals."[28] Faithful to their romantic creed—"All modern governments are pernicious"[29]—busy organizers on both sides of the Atlantic believed in the necessity to carve out new nonstate spaces for world-changing action.

Yet a more cosmopolitan perspective would have to concede that outside of the Western world things were different: while groups in India, for example, began to act on their disillusionment with forced modernization from above by seeking new transnational alliances, they still preferred the traditional "framework of nationalism" to a romantic vision of postnational life.[30]

A related intermediate social precondition for the rise of NGOs is the consolidation of a moral public brought about by sociostructural processes of change as well as by attitudinal changes in substantial portions of the population. To begin with, the spectacular growth of income and leisure time in liberal post–World War II societies has diversified the ways of life open to citizens and has reduced the formative influence of the social background particular to different social classes. This implies, among other things, that "politics" as an activity and subject matter has to compete for involvement and attention with an increasing range of other activities open to individuals, many of them seen as more exciting, pleasant, or significant. As a result, a higher level of resources available to individuals does not necessarily translate into higher levels of active political involvement. In fact, empirical research has found that among segments of the middle classes, high levels of subjective political interest are no longer matched by a desire to seek political involvement.[31] Conversely, low levels of political involvement do no longer always signal "apathy," because people may follow political developments closely without feeling obliged to spend their leisure time on political meetings and campaigns. The rise of this category of politically interested, well-informed, yet uninvolved "spectators" is an important precondition for post-traditional associations, which, unlike political parties or trade unions, can do without an engaged membership. What post-traditional civil associations need, however, is the capacity on the part of the public to process information about gross injustices and an emotional infrastructure that encourages people to feel and to show disgust at acts of senseless oppression or at humanitarian disasters, even when they are not themselves affected by them.

The spectator base for NGOs is no longer guided by frames for understanding and assessing conflicts in the world that justify almost any means if they contribute to achieving a predefined end state. Conflicts now merely appear as a series of abuses or "crimes" committed by the morally "evil" against the morally "good" and innocent. The old dualism of friends and foes, victors and vanquished, is replaced by the new dualism of perpetrators and victims. Political struggles that used to be read as being waged for justice, right, or honor are now seen as perpetuating senseless "cycles of violence" that call for therapeutic intervention instead of taking sides. Given the presumptive perniciousness of all political forces, the immediate situation of the victims is held to be all that matters. Morality becomes global and forsakes all political and national distinctions in favor of recognizing all humans as "needy creatures."[32]

This shift, which is at the root of the worldviews offered by NGOs and shared by their supporters, is captured well by one of the most original thinkers in this area, Michael Ignatieff, who characterized his own politics by quoting the disillusion of Don McCullin, a British war photographer: "I certainly take the side of the underprivileged. I could never say I was politically neutral. But whether I'm of the Right or the Left—I can't say . . . I feel, in my guts, at one with the victims."[33] Ignatieff astutely notes that this approach is very different from older forms of internationalism. These older forms were based on a scheme that interpreted different domestic and international struggles—of students, workers, or neocolonial subjects—as intimately related and converging. "Your Struggle Is Ours" was the rallying cry of social movements; conflict and intervention could be supported or opposed on the basis of a meaningful dichotomy of Left and Right.[34] Today we live in a very different world, in which, as Ignatieff puts it, "there are no good causes left—only victims of bad causes."[35]

These structural changes were crucial, although they would not have sufficed to lead to a truly new form of activism had they not been joined by more specific cultural changes. NGOs need a broad basis of interested spectators who confine their role to donating money without otherwise interfering in the day-to-day business of the organizations they help to keep going. Yet NGOs also depend on a critical mass of individuals with certain skills and dispositions from which they can recruit their personnel. The moral public that I have identified as a key condition for the rise of NGOs is not only composed of morally sensitive spectators, but also of potential activists willing to work for such organizations (for often low pay). Generally speaking, NGOs flourish in societies that value not only loyalty, but also initiative and outcome-oriented behavior and that do not attempt to confine the skills and virtues associated with "entrepreneurialism"[36] to the economic sphere. More specifically, the new organizations require a significant pool of people who are good at inducing cooperation and extracting resources from others by telling credible "stories" about situations that require urgent action. The ability to smoothly move from one social context to another, a principled openness, and "respectful curiosity"[37] toward other cultures and different people—all these traits need to be cultivated and institutionalized as ideals of personality.

Overall, these behavioral prerequisites are a far cry from those expected in traditional solidarist organizations. The social cohesion of Marxist political parties depended on organizational structures that were designed in such a way as to make it unlikely that "intellectuals" and "proletarians" would ever actually meet.[38] Furthermore, and unlike traditional charitable institutions such as Christian missions, NGOs are not predicated on the self-renunciation of their personnel, but tend to give room to the desire of their professionals to combine genuine moral motives with demands for expressive self-realization. Where moral activism requires taking personal risks, a precondition for success may even be that society encourages self-realization through "turning one's life into a novel," as two French observers have put it.[39]

Top-Down Internationalization

Nearing the end of our chain of causality, we need to take a look at two proximate conditions propitious for the growth and spread of NGOs: first, the roles of international organizations and donor states, and second, the professionalization of the new nonstate actors. Like the Culture Wars, these factors are crucial for characterizing the specific historical conjuncture that allowed certain opinions and moral attitudes to crystallize into concrete programs of organized actions.

We should begin by examining some top-down explanations for the growth and proliferation of NGOs, which are not without merits, but tend to exaggerate the causal role of international organizations with regard to the emergence and expansion of NGOs. Statistics show that from the 1970s, increasing portions of official development assistance and other forms of aid were channeled through NGOs. The 1990s saw a reversal of this trend with official aid flows from OECD countries to the rest of the world—and grants to NGOs—decreasing. However, private donations, including contributions from foundations and corporations, generally made up for this loss, so that NGO aid as share of all aid flows has not gone down.[40] Against the background of these trends, it has been argued that the expansion of NGOs can be explained by the expansion of funds and other opportunities provided by international organizations such as the World Bank and major UN agencies, plus donor states, the European Union, and a broad range of foundations.[41] In my view, however, it is tautological to say that NGOs have grown because funds earmarked for NGOs by international organizations have grown. The increase of funds available for NGOs *implies* their growth instead of *explaining* it. While superficially accurate, top-down explanations for the worldwide growth of NGOs fail to ask the more relevant question of how to explain the increase of funds for NGOs and the underlying normative shifts. Authors favoring this type of explanation also point to expanded political access within the UN system and other organizations as a reason for the global growth of the NGO sector.[42] Again, the real question is how to explain this expansion of access opportunities.

So, what accounts for increased funds and expanded political access? One general explanation is that differences in state capabilities have reached a point where some states are simply unable to provide a minimum of public goods for their populations, while others can easily take on social tasks far beyond their own borders. As a result of the growing gap in capabilities, the relationship between rich and poor countries is now often modeled as creating a situation in which the former are represented—often by their own citizens—as "bad Samaritans"[43] who choose to ignore the contemporary equivalents of the biblical roadside victim, although rescue would be easy. The line between "harming" and "withholding benefit," or between "acting" and "failures to act," is becoming blurry.[44] This increases the moral pressure on Western governments "to do something" about poverty, civil wars, epidemics, and other problems. In some developing countries, international NGOs such as CARE, World Vision, or Oxfam are the only agencies able to make sure that vulnerable populations have access to clean water, sanitation, seed multiplication projects or HIV/AIDS prevention measures. Unfortunately, the failures of public services in many developing countries are caused or further aggravated by corruption and the outright "criminalization" of the state.[45] The ineffectiveness and inefficiency of governments in the face of escalating crises and massive human suffering, combined with the Western urge to do something about other peoples' problems, have prompted states and international organizations to spend more money on these problems and to channel the money past corrupt or faltering governments directly to NGOs. Some observers have described this trend as the rise of a "non-governmentality" that is based on the belief that "the welfare of the population and the improvement of its condition can best be served by 'non-state' actors."[46]

Another general reason for growing international funds for NGOs has to do with changing norms regulating the exercise of power. With the demise of modernization theory and Malthusianism, top-down social engineering in areas such as development policy or the use of coercive means in population policy aimed at controlling the fertility of women have been replaced by policies that claim to be based on informed consent, persuasion, and the respect for human rights. This changing logic of power has led to a revaluation of forces associated with the formation of preferences in "civil society."[47]

This has meant that NGO access to decision-making bodies has been significantly expanded. At the UN level, NGOs now participate as observers at numerous Executive Board and Standing Committee meetings; they have access to all levels of deliberation and decision making at the Food and Agricultural Organization (FAO), the United Nations Environment Program (UNEP), and others; NGO representatives have seats on the Council of the Global Environmental Facility (GEF); agencies like the UN High Commissioner for Refugees (UNHCR) or the World Food Program (WFP) consider partnerships with groups such as CARE International or World Vision to be absolutely essential for the success of their emergency response systems; regular consultations have increased across the entire system including the UN Security Council with regard to humanitarian crises, the General Assembly, and the World Bank. On top of all this, NGOs have participated in various ways in the drafting of international treaties on topics such as climate change, biodiversity, landmines, or the establishment of the International Criminal Court (ICC). Since the 1990s, NGOs in the fields of human rights, development, environment, and humanitarian aid have continuously increased their portfolio of activities from the mere implementation of programs to the initiation and development of new policies.[48]

What is perhaps even more important is that NGOs were able to transform otherwise ineffective UN bodies, like the Commission on Human Rights, into a stage for their public advocacy. This crucial change is best epitomized by the exchange taking place in 1980 at the Commission on Human Rights, when the representative of Amnesty International for the first time—and only thanks to Canada and the United States—secured not only the right to speak on behalf of "disappeared" victims of political violence in Latin America, but also "the right . . . to attack a government by name."[49]

The expansion and transformation of access can be assessed from two different angles. First, what motivates NGOs to seek involvement with international organizations? And second, why are international organizations actively inviting and wooing NGOs? The first question is easier to answer. International organizations are bureaucracies with little democratic oversight. There is overwhelming evidence that weak democratic control attracts well-organized lobby groups, including those who are more or less morally motivated.[50] For these groups, it is attractive to enter centralized decision-making bodies that stipulate rules for international society without being accountable to electorates and parliaments.

Furthermore, as Michael Barnett and Martha Finnemore have demonstrated, international organizations are not handmaidens of the governments that create them. Rather, they assert their autonomy in a number of ways that make them ideal targets for NGOs: United Nation agencies, the World Bank, and the WTO sometimes take initiatives where states are indifferent; these organizations may fail to act as governments wish; in some cases, they may even opt for policies that run against the interests of member states. Oftentimes this autonomy works against the interests of weak states, but the expectations of strong states are occasionally frustrated as well.[51] If we further consider the idealistic and all-encompassing agenda enunciated in the UN Charter and various covenants and declarations, it is little wonder that NGOs see the world body as their venue of choice. In addition, there are many mundane reasons for NGOs to stay in touch with the UN. Humanitarian NGOs, for example, gain access to the logistical and security services provided by the UN.[52]

What is much less easy to explain is why international organizations should lower their guards and actively seek to be intruded by nosy outsiders—something that we have been witnessing for some time now. In some cases, international bureaucracies have directly paid NGO lobbies in order to be lobbied.[53] In the 1980s, the World Bank funded the entire administrative budget of the World Bank NGO Committee in which members of sixteen leading NGOs were laying the groundwork for critical "Bankwatch" activities. When in 2006 the government of Singapore banned accredited activists from entering the country to attend the annual meetings of the World Bank and the IMF, the Bank lobbied the government on behalf of the excluded NGOs.[54] Such findings do not square easily with the otherwise plausible assumption made by Barnett and Finnemore, that international organizations are bureaucracies—that is, hierarchical, rule-based structures that enjoy moral authority among the general public because of their expertise and their insulation from arbitrary political influences. External actors might have reasons for attempting to penetrate the boundaries of bureaucratic institutions, but why should such institutions themselves lower their guards and actively invite, fund, and favor nonbureaucratic organizational "parasites"?

The short answer to this question, to which I will return in the following two chapters, is that they seek alliances with globally connected NGOs in order to maintain their comparative advantage over member states. As bureaucracies, international organizations enjoy the moral authority to devise and enact impartial rules and norms based on expertise instead of material interests.[55] At the same time, however, they are beset by serious pathologies resulting, among other things, from their insulation vis-à-vis society, their structural insensitivity to changing situations to which rules are to be applied, and their fetishism of formal procedures.[56] The UN system, in particular, is in constant danger of losing its aura of moral superiority because of dismal failures, for example, to act in the face of genocide in Rwanda in 1994 and more recently in Darfur, Sudan, or its history of gross distortion of national human rights records produced by the now defunct Commission on Human Rights. With few exceptions, both governments and NGOs rate the performance of the UN in fulfilling its mission with regard to the promotion of democracy, the mitigation of social problems or the maintenance of peace and security as poor and disappointing.[57] Against this backdrop, some staff of international organizations are keen on cooperating with NGOs, which help them to live up to their professional self-image. Specifically, there are three things that NGOs are expected to provide: information, publicity, and sentimental attachment to common goals.

First, empirical evidence points to NGOs as having become reliable and sometimes indispensable sources of *information* for decision makers and other practitioners. Often it is their field-specific knowledge that works as a door opener. In policy areas organized around the consequences of the use of landmines, the effects of ozone-depleting substances on the stratosphere, or the release of genetically modified organisms, NGOs have provided credible information about the costs and benefits of different policies.[58] For example, the UN Mine Action Service uses a landmine-safety manual that was developed by CARE International. Moreover, some humanitarian NGOs hold a great deal of unpublished, "gray" information about conditions on the ground in weak, war-torn, or "failed" states, which makes them useful to the intelligence communities.[59] Given limited staff and budgets, and a fast-changing, fluid world where policy objects proliferate, international bureaucracies increasingly rely on external sources.

Second, NGOs assist international organizations in *publicizing* their activities and thus in bolstering their moral authority. This is crucial because citizens tend not to be interested in the work of organizations run by unelected officials in faraway places. Citizens are "rationally ignorant" about decisions taken by bodies they cannot effectively control.[60] In such a situation, NGOs can achieve two goals at once: they lower the costs of informing the world public about new treaties, reports, resolutions, or declarations; and due to their popularity, they may help to raise interest in these decisions and opinions. There is more to this. As transformative, intermediary agents, NGOs do not meet publicity needs in a neutral fashion. Rather, they often attempt to shame national governments into accepting standards or provisions promulgated by international organizations, something these organizations cannot do themselves.

A related third service offered by NGOs is their ability to introduce *passion* into the work of international organizations, in particular a sense of urgency, genuine concern, and enthusiasm. Emotions help to foster vivid, unique, intersubjective understandings that can be communicated and perpetuated in a way that often helps to achieve political results. An official involved at the international stage in the debate leading to the Ottawa Convention, which prohibits the use and production of antipersonnel landmines, explicitly stated that policymakers "wanted the enthusiasm that the NGOs could provide."[61] Even where motives and objectives are shared, NGOs are usually much better than officials at persuading others that their motives are "heartfelt" and hence trustworthy.

All this does not fit well into the classical model of a self-contained bureaucracy. We should therefore rather speak of *hybrid* bureaucracies. By this I mean bureaucracies that have to accommodate and act as host vessels for nonbureaucratic "parasites" in order to work. Many have echoed the complaint first made in the late 1990s by James Paul, former Executive Director of the Global Policy Forum in New York City, that relations of the UN with NGOs should not be placed under the Assistant Secretary General for External Relations, since NGOs "are not external but internal to the UN system."[62] In any case, we can conclude that international organizations function as proximate conditions for the growth of NGOs, because the latter are perceived as providers of key services such as information, publicity, and emotional attachment to common agendas. In addition, NGOs are often seen as efficient implementers of global health, education, and food distribution programs. However, neither funds nor access to decision-making bodies as such can explain NGO growth. Access opportunities do not create, but presuppose well-developed institutional capacities to collect and distribute novel information and to mobilize the public. Funding opportunities may encourage the formation of NGOs including efforts of all kinds of groups to *mimic* NGOs in order to appear eligible for external support (mutant NGOs). Yet, no major NGO has been directly created by an international organization or a donor state. Usually things work the other way round. It is the existence of vibrant and reliable NGO networks in a given country or policy area that encourages donors to invest in these networks.

PASSION AND PROFESSIONALIZATION

The final link in the causal chain is the professionalization of NGOs, which is driven by the multiple relationships entertained by NGOs with states and international organizations. "Professionalization" is an ambiguous term. For one, it is used to indicate a transition away from improvised, amateurish styles of engagement. It is also used as a synonym for process that is perhaps better characterized as "managerialization." Drawing on Emile Durkheim's concepts of the sacred and the profane, we may say that professions have two aspects. The sacred aspect of modern professions can be picked up and enlarged by practitioners in order to create strong value-oriented identities with no regard for the "impure" worlds of politics and markets. It is, in fact, striking to see how many of today's prominent post-traditional associations were started by lawyers, doctors, toxicologists, forensic scientists, or biologists who focused on the sacred aspects of their professional ethos. From this perspective, professionalization can mean the partial displacement and "pollution" of a purely value-oriented modality of professional existence by other, more goal-oriented and pragmatic modalities.

The history of NGOs illustrates both these trends: amateurs have turned into professionals, and groups stressing the sacred aspects of their profession started to hire managers in order to keep their growing organizations going. In order to understand professionalization as a development, it is instructive to study the origins of NGOs. They either started as breakaway groups from well-established institutions (such as the Sierra Club or the ICRC) or with no organizational prehistory at all. The first steps were made by passionate core groups who were united by a high degree of consensus, clan-like goal congruence, and the social glue of friendship.[63] The French founders of Doctors Without Borders were even inspired by the search for new forms of "masculine brotherhood"[64] to be forged in the midst of humanitarian disasters. In spite of their ethos of nonviolence, the language of the zealous first generation was often full of martial idioms. Bob Hunter of Greenpeace once declared, with no discernable trace of irony, that an emerging "nation of armless Buddhas" was about to protect whales and the oceans against "the equivalent of carnivorous Nazis equipped with seagoing tanks and Krupp cannons."[65] Bob Pierce, the first president of World Vision, was a gifted, well-traveled lay preacher who in the late 1940s had organized large "World Vision rallies" in major American cities to raise money and stir enthusiasm for the welfare of children worldwide—and for the tireless struggle against communism. In all these cases, the rhetoric conveys a sense of urgency to form new communities ready to face and get involved in epic struggles marked by extreme violence: ruthless enemies are contrasted with innocent victims in mortal danger—defenseless civilians, whales, children. Strong moral norms are invoked not to solve conflicts but to define and enable them on a global scale in a way that allows certain interventions to count as righteous.

Professionalization is the process by which much of what electrified early followers of emerging NGOs has changed to sounding musty. The shrillness of zealous public discourse has been toned down by a language that no longer precludes resolution and compromise. Professional organizations may continue to struggle against formidable enemies, but they also have to write reports, collect data, administer growing budgets, play with symbols, and package and sell a "product" to the public. In short, they have to make themselves understood among a host of non-zealots from very different backgrounds.

A primary driving force behind professionalization has been the competition for funds and the search for new sources of income. Professionalization is closely linked to the internationalization of NGOs.[66] In order to be eligible for funds, activist groups had to hire professionals with academic degrees, learn how to conduct various types of case and impact studies, and pepper their language with managerial euphemisms and words such as "sustainability," "partnership," and "empowerment." Externally funded organizations also need accountants in order to meet the financial transparency requirements of their donors and to survive financial audits by independent consultants.

Yet, it bears emphasizing that the overall process can not be accurately described as having led to a deradicalization of small activist groups into big mainstream public interest groups—although this clearly has been the perception of famous "zealots" like, for example, David Brower, who left his post as executive director of the Sierra Club in the late 1960s to start Friends of the Earth, which he left again as soon as they, too, became big and pragmatic. Instead, it can be argued that most organizations have retained a mixture of zealotry and managerialism without one aspect completely dominating the other. Modern NGOs hire people with transferable skills, but many of these people have a clear preference for working in an activist, noncommercial milieu.[67] Many have a religious background and are motivated by an ethic of universal benevolence rescued from the rubble of collapsed secular theodicies. They work for an NGO because they want a "meaningful" profession.[68] Balancing entrepreneurial and administrative skills with a strong ethical commitment, the full-time staff of the major modern NGOs are "exemplary value-oriented elites"[69] very much at the center of modern societies, although they do not always like to identify with such an account.

For the reconstruction of a chain of causality, it is important to note that professionalization improves both the effectiveness and the knowledge base of organizations. The growing capacity of human rights NGOs, for example, to provide reliable data on rights violations and to make accurate judgments about the behavior of states in light of human rights standards has significantly improved their *de facto* standing within the respective UN bodies.[70] The same is true for the relationship between NGOs and their funders. Professionals lend legitimacy to NGOs by smoothing the communication between activists, the public, and donor agencies. They have developed ways to resist efforts by funders to control their operations and are able shield the inner life of their organizations against overly curious outsiders.[71] For these reasons, professionalization must be seen as a precondition both for the independence of NGOs, for their proliferation, and for the strengthening of their transnational linkages.

Table 3.1 schematically represents the causal chain leading to what we see today as full-fledged NGOs. Causal arrows run from the left-hand to the right-hand side. The characteristics of NGOs are political independence, transnational linkages, and the prevalence of other-regarding orientations and policies. International organizations and a labor market of professionals are ongoing props of all these features, although the specific value component of NGO professionals points backward to other social preconditions. At the intermediate causal level, there are a number of crucial cultural factors such as the decline of national interests brought about by the Culture Wars in the West and the strengthening of a moral public. Even more fundamental are ultimate conditions such as the existence of a liberal democratic order, communication technologies, and the retreat of particularistic moralities that make us indifferent to the suffering of others.

SUMMARY

In the literature on the emergence and growth of NGOs, bottom-up explanations compete with top-down explanations. The first stress the role of societal and cultural factors in facilitating the rise of NGOs, whereas the second point to the role of international organizations and

Table 3.1 Conditions for the rise of NGOs

Ultimate conditions	Intermediate conditions	Proximate conditions	Aspects of fully developed NGOs
Liberal state	Decline of national interests		Political independence
Communication and transportation technologies	Culture Wars	Rise of international organizations	Transnational linkages
Affirmation of ordinary life	Moral public	Professionalization	Other-regarding policies
Decline of secular theodicies			

changing norms guiding the behavior of donor agencies. In this chapter, I have offered an account that rejects these alternatives as too simplistic. A much more promising way of understanding the recent history of this new organizational form is to differentiate between ultimate, intermediate, and proximate conditions. Thus, I have argued that NGOs are predicated on the existence of a liberal state and a liberal legal system as well as on the availability of basic communication and transport technologies. It is also important that the ordinary lives of others are seen as deserving some favorable attention at all. The affirmation of ordinary life, as Charles Taylor calls it, and the concomitant concern for the suffering of ordinary people were clearly among the general preconditions for the rise of NGOs and related social movements. More recently, aggressive ideologies that reduce real people to ciphers for power, class, or race have been drained of much of their venom. The same is true for more sophisticated secular theodicies such as modernization theories that frame the social world in such a way as to make the observable suffering of others meaningful and thus acceptable.

The widespread loss of self-confidence among Western political elites and the rejection of the politics of self-interest at both the national and the social level have further contributed to the idea of a "new politics" to be undertaken by new actors such as NGOs and new social movements. The Culture Wars of the 1960s have led to a political romanticism that celebrates the single human being as opposed to the citizen and the political community. They have created a moral climate that tends to replace the old dualism of friends and foes, victors and vanquished, by the new dualism of perpetrators and victims. Only against the background of these essentially technological, social, and cultural conditions, international organizations and NGO-friendly states play additional roles in spurring the growth and proliferation of NGOs. Increased funds and expanded political access at both the national and the international levels of decision making have been crucial for the capacity and visibility of NGOs (for which I have listed a number of reasons). The growing gap in capabilities between states has certainly contributed to refocus attention on non-Western regions and on new ways to channel funds and expertise from donors to people in need, bypassing as much as possible postcolonial governments. As "parasitical" intermediaries, NGOs have considerably improved their standing with international organizations, which increasingly need the information, publicity, and attention provided by the new actors. NGOs have become paradoxical "outsiders within" international organizations, in particular within many UN agencies and bodies that have actually become *hybrid* bureaucracies in constant need of their nonbureaucratic supporters from the imagined never-never land of "global civil society."

CHAPTER 4

WHAT ARE NGOS ACTUALLY DOING?

ABOLITIONISM AS A MORAL TEMPLATE

In the historical self-perception of Western societies, slavery has become to be seen as the epitome of injustice; to a lesser degree this also seems to be true in various non-Western societies that have their own checkered history of slavery and abolition.[1] The Atlantic system of slavery did enormous harm to some twelve million Africans who were transported to the New World, and to their descendants who for generations produced the bulk of the export staples in colonial America. In retrospect, slavery appears as one of the key symbols of evil in liberal democracies. By the same measure, the movement for the abolition of the slave trade and slavery in general, which began in eighteenth-century Britain and her American colonies, is something like the moral gold standard for contemporary struggles on behalf of others. The very concept of universal humanity was developed and made acceptable through the abolition of human bondage.[2] In this sense, one of the most positive things one can say about present-day NGOs is that abolitionism is their "most obvious forerunner."[3] I believe that this is true, although abolitionism is not a forerunner in the sense that most people working for NGOs today are directly inspired by the historical examples of the American Anti-Slavery Society or the British Society for Effecting the Abolition of the Slave Trade. Rather, the antislavery movement is interesting as a *model* that helps us to understand the mode of operation of post-traditional civil associations. I begin with three general observations, before I take a closer look at some of the political practices pioneered by abolitionists.

First, abolitionists were struggling for *cosmopolitan rules* that would prohibit a terrible harm inflicted on innocent victims by governments and private citizens. To be sure, abolitionists did not start that way. In the beginning, British antislavery advocates only wanted to keep the British Isles slave-free, similar to American Quakers who fought for purifying their own communities of the evil of slavery instead of abolishing it altogether.[4] Abolitionism as a principled and universalistic position emerged only as a result of subtle, but highly consequential interpretive shifts within various religious communities that moved from the vow to steer clear of any direct involvement with the slave system to the desire of preventing others from perpetuating that system. From a certain point onward, doing harm appeared to be as bad as *failing to prevent* harm. As the French-American Quaker Anthony Benezet declared in 1767, spectators were not "innocent" if they remained "silent" in the face of injustice.[5]

Second, unlike other historical movements, abolitionism was strongly *other-regarding*. In fact, it represented the prototype of a movement that focused on the liberation of distant strangers (or of strangers forcibly imported from distant places in Africa or the West Indies). As I have pointed out in chapter 2, it is implausible to claim that only people who themselves feel disrespected can muster the energy to fight injustice. This is a shortcoming of Honneth's critical theory of recognition. Honneth harks back to the examples of the labor movement and, to a lesser extent, the struggle against colonialism—examples that are tacitly assumed to offer the moral template for any modern emancipatory social movement.[6] He thereby ignores the alternative model of the nineteenth-century British and American crusade for the abolition of human bondage, which was based on the growing antislavery sentiment among mostly white *nonslaves*. This sentiment created a moral climate that encouraged slave rebellions and ultimately achieved sweeping legal victories from the Abolition of the Slave Trade Act in 1807 and the Slavery Abolition Act in 1833 in Britain, to the Thirteenth Amendment of 1865, which marks the abolition of slavery in the United States.

However, it would be incorrect to assume that abolitionism acted only as a catalyst for a movement of self-liberation. The historian David Brion Davis has demonstrated that the abolition of slavery cannot be explained by the resistance of slaves, which was motivated by moral experiences of being treated with utter contempt. Resistance including the mass exodus of people of African descent from Confederate plantations during the American Civil War did play a role; but overall slave resistance in Brazil, the Caribbean, and the North American mainland was much stronger *before* the abolitionist movement gained mass support.[7] The key factor for the abolition of slavery was that white nonslaves, with considerable help from black ex-slaves such as Frederick Douglass and others, empathized with others and acted *vicariously* for them, ultimately achieving a success that, according to Davis, "may have no parallel"[8] in the history of the Western world.

Third, the transatlantic antislavery crusade was not about the adequate application of already institutionalized norms of recognition, but about the very *definition* of these norms. People were not just struggling "for" but "over" institutional forms of recognition that were still in flux and heavily contested. Also, it should be noted that chattel slavery on the sugar, tobacco, and cotton plantations in the American South was not only seen as a violation of basic *rights*. Antislavery propagandists were equally eager to spotlight the two other elementary forms of denying recognition to others: the neglect of most basic affective *needs* and the denigration of the achievements and the *labor* of others.[9] Thus, in his influential 1839 compendium *American Slavery As It Is*, which even today makes for quite a harrowing read, leading activist Theodore Dwight Weld gave much room to describing the willful disruption of the emotional bonding between adults and between mothers and children. After the slave trade was prohibited, bonded laborers were literally ordered to "breed," children were given new names at the whim of slaveholders, women were constantly abused. As Weld put it, "Parents are almost never consulted as to the disposition to be made of their children; they have as little control over them as have domestic animals over the disposal of their young. Every natural and social feeling and affection are violated with indifference; slaves are treated as though they did not possess them."[10] Against all this, the abolitionists wanted to restore a protected sphere of intimacy and love for everybody.

Perhaps even more importantly, abolitionists were motivated by a strong desire to turn physical *labor* from an eternal punishment and animal-like exertion into a dignified and honorable activity. Only a few activists like Weld integrated manual labor in their personal lives of publishing and advocacy work, but all helped to generalize the idea of free labor as an activity that enhances the "sense of self-worth" in everybody engaged in it.[11] Abolishing slavery was thus a decisive step toward the institutionalization of the principle that labor deserves recognition. By institutionalizing the idea of achievement as a distinct principle of social recognition, the abolitionists made a crucial contribution to the moral foundations on which labor movements could be built and on which workers and employers could struggle over the value of their respective contributions to the well-being of society.

Besides these fundamental innovations, there are some innovative political aspects of the antislavery movement that deserve mention. Similar to more recent movements, abolitionists intended to change society by changing both what people knew and what people believed to be right. They wanted lawmakers and the public to face and *acknowledge* the sheer savagery of the slave system and its unfathomable human toll; and they wanted them to draw serious *moral and legal consequences* from what they were made to know. Both aspects are equally important. It has been pointed out that the abolitionists invented modern "information politics" by reporting undeniable facts and using testimonials of individuals to shake people out of their inertia.[12] The practice of signing a petition, the use of logos and graphic images of suffering, and the organization of consumer boycotts against things like slave-harvested sugar were all introduced by abolitionists. To many, the reported facts spoke for themselves in the sense that they were impossible to reconcile with fundamental moral norms intuitively held by large sections of the public. These were basic norms of universal benevolence, which were vaguely described as being laid down in "the laws of Justice, Mercy, and Truth."[13] What is important here is that the abolitionists could not yet refer to international human rights law to strengthen their case. They looked tirelessly for biblical condemnations of slavery, but in vain. The new argument had to be drawn from a different source: moral conscience. Believing that even slaveholders had some moral conscience, early opponents of slavery saw a chance "to shame them into better principles."[14]

An equally important innovation for the art of public protest was the distinction between evildoers and their knowing and unknowing accomplices. Generally speaking, abolitionism created a four-pronged strategy based on antislavery *advocates* appealing to a *moral public* on behalf of slaves who were represented as *victims* of a social system run by identifiable *perpetrators* including their accomplices. Regarding this last category, Christopher Leslie Brown has argued that antislavery enthusiasts during the era of the American Revolution actually "invented the notion of complicity."[15] Moving beyond blaming a faceless system or single slaveholders, activists began to target first, the entire social class of planters and traders as well as the laws allowing this class to act with impunity, and second, seemingly high-minded British officials who declared slavery to be only an American problem, despite the well-documented fact that their country continued to profit from the institution of bonded labor.[16] Thus for the abolitionists, the slave system was the outcome of choices made by identifiable actors as well as of the non-choices and bad faith of a wide range of accomplices. Ultimately even ordinary people who continued to buy goods made by slaves were blamed for inadvertently perpetuating an evil system. In this way, much of the contemporary moralization of everyday life can be traced back to abolitionism. One of things NGOs today are doing is precisely this: establishing and denouncing *degrees of complicity* of different actors in committing or soliciting injustices that frequently occur in place far out of sight.

It is interesting to note that the antislavery protest provoked two dominant counter-critiques from authors who either defended slavery or who thought of it as of minor importance. The first group comprises commentators in slave-trading nations such as France, Spain, or Portugal who denounced British antislavery initiatives as a "tool" of imperialism used with the intention to crowd out competitors from the world market.[17] A second group conceded that abolitionists did have a point in opposing slavery, but abolitionism was lambasted for its inconsistent preoccupation with distant strangers, which was allegedly blinding its proponents for injustices done in their own home country, for example, to coal miners and other workers.[18] Elements of both these counter-critiques can be detected in much of today's popular and academic anti-NGO discourse.

CHANGING NARRATIVES OF GOOD AND EVIL

Like their abolitionist forerunners, NGOs are active on two different fronts. They struggle to influence public opinion in order to broaden the appeal of issue-specific ideals of solidarity with some people (victims) against other people (perpetrators). And they work hard to crystallize normative expectations about desirable forms of solidarity into legally binding rules or self-binding commitments, not by filling official positions of power or by running for seats in parliaments, but by influencing the drafting of rules through lobbying, consulting, and advice. Another way to put this is to say that NGOs—post-traditional civil associations—act as "communicative" as well as "regulative" institutions.[19] This section is devoted to the role of NGOs in the first group of institutions, whereas in the next section I will look at NGOs as forces that shape rules in international society.

Much of the communicative energy of post-traditional associations is aimed at the "evocation of sympathy" for suffering strangers, which, according to Martha Finnemore, is "the very point of their activity. NGOs actively work to increase familiarity with the oppressed as a means of evoking sympathy and helping behavior."[20] This is but one side of the coin. NGOs are not only universal sympathizers but also global polarizers bent on creating *antipathy* for those who are deemed to be morally responsible for oppression and suffering. Like the abolitionists who denounced slavery as wicked and sinful, NGOs are exposing many evils, which are contrasted with as many human goods. As actors in civil society, they categorize persons, events, and institutions in terms of symbolic sets of value and antivalue, norm and counternorm. For members of contemporary society, some causes are worthy of their support, some people deserve to be included, and some events should be welcomed, while other causes, people, and events have to be dismissed, excluded, or feared.

Sociologists in the tradition of Emile Durkheim argue that these ascriptions are not made in a vacuum but according to a dominant binary civil discourse that establishes symbols of good and evil.[21] This dichotomy is not abstract; it becomes the real-life focus of what is considered emotionally desirable to achieve or to avoid. The contents of any civil discourse can, of course, be transformed by social actors. However, there is no way that individuals and groups could possibly avoid using binary codes altogether. These codes demarcate both the good and the evil, thereby creating powerful incentives to act in one way or another. The attempt to emphatically reject any symbolic division of the world would not supersede the binary scheme; rather, it would redistribute some groups across the same cultural scheme by tainting them as irrational, divisive, or exclusive. Rejecting a division as arbitrary or unjust implies drawing a line against arbitrariness and injustice and thus reaffirming the symbolic division.

In this way, throughout the nineteenth century, the struggle against the division of society into slaves and nonslaves was inextricably intertwined with the invention of new grounds for representing certain groups and events as evil, unwelcome, and un-American. Similarly in the 1960s, students around the world struggled against the binaries of the Cold War discourse in favor of alternative ways of representing the social and natural world and the threats facing this world. These symbolic struggles, which prepared the ground for many of today's prominent NGOs, aimed at subverting the self-descriptions of dominant elites. Motives that appeared rational and sane were unmasked as irrational and mad; relationships in the supposedly open society were redescribed as full of suspicion, greed, and conspirational trickery; liberal institutions were no longer represented as egalitarian and rule-regulated, but as hierarchical and driven by raw power.[22]

Like their forerunners, NGOs, too, are heavily engaged in struggles over how to apply the symbolic identifications of the civil discourse. At the same time, they are deliberately confounding existing definitions of good and evil in order to draw up new moral maps. In doing so, they use the symbolism of evil in sometimes radically new ways. First of all, they target actions rather than actors. Traditionally and throughout history, evil *actions* were reviled as illustrations of the evil *nature* of those who committed them. One of the major moral innovations in recent times consists in the ability to focus on actions as such, which is possible only after abstracting from the actor *behind* the actions. Environmental, human rights, or antipoverty groups eschew explicit causal narratives that explain harmful acts as predictable outcomes of the nature of existing groups, nations, religions, and so on. In contemporary society, NGOs represent the most radical break with the tradition of demonizing a mythical Other as evil incarnate. Evil is no longer projected onto any of the modern substitutes for Satan: dangerous social classes, alien races, or national archenemies. The important point here is that the disincarnation of evil changes the narrative of good and evil, but does in no way make the symbolism of evil itself disappear from public discourse.

In answering the question of what NGOs are actually doing, I wish to focus, above all, on their intellectual labor. Several researchers have observed that NGO staffers spend a lot of time deliberating and thinking, very much like the social movements from which they have emerged.[23] They connect events, identify causes and consequences, and distribute responsibilities. Since this activity precedes other practices like disseminating information, lobbying governments, or direct action protests, it deserves particular attention. Going one step further, I contend that the way NGOs think makes them akin to religious organizations. Let us recall the broad definition of "religion" given by Durkheim. According to the French sociologist,

> [The] real characteristic of religious phenomena is that they always suppose a bipartite division of the whole universe, known and knowable, into two classes which embrace all that exists, but which radically exclude each other. Sacred things are those which the interdictions protect and isolate; profane things, those to which these interdictions are applied and which must remain at a distance from the first.[24]

I contend that major NGOs are in the practice of symbolically dividing the universe along axes of good and evil; in doing so, they struggle to institutionalize legal and moral "interdictions" or, in other words, new sources of authority. While NGOs *do* all kinds of things, they *are* nontraditional or secularized religious organizations.[25]

With this in mind, I now turn to contrasting ways in which resonant symbols of evil are applied by international environmental NGOs. I select environmental NGOs to demonstrate that they are as eager as organizations in other fields to promote a polarizing discourse, although perhaps less obviously than Amnesty International, which sports a burning candle alongside barbed wire on its logo, or Transparency International, which distributes pictures showing anti-corruption "brooms" sweeping away the detritus of skulls and grim-looking fugitives with sacks of dollars.[26] I want to show that Western and non-Western organizations active in the field of environmental and natural-resource policy are no less engaged in the symbolic labor of polarization.

SYMBOLIC LABOR

Environmental organizations today promote activities and legal reforms aimed at protecting the oceans, saving ancient forests, eliminating genetically modified organisms, exposing toxic threats, and ending global warming. In addition, Greenpeace wants a nuke-free world. One way to look at these areas is to disaggregate them into two sets of things: sacred and pure things on the one hand, and things that are impure and polluting on the other hand. In light of Durkheim's definition, the campaign areas listed above comprise sacred things such as organisms, habitats, and life itself, as well as impure things such as intrusive technologies, pollutants, and lethal radiation. This is the first aspect I wish to highlight: much of what NGOs actually do is about inventing and disseminating symbols.

NGOs must be analyzed in the context of broader social movements that over the last fifty years have tried to make banal, inconspicuous, or remote threats that had not been on anybody's radar before, a matter of popular debate, anxiety, and excitement. An important beginning was the antitoxics movement that emerged in the late 1950s with the discovery of high concentrations of the radioactive isotope strontium-90 in mothers' milk in the United States and Canada. The 1960s spawned a much broader range of "quality-of-life"-movements concerned about the industrialization of the agrofood system, questions of environmental justice, and the long-term consequences of waste-intensive Western lifestyles.[27] Over the decades, these developments have stimulated new ways in which people were beginning to perceive risks and organize their everyday lives.

In this context, emerging NGOs have contributed to the transformation of organisms and habitats like the rainforests into resonant symbols of ultimate moral purity. The best example is perhaps "biological diversity," a term introduced by Thomas Lovejoy of WWF-USA in 1980, which replaced the older idea of wilderness while invoking the same sacred values.[28] During the lead-up to the 1992 United Nations Conference on Environment and Development (UNCED)—or Earth Summit—Lovejoy organized guided tours into the Amazon for senators, members of Congress, celebrities, and students to make them sense the wondrous and *paradisiacal* qualities of the rainforest. As he explained in an interview,

When you go into the forest, it's not what you think it is. It's not a bunch of animals just leaping around that you can't possibly miss. It's all this subtle stuff. Telling one tree from another is not a simple thing to do. It's the insects and the ants and the termites and the butterflies. And they [the visitors from the United States] will have spent the whole night listening to all these voices. That becomes biological diversity in their brains.[29]

Biodiversity was no longer meant to be simply a concept used by conservation biologists. The term has a literal meaning, but has also been invested with seminal depth and resonance; it connotes variety, subtlety, sensuality, sentiment, and the fragility of life itself. Lovejoy's word has become shorthand for the Western idea of nature as "source" and "voice."[30] Biodiversity is both: an indispensable resource, but also a concept with strong moral connotations.

Simultaneously, new symbols of evil were circulated by activists. Most importantly, the religious metaphor of pollution was secularized and blended *with its literal referent*. This has perhaps been the most truly innovative move of organized environmentalism. Essentially, Western environmentalists strive to shield parts of the world such as the rainforests, whales, genetic material, or the polar regions of the Arctic and the Antarctic from any kind of encroachment and utilitarian calculus. These phenomena are envisioned as "pristine" or "untouched" and thus, in a sense, as sacred. On the negative side, there are physical threats that are not only materially but also symbolically polluting in that they are seen to be harmful to a generalized sense of living in tune with strongly felt, meaningful supra-individual ends symbolized as Nature. Countless visual stereotypes published by environmental groups reinforce this dichotomy by playing with contrasts that have both a literal and a symbolic meaning. Ocean waters, for instance, evoke connotations of awe-inspiring eternity and innocence, whereas crude oil spilling out of the ruptured hull of a tanker symbolizes the fearsome downside of our civilization: materialism, greed, war, and dependence on foreign powers. Given these stark dichotomies, it is not surprising that early activists such as the founders of Greenpeace were under the impression of being engaged not in mundane politics but in campaigns with "the flavor of a crusade, or *jihad*, a sacred undertaking."[31]

A second aspect of the symbolic labor of NGOs is related to what I have called their aloofness from conventional politics. Thus, the normative "interdictions" lobbied for by NGOs are not directed against an enemy on whom responsibility for all polluting activities can be immediately pinned. Of course, certain countries or corporations draw more fire than others because of regulatory slack or poor environmental records. But there is nothing in the structure or essence of these entities that prevents them from changing their practices and becoming "good." The enemy is neither capitalism nor corporations as such, but only their "products and behavior."[32] Here is how the British branch of Greenpeace describes its approach toward multinational oil and food corporations:

> Our relationship with most companies is schizophrenic anyway. We do not have clear "opponents" or "friends." We support BP's solar and renewable energy activities, but totally oppose their plans for future oil exploration (especially in the Arctic region and Alaska). We have worked with Unilever on "greenfreeze" technology and against them on the issue of GM [genetically modified] foods.[33]

This quote nicely summarizes the paradox at the root of nongovernmental politics in the West: NGOs "totally oppose" certain actions without having "opponents." In line with this paradox, environmental NGOs have radicalized the *idea of complicity* that was introduced as a new category of moral discourse by the abolitionists: as long as we do not transform our lifestyle and reduce our "ecological footprint," we are all accomplices in a crime that has no longer one main identifiable culprit. This is why environmental NGO leaders often call on the public to engage in self-scrutiny, change old habits, and respect the values of a redefined civil culture. As "value-oriented elites"[34] in contemporary democratic societies, NGOs are deeply involved in symbolic struggles over the criteria that allow citizens to see themselves as either included in society and "socially saved," or excluded and "damned."[35] As soon as these values have been accepted into public life, people wish to endorse them in order to feel as legitimate members of society.

It is clear, then, that the first answer to the question of what NGOs are actually doing is not that they struggle to save the oceans or persecuted minorities; they rather struggle, above all, to change the way in which the symbolism of good and evil is applied to actions that are harmful to distant others—or to beings from whales to slaves who are (or were) perceived solely as natural resources. Once the civil discourse has been changed, members of society are motivated to "save the rainforests" (and other sacred things) because they know that their own "secular salvation"[36] and sense of belonging are at stake.

PARKS VERSUS PEOPLE

The idea that there is no clearly identifiable group of evildoers, but a sea of accomplices in environmental destruction often shades into a misanthropic denunciation of humans as such. Until recently, conservationists have called for marking out areas that they wished to "protect and isolate" from human interference, thereby turning them into sacred things. The environment was to be protected not *for* humans, but *from* them. Traditionally, this attitude was strongly influenced by Malthusian ideas. But a world-weary posture of "giving up on humanity" was also common among influential protagonists of the 1960s counterculture such as Kurt Vonnegut and others. Whatever the sources of misanthropy, the troubling fact is that in some cases the other-regarding ethic inspiring modern NGOs has taken a paradoxical turn, passing almost instantly from an expansive politics of intersubjective recognition to despair about humanity as an ongoing project. The critical juncture of global environmental activism was reached with technocratic conceptions aiming at the protection of "virgin areas" all over the world, either by cleansing the local population out of areas earmarked to become nature reserves or, in the long run, by lowering the birth rates in "poor nations."[37] Both the longstanding policies of the WWF with regard to protected areas and the Greenpeace stance against the Arctic hunting communities in Canada and Alaska have been seen by many as examples of a politics of recognition gone awry.

Throughout the last decades, the dominant opposition structuring the WWF worldview used to be between species-rich nature parks and human intruders. This opposition can be traced back to a colonial game-reserve ideology and popular metaphors of paradise that since the late seventeenth century were stereotypically associated with Europe's first tropical colonies.[38] The WWF has also been a major force in translating this opposition into material policies, for example, by supporting the training of armed game rangers in third world countries who are routinely using force to keep not only commercial poachers but also traditional local hunters out of protected areas. This process has in some cases directly contributed to the suffering of pastoral peoples like the Maasai in East Africa. The creation of the Serengeti National Park alone was made possible only after fifty thousand Maasai had been displaced from their land. More recently, WWF, IUCN, and other agencies supported the World Bank and the ruling party in Laos in resettling indigenous mountain populations in the Mekong region in order to ensure that large swaths of land can be used for biodiversity conservation projects, hydroelectric power plants, and ecotourism.[39]

For a long time, such NGO-supported programs were seen as exercises in balancing trade-offs between a number of significant benefits and fairly negligible human needs. Protected areas safeguard wildlife, plants, and freshwater reserves; generate new sources of income; and benefit the public at large, including future generations. This perception of the benefits of conservation has been further enhanced with the discovery of the value of biodiversity. The protection of biodiversity at the genetic, species, and ecosystem levels is today, in fact, universally accepted as critically important for safeguarding the livelihoods of all human communities on earth. What makes things complicated is that biodiversity is not distributed evenly across the planet. The most vital hotspots of global biodiversity happen to be located in tropical and subtropical regions that are home to a significant percentage of the global poor, who often depend on using the species-rich areas as grazing lands for their sheep and cattle and many other activities. This makes protection in the Western sense of fencing in large swaths of land as "parks" a difficult proposition. Still, for those who see the "future of nature" at stake, it has become even easier to gloss over the fate of short-term losers of protection measures such as local subsistence farmers, pastoralists, or hunters who seem to be on their way out of history anyway.

However, this perspective vastly underestimates the extent to which the protection of land from human habitation and use has created an entire new category of victims of modernity: "conservation refugees." Charles Geisler, who has coined this term, describes conservation refugees as "victims of planned human interventions at the landscape level, a form of macro-zoning stipulating . . . which human activities are legally permissible and where."[40] Communities affected by protection programs usually have neither the time nor the resources to adjust to the new situation, and are thus often driven into poverty. This problem may get even larger with the importance attributed to protect global biodiversity and the shift in growth in protected areas from rich to poor countries.[41] Although they have somewhat softened their stance, many conservationists still show little patience with locals in remote areas who do not share their expert views on global imperatives and eco-efficient resource management.[42]

From the point of view of concerned citizens in Europe or North America, all this seems of marginal relevance. Many who support the policies of conservationist NGOs believe that the zones of wilderness on earth are shrinking due to industrial development and population pressure. Yet the opposite is true. According to IUCN and the United Nations Environment Program (UNEP), the number of protected areas worldwide grew from around 28,000 in 1982 to 102,000 in 2003. In the same period, the land shielded from any kind of human interference and economic use grew from 8.8 million to nearly 19 million square kilometers, which comes close to the size of the entire United States plus Canada.[43] By multiplying the size of protected areas with human density figures, Geisler estimates that the number of conservation refugees is likely to be higher than the 20 million political refugees counted by the UN a few years ago.[44] Seen from this angle, the global map of "spectacular places," which the WWF considers to be high-priority areas for future conservation efforts, conveys a mixed message: it testifies to the ambition of securing crucial ecological benefits to future generations, but it does not hold out much promise for poor people living today in those areas. Yet these people, too, "are deserving of recognition."[45]

WHALES VERSUS INDIANS

A similar matter fraught with ambivalence is the protection of marine mammals, some of which are threatened by extinction; some, like harp seals in Canada, are not. The moral impulse of modern conservationists is to treat these animals as sacred things, or even, in the case of whales and dolphins, as "people," although "strange people."[46] In this, North American activists always felt close to the worldview of native communities who also revere many animals—although they hunt, kill, and eat them.

Since the 1970s, this apparent contradiction gave rise to a series of unexpected social conflicts. Greenpeace, in particular, had to face a twofold conundrum. A dilemma emerged, first of all, from the desire for a total ban on whaling, which competed with the desire not to antagonize the Alaskan and Canadian Inuit whose livelihood traditionally depends on hunting especially the bowhead whale. Thus, when the decision to campaign for a ban on the bowhead hunt was made, Greenpeace—an organization that loves to display Indian symbols such as the killer whale crest on T-shirts and bumper stickers—became an accomplice in the ongoing process of marginalization and disenfranchisement of some of the last native communities in North America. This situation was further compounded by the fact that the Inuit both in the United States and Canada had achieved a number of political and legal victories that granted them special hunting rights. The U.S. Endangered Species Act of 1973, for example, exempts Alaskan natives from certain conservationist provisions, as long as animals are taken for purposes of consumption or traditional manufacture. As a result, Greenpeace staffers found themselves in the thankless situation of having to argue not only against the practice of whaling, which happened to be a key element of the way of life of native communities, but also against officials in Washington, DC, who appeared to be much more attuned to the voices of indigenous peoples than the self-appointed green activists.

Greenpeace was not prepared to place the Inuit and other hunting peoples on the side of "the evil." Instead, it was argued that science and ethics as understood by Greenpeace was more important than the "short-term cultural priorities" of native communities who hopefully would adjust to the new circumstances. In 1978, a leading campaigner assured the Inuit that they were likely to survive the end of the hunt for bowhead whales, which would always "remain an important part of native cultural history . . . to be recalled in dance and legend rather than in the act itself."[47] What is remarkable about these statements is that they were made by environmentalists from a monological position of power that did not allow them to ask whether their *own* values might be the expression of short-term cultural priorities. From the perspective of indigenous rights advocates, this attitude amounted to an insult. It was not well received that NGOs appeared to pillage native cultures for trendy symbols; and it was seen as a sign of contempt to express hope that First Nations peoples, once they were made to conform to values of the white urban middle class, would continue to produce "dance and legend."

In the meantime, Greenpeace has modified its stance on native hunting practices that are no longer considered necessarily wrongful, if they are sustainable and serve the needs of subsistence. This turn, however, has prompted dissidents to split from Greenpeace and to set up new organizations such as the animal rights group Lynx or the militant Sea Shepherd Conservation Society—groups that do not budge an inch from their principles. During the 1980s, new global campaigns against the import of seal pelts from Canada resulted in the almost complete devastation of some seal-hunting communities in Canada's Northwest Territories. As prices for skins and furs collapsed, welfare payments to these communities went up steeply, together with the rates of domestic violence, suicide, and alcoholism. "In the grip of moral righteousness," Hugh Brody concludes in *Living Arctic: Hunters of the Canadian North*, "animal rights activists have been slow to recognize that their campaign had become a new example of southern, imperialist intrusion."[48]

Once in while, this smoldering conflict between environmental NGOs and indigenous peoples is reignited. In 1998, twenty years after the bowhead controversy between Greenpeace and the Inuit, the Makah Indian tribe, whose members live in the northwestern corner of the state of Washington, decided to resume their ancient custom of hunting a few gray whales—animals that are no longer on the endangered species list. Although this decision was perfectly legal and in spite of the irony that the Makah are the only tribe in the United States whose whaling rights were guaranteed by a federal treaty signed as early as 1855, the hunters had to face stiff and ultimately successful resistance from Sea Shepherd and other conservationist groups. "They want us in the museum," as a member of the tribe's whaling commission complained.[49]

From the foregoing examples, it appears that being other-regarding is perfectly compatible with showing disregard for particular lifestyles of indigenous peoples, even if it is by no means certain that these lifestyles are damaging a public good such as an endangered species. To some extent, the coexistence between a principled other-regarding ethic and the disregard for cultural lifestyles can be traced to the fundamental conflict of human goods, many of which we pursue simultaneously, although they are in conflict or even incommensurable. However, neither the confluence of different goals nor their "tragic" incompatibility is set in stone. In the 1980s some environmental NGOs began to understand that indigenous peoples often have a detailed ecological knowledge that could be helpful in preserving biodiversity and natural resources. To some extent, even the WWF gave in to pressures from indigenous rights movements and advocacy-oriented ecologists and has partly reconsidered its misanthropic view of humans as a calamity befalling a paradise-like nature.[50]

Another problem is internal to the ethics of other-regarding organizations. Staff-driven NGOs with global ambitions are speaking for absent others without a mandate from them. The greater the cultural distance and the knowledge gap, the higher the risk that NGOs advocate causes that are not shared by their supposed beneficiaries, or that they deliver services that are not needed. How can the risk of pointless advocacy and useless service be reduced? One answer is by listening to the dispersed voices of Asia, Africa, Latin America, and Eastern Europe.

NON-WESTERN CONSTRUCTIONS OF EVIL: CORPORATE PIRACY

The emergence of some powerful NGOs in developing countries since the 1990s has often added authenticity and depth to the diagnosis of global social crises. However, insofar as we are talking about NGOs, non-Western organizations share certain structures and passions with their Western counterparts. In particular, they also speak for others, act vicariously, and are deeply engaged in the symbolic labor of representing good and evil. In order to get a sense of similarities and differences between Western and non-Western symbolic practices, I now discuss some prominent environmental groups in India that are active in conflicts over the conservation and use of biodiversity.

A powerful symbol of evil that unites many Western and non-Western groups is "biopiracy." The term was introduced in 1991 by Pat Mooney, director of the Rural Advancement Foundation International (RAFI), in the context of the Uruguay Round of trade negotiations that lasted from 1986 to 1994. The single most controversial issue of these negotiations concerned the establishment of a strengthened and globally uniform intellectual property regime, the key provisions of which have been laid down in the 1994 Agreement on Trade-Related Aspects of Intellectual Property Rights (TRIPS). By expanding both their scope and their authority, TRIPS guarantees property rights in trademarks, copyrights, industrial designs, geographical indications, patents, as well as in plant varieties on a global scale. In this connection, "biopiracy" was introduced as a polemical charge against the concerted efforts by the newly emerged life sciences industry to seek strong intellectual property protection for an increasing range of seeds, pharmaceuticals, and other biotechnological innovations including the human genome itself. Many see these efforts as ultimately aiming at the wholesale privatization of the first links of the food chain and key medical resources. It is feared that, in the long run, this would leave the global poor totally dependent on big business and the vicissitudes of international markets. To make things look even worse, pharmaceutical and agro-chemical companies are using living organisms found on public land in southern regions for the genetic information those organisms contain, thereby creating the impression of turning resources against those who claim to own them.[51] This complex field of intersecting struggles over biodiversity can be broken down into three distinct but closely related conflicts that are fought out in various international fora such as the Conferences of Parties to the Convention on Biological Diversity (CBD), the World Trade Organization (WTO) and the UN Food and Agriculture Organization (FAO). First, there are conflicts over how to best protect biodiversity against ecological degradation. Second, countries like India and many others wish to protect themselves against "biopiracy" and regulate access to genetic resources and plant breeding material, which is of vital importance for the burgeoning biotechnology industry. Third, southern countries have struggled to get privileged access to new biotechnologies in exchange for their genetic resources.[52] Many current attempts to develop a new, postcolonial civil discourse and a new conception of "the good" are revolving around these themes. The "biopiracy" critique inverts the standard critique against infringers of intellectual property rights (IPRs) who in the context of the negotiation of TRIPS were labeled "pirates" by business spokespersons. By using this loaded expression, advocates of a stronger patent regime transformed the mundane economic issue of IPRs into a symbol with powerful moral meanings. Since ancient times the pirate was declared an enemy of mankind itself—*hostis humani generis*—and even relatively recent court rulings in the United States placed the pirate under the same rubric as the "torturer" and the "slave trader."[53] The critics of "biopiracy" are trying to evoke the same connotations with the public.

Although the term "biopiracy"—like the term "biodiversity"—has Western origins, there is a strong South Asian component to its success as a symbol. In 1986, the Indian journalist Claude Alvares, a correspondent for the Third World Network (TWN), published an article titled "The Great Gene Robbery" about a "hostile takeover" of thousands of Indian rice varieties by the Philippine-based International Rice Research Institute (IRRI), an institute that has served to promote agricultural modernization in South and East Asia.[54] The role of the villain in this story is played by the Ford Foundation and its Indian ally, M. S. Swaminathan, distinguished plant geneticist, father of the Green Revolution in India, and a member of the Indian government before being made director of the IRRI in 1982. At the time, word had already been circulating that crops grown in monoculture were, contrary to initial expectations, genetically vulnerable, so that breeders would have to continue to use wild relatives of these crops as sources of disease resistance, vigor, and other traits that are worth billions of dollars in benefits to global agriculture. These traditional crop varieties or "landraces" were maintained and preserved on the fields and in the research institutes of individual countries. Alvares tells the colorful story of the closing of a national agricultural research institute in the Indian state of Madhya Pradesh, the harassment of its patriotic as well as exceptionally gifted director, and finally the removal of some of the institute's nineteen thousand rice varieties by a number of Indians and foreigners at the bidding of the Ford Foundation and the IRRI.

The story, which we are not examining in terms of its veracity,[55] contains almost all aspects of a highly influential civil discourse developed by TWN and its various national affiliates such as the Indian Research Foundation for Science, Technology and Ecology (RFSTE). To begin with, this discourse is directed against the Green Revolution and the modernization consensus found among the Western-educated elite in research and politics, namely those who set the tone in India and other ambitious developing countries. From the very beginning, the modernization consensus in India was fragile, as there was a powerful Gandhian streak of critique of technological progress, consumerism, and other supposedly Western values. Iconic events like the horrific gas leak disaster in the city of Bhopal in 1984, blamed on a subsidiary of an American multinational, have been turned into a powerful symbol of the evil nature of foreign companies in India.

Accordingly, the Green Revolution was not criticized for failing to achieve its promised goals. Instead, Vandana Shiva, a holder of the Right Livelihood Award (the alternative Nobel Prize) and one of its most vocal critics, condemned agricultural modernization as a project based on "foreign" methodologies that were propagated by "foreign" experts.[56] Alvares had left it open whether the "modern" is always "foreign" to India. In contrast, Shiva equates India, the traditional, and the good, and contrasts these symbols with foreigners, the modern, and the evil. Shiva's well-connected, Western-funded Research Foundation popularized the term "biopiracy" and used it to highlight an issue of not only global, but also national concern. In the mid-1990s, major newspapers in India began to arouse public interest with chilling headlines, warning the nation of barbarians at the gate. As the *Times of India* once alarmingly titled a news article, "Biopirates eye $147 billion stake in forests."[57]

Over the years, the symbolic labor of Shiva's NGO consisted mainly in elaborating on the two antagonistic poles of her nationalistic discourse, while insisting on the impossibility of any reconciliation between the forces of good and evil. India is feminine, diverse, creative, caring, life-enhancing; non-India is masculine, monocultural, destructive, predatory, and death loving. Referring to the project of the so-called genetic use restriction technology (popularly known as "terminator" technology) that would prevent farmers to use genetically modified seeds more than once by causing second generation seeds to be sterile, she explained

> There can be no partnership between the terminator logic that destroys nature's renewability and regeneration and the commitment to continuity of life held by women farmers of the Third World. The two worldviews do not merely clash—they are mutually exclusive. There can be no partnership between a logic of death on which [the U.S. corporation] Monsanto bases its expanding empire and the logic of life on which women farmers in the Third World base their partnership with the earth to provide food security to their families and communities.[58]

We are confronted with a public discourse that permits absolutely no shades of gray and, in the process, denies its own ideal of a nonreductionist interpretation of the world. Here is an NGO that has given us almost a cartoon version of Durkheim's definition of religious beliefs. Little wonder that its protagonists did not hesitate to primordialize the Global South as the true source of "life itself."[59]

Initially, the scathing critique leveled by groups of Asian intellectuals against agricultural modernization was only indirectly felt by transnational private companies, as the Green Revolution was a project financed by public institutions and supported by intergovernmental agreements. The situation changed in the late 1980s, when large companies began to press for a strengthening of patent rights and the aggressive implementation of innovations in biotechnology. In response to that, the discourse of the Research Foundation was slightly modified; transnational companies now occupied the role of the principle evildoer. At the 1992 Earth Summit in Rio de Janeiro, multinational corporations were, for the first time, identified as the main culprits behind the global environmental crisis and branded as enemies of "life itself"—enemies in the literal sense that they were suspected to be involved in the "*planned* destruction" of biodiversity.[60]

Curiously, this nationalistic and populist discourse draws on semantic conventions that strongly resonate with the classical discourse of British colonialism. The historian Thomas Metcalf has shown that British colonial literature constantly portrayed India as an irresistible, feminine, and threatening force able to derail the progress set in motion by cool, masculine reason. Also among the obsessions of colonial officers was the view that simple subsistence farmers were gentle and open, unlike city dwellers.[61] Outside of the cities and administrative offices, many Europeans were incapable of seeing the rural female population as anything other than "sinless," "pure," and "innocent" custodians of heavenly gardens.[62]

This is the starting point of the civil discourse popularized by the Research Foundation. The images displayed in its brochures and pamphlets show pastoral settings, located in rural India far removed from big cities; Shiva talks of rustic farmers who invoke the village deity before sowing, offering her the same rice varieties that deceitful patent lawyers are now trying to steal for multinational corporations.[63] Yet all this, and in particular the equivalence of nature, femininity, and the South, forms one of the most persistent components of the colonial imaginary. It is one of the ironies of the emergence of at least a few non-Western NGOs that this imaginary continues to live on in their contribution to a new civil discourse. This irony may also explain some of the strong positive resonance that the South Asian nativism of the Research Foundation and the TWN evokes among Western activists and funders. Thus, the "clash of cultures" conjured up by Shiva does not exist. The Indian affiliate of the TWN projects the image of tropical landscapes unspoiled but mortally threatened by Western technology and vices; those landscapes are populated by people who are essentially different from and superior to the faceless functionaries of the aggressive West. The discourse reaffirms dichotomizing orientalist clichés by simply inverting them and assigning a negative value to everything "Western." My point is that this orientalism in reverse meshes well with the other-regarding ethic prevalent among Western elites and with a popular undercurrent of self-loathing in the West. This constellation also explains the paradox that Western funders see the Research Foundation as an "authentic voice"[64] of Indian protest movements, while Indian agricultural experts characterize the leader of the Research Foundation as a foreign-funded charlatan with no popular basis in her own country.[65]

Non-Western Constructions of Evil: Wicked Officials

It is interesting to observe that the identity-political discourse of the Research Foundation, which perpetuates the colonial cliché of an India forever different and eternally feminine, meets the strongest opposition not in the West, but in India itself. Groups like Gene Campaign or the Centre for Science and Environment (CSE) in Delhi are no less nationalistic, but have chosen to identify "the evil" not (or not only) as originating from outside, but within India. With regard to Western technologies and agricultural progress, the views of Gene Campaign are diametrically opposed to those held by the Research Foundation. While the latter regards genetic engineering and synthetic fertilizers as foreign to Indian culture, Gene Campaign conversely criticizes the idea of "ethical" restraint in using new technologies as pusillanimous and, again, foreign to Indian culture. According to Suman Sahai, director of Gene Campaign, bioethical scruples are in essence a recent Western phenomena and a luxury that developing countries cannot afford. Following this reading, all three historical reasons that have led to the ethical objections to biotechnology currently fashionable in the West are not applicable to South Asia: the history of eugenics and its racist radicalization culminating in the Holocaust; the theological conception of mankind created in the image of God, including the idea of a radical discontinuity between human and nonhuman beings; and the economic prosperity that creates the latitude for ethical consumerism in the first place.[66]

Thus, similar to the Research Foundation, Gene Campaign also detects "fundamental differences"[67] between East and West. Both organizations stress the necessity of doing things differently and better than in the West. Both NGOs are fiercely nationalistic and refer to the same basic set of oppositional terms of pro-farmer versus anti-farmer policies, true science versus junk science, *swadeshi* (self-reliance) versus foreign control.

Yet they come to opposite conclusions about how this symbolic set of Indian civil society should be applied—to the point that they perceive each other as mutant extensions of the evil to overcome. Each organization accuses the other of drawing on discursive imports from the West instead of being based on the *truth* of South Asian culture. In each discourse, the West is ascribed conflicting negative attributes: on the one hand, the propensity to unleash destructive technological forces on the world, and on the other hand, the tendency to overmoralize about technical innovation.[68]

Gene Campaign is an organization that relies on the independent rationalist and modern traditions of South Asia. Whereas the identity politicians of the Research Foundation regard new biotechnologies and the expanded application of property rights to "life" as an infringement on local traditions and values, Gene Campaign repeats the same basic arguments against strict intellectual property rights (IPRs) that were voiced up until around the 1870s by liberal propagandists of free trade in Europe and the United States. The Western discourse on patent protection is rejected as an internationally imposed hurdle against India's economic development. But who is to blame? In retrospect, Gene Campaign largely welcomes the Green Revolution, which has led to an increase in prosperity on the countryside and a reduction in dependence on foreign imports, although it did not result in greater political participation. Similarly, the policy of India's political class to open the country to the global market in line with the requirements of the World Trade Organization (WTO) is not criticized on the ground that India should stay aloof from the rest of the world. Rather, the current model of one-sided market liberalization is seen as an attempt to secure the economic and political monopoly position of the Indian elite. Gene Campaign provides a complex critique of the *sellout* of Indian interests to international organizations by the Indian elite. The central problem consists not of the expansion of Western modernity to non-Western regions, but rather in the withholding of the West's technological achievements through the restrictive practices of intellectual property protection and technology transfer—practices that are harmful to the rise of an independent Indian business class, but benefit the entrenched *bureaucratic* elite of the country.

For Gene Campaign, American and other Western business interests are a threat, but the truly "evil" force is the Indian civil service. A while ago, the director of Gene Campaign depicted this powerful institution in polarizing language. The officials of the Indian Administrative Service were not only declared to be "stupid," "corrupt," and "pompous"; the whole institution was portrayed as irredeemably particularistic and pernicious to the solidaristic core of the nation. Therefore, "they are really deserving the most utter and complete contempt of anybody who is interested in this nation's wellbeing. . . . If there is one group of people who has damaged this country's interests *fatally*, it is *this* group."[69] Similarly, Anil Agarwal, the well-known environmentalist and founder of the Centre for Science and Environment (CSE), who died in 2002, formulated his opposition to the Indian bureaucracy in an interview:

> What CSE is trying to do now is to push for better governance. Better governance in the sense of changing the way our government works in terms of accountability, transparency, devolution of power, in terms of changing the power of the bureaucracy over natural resources. I think the *biggest obstacle* in this country would be the Indian Administrative Service, the IAS. If we get rid of them, we will have a clean environment.[70]

Both Gene Campaign and the CSE see the key evil not in multinational corporations, but in India's corrupt and inefficient civil service, which is repeatedly described as a monstrous, anticivil force. This line of critique goes back to the much older motif of "the wicked official"[71] and the indigenous tradition of peasants and tribals in India to attack representatives of the state whenever they feel the need to defend their livelihood.

Moral Geographies

I propose to wrap up the above discussion by specifying three basic moral geographies that emerge from the symbolic labor of NGOs. Post-traditional moral geographies no longer primordialize the citizens of other countries as uncivil or threatening.[72] Yet, they still distribute victims, evildoers, accomplices, and moral publics along imagined geographical axes.

We have seen that NGOs are involved in larger struggles over universalistic standards of recognition to be applied to others. From a slightly different point of view, they are in the business of identifying harmful acts and conditions as well as those who are responsible for these acts and conditions. Sometimes evildoers are identified as well-defined groups like, for instance, the oil industry or the U.S. government; sometimes they seem to dissolve into much larger, diffuse groups of accomplices. NGOs thrive in societies that have been subjected to phenomena like the Culture Wars in the United States and elsewhere—societies where the elites no longer believe in the transcendent certainties of a national interest or a civilizing mission. Against the background of a culture of institutionalized self-criticism, many NGOs locate evildoers *at home*, in their own domestic societies, while advocating the cause of victims located *abroad*, often in poor, abused or war-torn countries. Campaigns against global warming, landmines, sweat shops, Western oil and mining industries in third world countries, or the rendition of terrorist suspects to countries where they are likely to be tortured are expressions of a firmly institutionalized pattern of Western self-criticism. Self-criticism implies that both the evildoers and the public, which is made to see the evil, are members of the same political community; furthermore, it implies that the evildoers themselves can be "shamed" and thus transformed by virtue of their implicit knowledge of good and evil.[73]

It would be a grave mistake, however, to fit all Western NGOs into this model. I have given examples from the history of the WWF and Greenpeace that suggest that occasionally even reputed organizations have targeted vulnerable and marginalized groups like African pastoralists or Arctic hunters as accomplices in wrongdoing. The model can also degenerate in various forms of paternalism and self-loathing. Blaming our own society for all evil in the world implies that it is exclusively "up to us" to change the world; treating other societies or distant groups like third world farmers or refugee populations only as victims means robbing them of agency and responsibility. On the other hand, the discourse of the Research Foundation in India presents something like the mirror image of a bastardized version of Western self-criticism. The anti-modernism of this organization frames India as a victim and all evil as coming from abroad. From the fact that the language of the organization is English, which is read and spoken only by a small minority of Indian citizens, one can learn that the key public is also being located abroad.

Interestingly, to the extent that they criticize unjust institutions of *their own* society, the two other Indian organizations briefly discussed above escape the grid of table 4.1. However, self-criticism is only a subordinate

Table 4.1 NGOs and their moral geographies

	Located at home	Located abroad
Western self-criticism	Evildoers and key publics	Victims
Third World anti-modernism	Victims	Evildoers and key publics
Western neo-interventionism	Key publics	Evildoers and victims

aspect of the discourse of these groups that are funded by Western agencies for attempting to mollify the effects of reforms imposed by *other* Western agencies.

The bottom row in table 4.1 represents the moral geography of yet another type of contemporary NGOs, which I will further discuss in the next chapter. Groups that I call "neo-interventionist" locate both victims and evildoers mainly abroad, whereas the public to be addressed, informed, and awakened is composed of fellow citizens. This is the classical model of Doctors Without Borders and other post–Red Cross humanitarian organizations. In addition, many human rights and some environmental campaigns fall under this category. In line with the dominant pattern of Western self-criticism, these campaigns also emphasize the facilitating role of willing accomplices and the spineless behavior on the part of mainstream of society, which allows evil things to happen.

(RE)WRITING RULES FOR THE WORLD

Although NGOs typically stay aloof from the divides of conventional politics, their normative discourses are no less divisive. NGOs polarize the public, although usually not along the familiar difference between Left and Right. Polarization in public life is inescapable; the question is only where to draw the line between "us" and "them." Communication in society must be balanced by *regulative* institutions such as the law for two reasons. One reason has to do with the boundlessness of human imagination and the constant need of social groups to affix blame on outsiders, often regardless of the facts and with disastrous consequences for those who are portrayed as responsible for evil. Regulative institutions respond to the unavoidability of polarization and the passions and forces of imagination stoked by it. They help to prevent the disintegration of public life by devising and imposing *rules*—standards of behavior or norms—that are designed to tame the unruly and potentially destructive dynamics of motives and relations shaped by binary codes and symbolizations of evil.[74] NGOs would be much less significant if they were only communicating. Yet, they live in both the worlds of public communication and of rule making: they define, explore, and publicly denounce contemporary forms of evil; and they seek access to international organizations and other decision-making bodies to make evil activities illegal.

Besides the *boundlessness* of human imagination, the *limitations* of human sympathy are a second reason why regulative institutions are essential. Advocates for the global poor have learnt that the publication of statistics on global poverty, diseases, or war casualties does little to shock people into action. Often the opposite is true: the more victims, the less sympathy and compassion. The phenomenon of "psychic numbing" in the face of reported or witnessed mass atrocities teaches us that we cannot rely on the innate morality even of a well-intentioned public.[75] Communicating problems is not enough to effect change; NGOs also work to develop regulative mechanisms to confront violations of rights and the avoidable neglect of basic needs.

In this sense, NGOs are agents of legal and moral change within international society; at a declaratory level, normative changes are often brought about by the United Nations and other international organizations. In some cases, NGOs bypass international organizations in favor of working with broad coalitions of friendly states; the forging of "coalitions of the willing" is not only a prerogative of the last remaining superpower. Frequently NGOs struggle for the creation and enforcement of rules where there are none. Rules are important because victims of broken rules are, as Judith Shklar has remarked, "recognized as such"; whereas victims who "fall entirely outside the reach of public rules"[76] are without status and often not even visible.

This does, of course, not mean that NGOs are happy with any kind of rule. Sometimes they criticize the absence of internationally binding rules, whereas on other occasions they decry the burdens imposed by international rules on distant strangers. In these cases, NGOs do not fight for universal rules, but for flexible thresholds, differential treatment, and exemptions from universal rules. Taking the whole spectrum of approaches to rule making into account, it seems that NGOs follow an old script of civil society in light of which the *loss* of order is to be feared as much as the *excess* of order.[77]

The common denominator of these different strategies of making (and breaking) rules can be found in the pursuit of more and better "harm conventions" that protect others against all three forms of misrecognition: the denial of basic rights, the systematic neglect of needs, and the denigration of ways of life and contributions to the common good. As Andrew Linklater and Hidemi Suganami explain,

> The pluralist society of states can be regarded as the global expression of an ethic which privileges negative over positive obligations in the attempt to reduce the Hobbesian features of international life. What might be called *international harm conventions*—conventions which are designed to prevent harm in relations between states—can work to the advantage of the inhabitants of those states, but this is not always the case and it is therefore essential to develop *cosmopolitan harm conventions* which protect individuals in and of themselves.[78]

This distinction reflects Hedley Bull's more fundamental distinction between international society, which is composed of sovereign states, and a world society composed of individuals as ultimate units. Cosmopolitan harm conventions are not essentially the result of interstate bargaining, but draw also from networks of NGOs and other private actors who are attempting to win over and "infect" states with their messages.[79] Unlike international harm conventions such as arms control or nonaggression treaties, cosmopolitan harm conventions are intended to give moral and political priority to individuals over states. Linklater concedes that the distinction between the two is not always clear-cut. The laws of war, for example, protect states; but they also stipulate that wounded and captured soldiers as well as civilians should be treated simply as humans, regardless of their belonging to any political community.

NGOs are inextricably bound to international organizations in the process of drafting global rules that are supposed to reflect normative ideals of universal justice. Thus, NGOs are neither fully external nor properly internal to the functioning of international organizations, which is the reason why I have called international organizations *hybrid* bureaucracies. On the part of NGOs, rule-making efforts are backed up by a special knowledge about situations of blatant injustice and avoidable suffering. In this section, I examine a number of cases in which NGOs— on the basis of their strategically disseminated specialized knowledge— have contributed either to new *rules*, or to *exceptions* from existing rules. This survey elucidates certain ironic reversals in the pas de deux of rule making between NGOs and international organizations.

Barnett and Finnemore have correctly pointed out that as bureaucracies, international organizations "necessarily flatten diversity because they are supposed to generate universal rules and categories that are by design inattentive to contextual and particularistic concerns."[80] This is mostly true, but not always. On various occasions, delegations in UN treaty negotiations tried hard to customize rules by accommodating differences among states or industries, whereas NGOs struggled for uniform rules. The policy debate about trade in genetically modified seeds or foodstuffs is a case in point. Oftentimes, and in spite of being nonbureaucracies, NGOs helped to generate rigid, uniform, and comprehensive rules or blanket prohibitions of certain practices that were considered harmful. To this day, many NGOs are "abolitionists" in one way or another. Yet there are also cases, as I will show, in which NGOs prefer customized over uniform rules, or exemptions from rules imposed by powerful agencies like the WTO. In a nutshell, it is not that states and international bureaucracies always favor one type of rule while nonbureaucracies favor another type.

From an NGO perspective, the campaigns for the International Criminal Court (ICC), the ban on antipersonnel landmines, and a framework treaty regulating the release of genetically modified organisms (GMOs) have shared the goal of establishing a stiff set of universal rules to be applied rigidly. Advocacy efforts on global greenhouse gas emissions, intellectual property rights (IPRs), or the sanctions policy of great powers, on the other hand, have been about relaxing or customizing rules in light of particular circumstances that were said to warrant a departure from uniformity. Thus, NGOs have lobbied for cosmopolitan harm prevention either by new treaties or by measures designed to mitigate the potentially harmful consequences of existing treaties or policies.

These alternating stances can be demonstrated by briefly examining NGO strategies with regard to the Rome Statute of the ICC (1998), the Mine Ban Treaty or Ottawa Convention (1997), the Biosafety Protocol to the Convention of Biological Diversity (2000), the Kyoto Protocol to the United Nations Framework Convention on Climate Change (1997), the campaign for amendments to the TRIPS Agreement with regard to essential medicines, and various initiatives on economic sanctions and trade embargoes against hostile or rights-violating countries. This list is by no means exhaustive, but it provides an overview of the ways in which NGOs attempt to (re)write rules for international society based on harm assessments and covering a range of recent cases in the fields of human rights, environment, and trade. In all cases, these mechanisms were strongly influenced by NGOs. In some instances, NGOs were crucial for the very definition of the problem to be tackled by these new agreements.

THE INTERNATIONAL CRIMINAL COURT

If NGOs respond to situations in which evil things happen to the innocent, they respond even more strongly to situations in which agents who are liable to blame for causing those evil things can be identified. War crimes or crimes against humanity such as genocide are the most obvious examples.

An international criminal court was on the agenda of human rights NGOs for some time because it is seen as a chance to recalibrate the relationship between state sovereignty and universal justice. Activists such as Aryeh Neier, president of the Open Society Institute and former director of Human Rights Watch, or William Pace, director of the World Federalist Movement, envisioned the international court as a truly supranational institution that would go beyond its predecessors—the post–World War II military tribunals of Nuremberg and Tokyo and the more recent UN sponsored war crimes tribunals for the former Yugoslavia,

Rwanda, Sierra Leone, or Cambodia—in being independent from the Security Council and the corrupting influence of great power meddling. This vision did not materialize. The Statute of the ICC as it was negotiated and adopted in Rome in 1998 constitutes an international institution that preserves the primacy of national legal systems and offers a jurisdictional resort of convenience for the Security Council, whose members can decide to refer a particular "situation" to the ICC. In addition, it empowers a prosecutor who can initiate investigations *proprio motu*, that is, on his or her own authority, independently from the Security Council and even on behalf of nonstate parties who wish to submit relevant information about gross human rights violations and prompt the court into action. Yet this does not entail universal jurisdiction in the sense that the court can prosecute alleged offences anywhere. Only crimes committed in the territory of a state that has ratified the Rome Statute or crimes committed by citizens of a state that has ratified this statute can be prosecuted—unless, as mentioned before, the Security Council refers a case to the court.

Still, the NGOs united in the Campaign for the International Criminal Court have endorsed the outcome of the negotiations as a success, which they believe is at least partly due to their own sustained efforts over many years. The level of access of NGOs to the meetings in Rome has, in fact, been described as "unprecedented" and their influence as "trend-setting."[81] The doors were wide open mostly because NGOs were backed by a coalition of about sixty "like-minded states" from Australia to Venezuela. Why is the ICC considered a success despite the lacking universality of jurisdiction? I see three main reasons.

First, the Rome Statute has strengthened the consensus that certain acts are criminal without exception in all circumstances. Some rights are held by anyone, in any situation, and neither emergencies nor unjust laws or commands absolve individuals and states from the responsibility to respect them. Accordingly, and unlike with other treaties, the statute does not allow reservations. States cannot declare that certain articles do not apply to them, or that they apply only in normal circumstances.

Second, some definitions of crimes have been expanded. As soon as massive human rights violations are "widespread or systematic," they can be read as crimes against humanity.[82] Also, violent sexual acts and imposed conditions such as "rape, sexual slavery, enforced prostitution, forced pregnancy, enforced sterilization, or any other form of sexual violence of comparable gravity"[83] have been outlawed. The same is true for attacks on aid workers or attempts to cut off civilian populations from international aid. While these prohibitions are not without precedent, the statute breaks new ground by defining the military recruitment of children under the age of fifteen as a war crime.

Third, the ICC is institutionalizing the expectation that the uniform rules laid down in its statute will be increasingly respected, even if they cannot yet be enforced universally. The statute is perceived as a *promise* of universal justice, if only because the public salience of the protection of particular rights has been raised. This, it is hoped, will encourage angry forms of public denunciation whenever those rights are violated, which in turn might trigger successive cycles of their legal consolidation.

THE MINE BAN TREATY

NGOs have provided ample evidence that antipersonnel mines are harming innocent victims mostly outside of any conflict. They are designed and used to deny enemies access to certain areas, but remain lethal long after hostilities have ceased. Unlike many other campaigns, the International Campaign to Ban Landmines has focused on odious *things* rather than on *agents* responsible for harming others. Landmines are mostly buried and detonate by foot pressure, causing devastating injuries not only to soldiers but also to civilians. Thousands of children have been killed or sentenced to a lifetime of suffering while at play and roaming; thousands in poor countries have suffered the same fate while farming or collecting firewood. It is for a reason that the initiative to fight landmines came from surgeons of the International Committee of the Red Cross (ICRC) who were shocked at the increase of horrendous landmine victim injuries during the 1980s.

It is important to note that the issue of landmines has not been presented as being primarily about the denial of rights, although many human rights NGOs took up this cause. Despite the powerful tendency in public discourse to translate the fulfillment of every basic need into a right, it was implicitly acknowledged that elementary needs must be fulfilled even they are not covered by enforceable rights. Rights are being invoked whenever people search for somebody who is assigned the duty to do something for the rightholder. Yet, some of the most basic needs of humans are not matched by corresponding legal duties to cater to those needs. There is no legal duty to care for, to love, or even to like somebody, no matter how desperately he or she needs it.[84] This difference between rights and needs is mirrored by the different strategies of human rights and humanitarian groups. The campaign against landmines was above all a humanitarian effort, motivated by an ethic of benevolence.

Accordingly, the main difference between the campaign for the ICC and the International Campaign to Ban Landmines (ICBL) is that divisive issues of responsibility and liability were bracketed out, at least until recently. Instead, every effort was made to focus the attention of the public and of as many decision makers as possible on the humanitarian situations of people who live, work, and move in areas infested with landmines.

The Mine Ban Treaty illustrates the fact that one and the same source of harm can be tackled by either an "international" or a "cosmopolitan" harm convention (as defined by Linklater and Suganami), depending on whether landmines are framed as an arms control issue or a humanitarian and human security issue. The first success of the activists was, in fact, that landmines were made to be seen not as arms with some military value, but as indiscriminate killers.[85] Once this view was widely shared, it was plausible to call for the issue of landmines to be removed from the agenda of arms control meetings, such as the review conferences of the 1980 Convention on Prohibitions or Restrictions on the Use of Certain Conventional Weapons (CCW). Next, a new space for negotiation had to be created in which the goal was no longer to regulate the use and production of antipersonnel mines, but to impose a complete and comprehensive ban on the production and use of landmines.

By this standard, the campaign was a huge success. NGOs persuaded a core group of ten countries (Austria, Belgium, Canada, Germany, Ireland, Mexico, Norway, Philippines, South Africa, and Switzerland) to not allow the call for a total ban to be watered down by concessions to the rest of the world, and they succeeded in getting the majority of states to ratify the new treaty. This was due to the pressure from international NGOs, but also from the desire of a number of small and medium-sized states to increase their moral prestige at the expense of great powers like the United States and others, who at first were reluctant to join the treaty.

THE BIOSAFETY PROTOCOL

The Biosafety Protocol to the UN Convention on Biological Diversity (CBD) deals with the potential risks associated with genetically modified organisms (GMOs) such as transgenic crops that are planted and traded at an increasing rate in the global economy.[86] As a cosmopolitan harm convention, the Biosafety Protocol (or Cartagena Protocol on Biosafety) differs from the aforementioned cases in two respects. First, there is considerable controversy about whether commercially available GMOs are harmful at all and what kind of harm could potentially be caused by the rapidly growing number of biotechnological applications. While proponents of biotechnology tend to downplay risks, many NGOs have warned against adverse environmental consequences that might be triggered, for example, by gene flows from modified organisms to their wild relatives. Much uncertainty also surrounds the question whether and how the use of transgenic seeds could lead to wider and irreversible changes in the dynamic of ecosystems. These changes would be the result of indirect effects that are obviously difficult to predict. Other groups have focused more on possible health risks caused by genetically modified food ingredients. Here again, there seems to be little conclusive evidence about the character and level of risks.

Second, given the uncertainty of the harm caused by GMOs combined with the equally controversial benefits of biotechnology, especially in agriculture, only a few groups called for an outright ban on the trade of transgenic seeds or foods. Instead of a prohibition regime, most actors favored more or less comprehensive regulative schemes.[87] The main fault line during the complex negotiation process ran between exporters and potential or actual importers of transgenic crops and products derived from them, with NGOs taking the side of the importers who were seen to be in harm's way.[88] It is important to realize that this fault line did not simply pit developed against developing countries. Some developing countries such as Uruguay, Chile, and Argentina joined the United States, Canada, and Australia as advocates of general rules designed to facilitate the global trade with GMOs, while the European Union and most of the developing world championed the so-called precautionary principle. This principle stipulates that the burden of proof that a new products or technologies offer no severe harm falls on the proponents of those innovations, unless there is already a scientific consensus that harm would not ensue.

NGOs as different as Greenpeace and the Third World Network have welcomed the protocol because it includes the concept of precaution in its operational provisions. The treaty text stresses the need to carry out risk assessments on modified organisms that are deliberately released into the environment. In order to make this possible, it declares to support developing countries in building regulatory capacities for assessing the biosafety of GMOs. Exporting countries have agreed to the so-called Advance Informed Agreement procedure, which obliges exporters to fully inform importers about possible risks of GMOs and also entitles the importing country to ban genetically modified products from their market, if they consider them hazardous in accordance with established risk assessment procedures.[89] To date, it is not clear who will benefit the most from the vagueness of what constitutes an established risk-assessment procedure. The Biosafety Protocol does not establish the restrictive global framework many NGOs have struggled for. Specifically, it exempts pharmaceuticals and products derived from GMOs (like, for example, GM tomato sauce) from risk assessment provisions; it does not require the labeling of GM foods; and it has so far not established binding rules on liability and redress.

THE KYOTO PROTOCOL

If the issue of war crimes and crimes against humanity to be judged by the ICC lies at one end of the spectrum of NGO concerns, global warming is at the other end. In the first case, there are identifiable perpetrators who harm innocent victims; a complete ban of those crimes seems both feasible and morally imperative. In the case of greenhouse gas emissions, which are believed to be responsible for current changes in global temperatures, we are facing a completely different situation. Responsibility for the harm caused by global warming cannot be pinned on a clear-cut group of perpetrators opposed to groups of innocent victims; perpetrators are likely to become victims themselves, and victims are complicit in the harm that befalls them. Furthermore, most of those who will be most harmed by global warming are not even born yet; climate activists are *other-regarding* in the strongest possible sense as they act vicariously for future generations in the name of intertemporal equity. Another feature of climate activism is that nobody—including the Kyoto Protocol to the United Nations Framework Convention on Climate Change (UNFCCC)—calls for a blanket prohibition of greenhouse gas emissions in spite of the well-established fact that concentrations of these gases in the atmosphere have harmful consequences, such as more frequent floods and droughts. In the face of war crimes and crimes against humanity, abolitionism is the only morally consistent option. It would be ludicrous to suggest that under certain circumstances, massacres or similar actions ought to be contemplated. In contrast, a complete ban on greenhouse gas emissions is no option at all, if only because some potent gases like methane are emitted even from rice paddies.

Thus, climate change activism is about regulating activities that produce, in the long run, accumulative harm without being intrinsically wrong. Global warming also offers a paradigm case for a harm that cannot be interpreted as constituting a denial of rights. Persons do not have rights to particular levels of the seas and oceans, or to particular patterns of rainfall and wind, for two reasons: first, since these goods cannot be delivered at will, there can be no duty to do so; and second, even if there were a duty of some sort, it would be difficult to draw a line between rightholders and dutyholders, because almost everybody contributes to and is likely to be adversely affected by the consequences of a rise in global temperatures—although, of course, to vastly different degrees. Predictably, it has nevertheless been tried to frame global warming as a human rights issue. Together with a group of indigenous Arctic hunters, the Inuit representative Sheila Watt-Cloutier filed a petition in 2005 with the Inter-American Commission on Human Rights claiming that greenhouse gases threatened the existence of Inuit culture and thus violated their "right to be cold."[90] Presumably for the reasons stated above, the commission declined to consider the petition. The harm done by global warming is one that leaves certain needs of people unaddressed, thereby undermining the basic conditions of self-confidence; yet it does not constitute a human rights violation.

In proposing elements of a cosmopolitan harm convention, the Climate Action Network (CAN), a global coalition of environmental NGOs, subscribed to the "principle of historical responsibility": industrialized countries, which have produced most of the greenhouse gases accumulated in the atmosphere, must act first to reduce their emissions. This principle exempts the G77 group of developing countries plus China from reduction obligations. Thus, CAN welcomed the United Nations Framework Convention on Climate Change (UNFCCC), which has called for a stabilization of greenhouse gas emissions at 1990 levels for all industrialized countries. Subsequently, CAN was also successful in its push for fixed targets and timetables. Under the Kyoto Protocol, industrialized countries committed themselves to emissions reductions of an average of 5 percent by 2010. This was widely celebrated as a victory over the fossil fuel industry and its allies among governments and trade unions. NGOs such as WWF and Greenpeace have criticized and promised to plug a number of perceived "loopholes," such as possible accounting tricks on carbon sinks. The other major concern of climate activists was how to deal with cases of repeated noncompliance with the targets and timetables of the protocol in the absence of strong global enforcement mechanisms. To date, this problem has not been resolved.

TRIPS REVISION

So far I have sketched a few examples of cosmopolitan harm conventions to showcase key areas of NGO activity. My last two examples illustrate cases where NGOs have become active in order to mitigate potentially harmful consequences flowing from established global economic rules. Recent attempts to amend the 1994 Agreement on Trade-Related Aspects of Intellectual Property Rights (TRIPS), which is overseen by the

World Trade Organization (WTO), are a case in point. During and after the negotiations leading to this agreement, many activists have claimed that intellectual property rights (IPRs) on medicines and plant varieties may threaten the enjoyment of human rights, like the right to health, food, or even self-determination.[91]

In the 1990s, these ideas about the potential antagonism between IPRs and human rights were turned into a tool for mobilization. Interestingly enough, this process was spurred by one particular crisis that had repercussions not foreseen by the drafters of the TRIPS Agreement: the global AIDS epidemic. In 2005 alone, HIV/AIDS killed more than three million people, most of them in the developing world, particularly in southern Africa. Yet the protest against possible negative consequences of the TRIPS Agreement started first as a local concern in the West. In the mid-1990s, consumer activists in the United States began to protest the TRIPS Agreement, which they saw as leading to further price hikes for medicines, thereby making health care even less affordable for poor citizens. This initial campaign gained enormous momentum and became global when, shortly afterwards, the South African Treatment Action Campaign (TAC) in alliance with Doctors Without Borders (MSF), Oxfam, and others began to draw a connection between the granting of product patents for pharmaceuticals, the ban of parallel imports of cheaper generic substitutes for patented AIDS drugs, and the avoidable death of people living with the virus. Overall, the Campaign for Access to Essential Medicines, as it soon became known, was remarkably successful in drawing attention to the human rights implications of stronger patent regimes for the treatment of HIV/AIDS, in naming and shaming powerful pharmaceutical lobbies, and in encouraging poor countries to seek amendments of the TRIPS Agreement.[92]

The conventional humanitarian narrative is modeled after the analogy of the good swimmer (the West) who is morally obliged to rescue the drowning child (innocent third world victims) who fell into the swimming pool, because it is easy for him to do so. Yet the Access Campaign has modified this analogy by accusing the industrialized countries of not just *failing to benefit* the drowning child, but of actively *harming* her, without being responsible for the bad situation she was already in. Instead of pulling the child out of the water, the good swimmer has (perhaps inadvertently) switched on the one-hundred-horsepower pump for artificial wave generation, making it more difficult for the child to reach the rim of the pool. That is why Zackie Achmat, director of TAC, has stirred the global public against a looming "holocaust against the poor."[93]

Treatment of people suffering from HIV/AIDS is possible thanks to drugs, in particular, antiretrovirals. Product patents tend to increase the price of antiretrovirals, which results in fewer people being able to afford them. Some countries like India produce generic equivalents of patented antiretrovirals that are much cheaper, yet TRIPS has made the "parallel import" of generic versions of patented drugs illegal or very cumbersome. In late 2005, however, member states of the WTO, including the United States, decided to make permanent a waiver enabling poor countries, in particular those with inadequate production facilities, to obtain such generics by setting aside the original TRIPS provision. Among other things, competition from producers of generics is likely to force brand name firms to lower their prices, which allows for more people to be treated. In fact, prices for antiretrovirals in poor countries have *fallen*; the number of people on antiretroviral therapy has massively *increased*; and overall access to AIDS drugs is *expanding*.[94] All this amounts to a limited success for the NGOs involved in the Access Campaign. Other NGOs have made some headway in helping to institutionalize two new rights that are still largely aspirational, but might be developed into creating further exemptions from global IPRs: farmers' rights and traditional resource rights.

The concept of *farmers' rights* emerged from discussions in the late 1980s in the UN Food and Agricultural Organization (FAO) in response to strengthened legal protection of plant varieties and breeders' rights, sometimes explicitly with reference to the right to food. The concept also entered the 2001 International Treaty on Plant Genetic Resources for Food and Agriculture. Farmers' rights are socioeconomic rights invented to entitle farmers—particularly small farmers in developing countries—to measures in support of their, so far, largely underrated contributions to the conservation and cultivation of agricultural plant varieties. The concept of *traditional resource rights* was developed by Western activists in collaboration with indigenous groups, again mostly in response to imbalances in the modern patent and plant variety protection systems that recognize certain forms of creative activity but not others.[95] Resource rights, which are also still largely aspirational, have moved to center stage recently. This is partly because of cases that proved the usefulness of indigenous knowledge in identifying compounds in plants that were later used to develop potentially lucrative pharmaceutical drugs.

SANCTIONS AND EMBARGOES

Trade embargoes and economic sanctions against states have been used throughout modern history, either as an accompaniment or a substitute for the use of military force. In the list of examples I have discussed so far, sanctions and embargoes occupy a special place because they are designed to *inflict* harm on states and national economies, but only in order to encourage compliance with established rules, which are often international harm conventions such as nonproliferation treaties or peace accords. Thus, we are dealing with planned "harmful" actions that are undertaken for "good" reasons. In such situations, it seems, harming is quite different from wronging.

Yet during the 1990s, sanctions increasingly drew fire from churches, medical experts, and NGOs. MSF openly began to challenge some international sanctions, even risking violent clashes with peacekeeping forces. For instance, MSF interpreted the 1993 UN embargo on a territory in northern Liberia, which was controlled by an infamous rogue militia, as an illegitimate attempt to withhold even the most basic relief goods in order to achieve a political goal. Following their creed, MSF operatives entered the forbidden territory in April that year with two aid convoys that were then attacked by Alpha Jets of the peacekeeping forces.[96] Somewhat less spectacularly, European Caritas organizations tried to open a chink in the Western sanctions regime against the Serbian dictator Milosevic by supplying heating oil to Serbian towns in 1999, thereby defying the "oil for democracy" plan agreed on by EU foreign ministers, which had made the supply of oil contingent on the readiness of Serbian communities to turn against the government.

The single most important catalyst for questioning comprehensive sanctions was the worsening humanitarian situation in Iraq after the 1991 Gulf War. Networks like the Campaign Against Sanctions on Iraq (CASI), which was founded by students at the University of Cambridge, England, bolstered their case by citing extremely worrying health assessments on the situation in Iraq. In the late 1990s, the U.S.-based group Peace Action flatly called for the "abolition" of comprehensive sanctions. Many others, including a number of United Nations officials, shared the view that the imposition of nonmilitary sanctions against Iraq was to a large extent responsible for deepening the suffering of the civilian population without achieving lasting changes in the behavior of the regime. Interestingly, most NGOs blended utilitarian and principled lines of critique: one line of critique was directed against the ineffectiveness of comprehensive sanctions in bringing about the desired political changes, which implies that people were seen as being made to suffer for nothing; the other critique invoked human rights and criticized the sanctions policy of the UN Security Council and the United States on the ground that no international treaty regulates the use of sanctions. Consequently, their imposition was said to be an expression of the arbitrary rule of great powers and their willful neglect of the needs of defenseless human beings. Some groups have lambasted comprehensive sanctions as a "weapon of mass destruction" and the United States as a "baby killer," while others confined their critique to stating the complicity or "indirect responsibility" of the American government for creating avoidable and senseless suffering.[97]

To date, all these campaigns have achieved only limited success in light of consistent efforts toward "smart sanctions" that try to exempt the civilian population or certain goods such as food and medicine from unilateral or multilateral sanction regimes. However, the abolition of sanctions and trade embargoes is not on the horizon; nor is any great power willing to subject its sanctions policy to a universal treaty.

Table 4.2 presents key elements of the six cases sketched above: the type of harm NGOs struggled to prevent, the type of goal to be achieved by proposed new rules or exemptions to established rules, and the extent to which this goal could be realized. I have questioned the assumption that only international organizations, by virtue of their bureaucratic character, are devising uniform rules for international society that do not accommodate differences among those who are supposed to follow those rules. Sometimes this is the case, and NGOs seek to influence rule-making bodies with the goal of mitigating the pathologies that inevitably result from applying rigid universal rules to an increasingly diverse and multifaceted social reality (the examples of the Kyoto Protocol, TRIPS, and various sanction regimes). But sometimes it is the other way around, and NGOs take the initiative to propose uniform rules or prohibitions that do not allow for individualized solutions or any fine-tuning (the examples of the ICC, the Mine Ban Treaty, and the Biosafety Protocol). In chapter 6, I will get back to the question of what accounts for the different levels of success of these campaigns.

TAMING AND BACKING THE SOVEREIGNS

At this point, I wish to take up again the concepts of "global civil society" and "Empire" as ways of framing the activities of post-traditional associations. The global civil society literature describes NGOs and transnational social movements as independent agents capable of taming sovereign states and other powerholders. The neo-Marxist literature, by contrast, casts NGOs as backers and instruments of hegemonic states. Each of these theories contains a kernel of truth; both have, with repetition, become clichés. Are NGOs taming or backing, weakening or strengthening states? The short answer is that NGOs do both, depending

Table 4.2 Cases of cosmopolitan harm prevention: The NGO perspective

	Harm	Goals	Goals achieved
ICC Statute	Denial of rights	Uniform and universally enforceable prohibitions	Uniform, but not (yet) universally enforceable prohibitions
Mine Ban Treaty	Neglect of needs	Uniform global prohibition	Uniform regional prohibition
Biosafety Protocol	Neglect of needs	Uniform global prohibitions; comprehensive regulatory rules	Regulatory rules with loopholes
Kyoto Protocol	Neglect of needs	Exemptions; enforceable regulatory rules	Exemptions; non-enforceable regulatory rules
TRIPS revision	Denial of rights; denigration of ways of life	Customized rules; exemptions from prohibitions	Some exemptions from prohibitions
Sanctions and embargoes	Neglect of needs; denial of rights	Uniform global prohibitions; exemptions	Some exemptions

on the circumstances. Taming the sovereigns by making them subject to clear and consistent rules is obviously a priority concern for many organizations, campaigns, and initiatives. Yet taming is not necessarily the same as weakening. The global civil society model posits that NGOs and new global social movements flourish against the horizon of a sovereign state that is "passing away"[98] into the sunset. But this assumption is wrong on two counts. First, the fact that states cannot control everything they want to control does not mean that they are no longer the ultimate units of international society; transnational flows of goods, people, and ideas do not lead to the erosion of the *norms* of sovereignty and territorial integrity, which in some respects have even been reinforced in recent decades.[99] Second, theorists of global civil society often ignore evidence indicating that NGOs often empower, support, and legitimize state action. This counterintuitive claim is at odds with the conventional wisdom that NGOs are gaining influence *at the expense* of states.

In order to understand how NGOs support states, either consciously or inadvertently, it is important to start from the observation that a central part of the activity of NGOs consists in assigning different kinds of responsibilities to different actors. We know already that NGOs are eager to identify evildoers who are blamed for having caused the suffering of others. They are held morally responsible for harming innocent victims. Since the time of the antislavery movement, activists have tended to erase the distinction between moral and causal responsibility, or between harming as wronging and behaviors that are harmful, but justified.[100] For instance, there seemed to be nothing more harmless than buying an ounce of pipe tobacco in early nineteenth-century London, although every such local act contributed through a long and convoluted chain of transactions to the perpetuation of the Atlantic system of slavery, as abolitionists were anxious to point out. The notion of unknowing complicity was invented by abolitionists precisely to narrow down the difference between those who were morally responsible for the slave system and large sections of the general public who bore at least a share of causal responsibility for that system.

At this point, it is helpful to introduce the related concept of *remedial* responsibility. According to David Miller, "[to] be remedially responsible for a bad situation means to have a special obligation to put the bad situation right, in other words to be picked out, either individually or along with others, as having a responsibility towards the deprived or suffering party that is not shared equally among all agents."[101] In real life, the remedial responsibility often falls on the shoulders of those who are morally (and causally) responsible for the creation of a bad situation. A good example is the Polluter Pays Principle, which says that whoever causes environmental damage has to pay for the cleanup. However, moral activists are frequently confronted with situations where the responsibility to remedy a harm cannot be assigned to the individuals or groups who have done the harm. This is obviously the case whenever not only the victims, but also the perpetrators of crimes are dead. Memory activists in post-totalitarian societies (for example, the Russian group Memorial) are seeking remedies for the wounds of the past without being able to point to living perpetrators. In other situations, NGOs themselves take on certain remedial responsibilities by delivering aid to earthquake victims or by saving oiled seabirds after tanker spills. Or they pin these responsibilities on the larger public, which is called upon to engage in boycotts or help fund relief efforts.

All this does not work, however, in much of the field of human rights activism, where the disjunction between moral and remedial responsibility is particularly visible. Here the familiar situation is that those who are most responsible for gross violations of human rights are the least likely to prosecute the crimes, to compensate victims, and to repair the moral fabric of the society.[102] What makes things worse is that in international society there is no legal mechanism that automatically assigns the task of dealing with the situation created by massive human rights violations to a court or a police force. Under such circumstances, in which nobody is formally in charge to act, NGOs set out to create the normative conditions for powerful states to fill the vacuum by intervening from the outside. In other words, NGOs contribute to the redefinition of the norms regulating the use of force. The power of the United States, in particular, is perceived by many NGOs as a reality to be harnessed, not resisted.[103] The humanitarian interventions in the 1990s in Somalia, Bosnia, and elsewhere, for example, were partly the result of lobbying efforts that helped to overcome the reluctance against using military force for other-regarding, cosmopolitan purposes.[104] This is true for the United States, but also for France. When a parliamentary commission in Paris investigated the behavior of the French government during the 1994 genocide in Rwanda, the program director of MSF-France for Africa, Jean-Hervé Bradol, stated that when confronted with crimes against humanity, foreign democracies should intervene to stop them. And as if he was afraid of being misinterpreted, he specified the kind of intervention he had in mind: "We asked for a military operation to stop the killers, not for a military-humanitarian one."[105] Again, during the Bosnia crisis, MSF was not opposed to the deployment of French or other troops. Rather, the organization was interested—particularly after the fall of Srebrenica in 1995—in ensuring that never again soldiers will be deployed who are then "destined to remain tied, hand and foot, in the face of criminal policies."[106]

Less exceptional (and hence less widely reported) situations arise when international NGOs put pressure on target states to reassert their sovereign power in the face of domestic wrongdoing. Greenpeace, for example, wants governments to crack down on "illegal loggers," "corrupt officials," and other evildoers—and sometimes governments have indeed responded to such pressure.[107] The WWF assists national governments in conservation efforts by providing resources to survey and monitor endangered species, migration patterns, and the illicit trade in them. Some groups critical of the WTO and the World Bank want their own countries to withdraw from or curb the power of international organizations that are perceived as threats to the sovereignty of the nation-state. The anti-corruption NGO Transparency International fights for the consolidation of rational administrative structures throughout the world by publishing a highly influential Global Corruption Barometer and a Bribe Payers Index, among other things. Human rights organizations have demanded that European governments get tough on Rwandan genocide suspects living in Europe by tracking and prosecuting them.[108] Women's rights groups have promoted a wide range of measures from the stricter regulation of travel agents to the training of law enforcement officers and border-control personnel in order to combat trafficking of would-be prostitutes or sex slaves.[109]

All these examples are about NGOs struggling either to legitimize corrective state action for remedying gross injustices or to improve the capacity of states to take such action. In light of this, it is difficult to accept the much-repeated claim that NGOs "oppose" or "challenge" sovereign states. At best, this appears to be a half-truth. The reality is that as they are searching for qualified agents who are capable of taking on remedial responsibilities; NGOs regularly pick powerful sovereign states as the most promising candidates. The first reason is that past perpetrators are often unable to remedy the bad situation they have created, so a "forward-looking" approach is needed.[110] The second and most basic reason is that NGOs cannot enforce the good rules they help to devise. Occasionally, fringe conservationist groups have made quixotic attempts at using force against whaling vessels by throwing smoke bombs and bottles on the decks, but this has been an exception. For NGOs to win, it is not enough for them to generate new rules for international society; they also have to change the secondary rules that regulate the use of force by sovereign states.

Again, saying that NGOs encourage states to assert their power does not mean that they are subservient to the predefined interests of the powerful. Rather, post-traditional civil associations influence the norms of state conduct in an age where the "national interest" has ceased to be a self-evident guidepost. While NGOs mobilize to change the minds of those who are, often unwittingly, complicit in evil, they demand forceful approaches from states against corrupt officials, poachers, human traffickers, and *génocidaires*. This peculiar dialectic of challenging and bolstering sovereign statehood becomes clearer if we take a brief second look at several of the NGO-influenced treaties and protocols discussed above.

THE ICC AND THE INDISPENSABILITY OF THE USE OF FORCE

NGOs lobbying for the ICC hoped to create an institution powerful enough to send a strong signal to states and individuals responsible for massive atrocities and human rights violations. The normative vision was one of taming sovereignty by ending the international consensus that sovereignty means impunity for certain kinds of harm done to others. It was further hoped that the prospect of punishment would serve as a deterrent to ruthless political powerholders in the future. NGOs successfully lobbied for a strong prosecutor who has the authority to initiate prosecutions. The ICC is, in fact, a court that is authorized to indict suspects without or against the will of states.

Two cases help to illustrate the enormous practical difficulties bedeviling the court. The first case regards the investigation against the leadership of the Lord's Resistance Army (LRA) in northern Uganda that was undertaken by the ICC beginning in 2004 at the behest of the Ugandan government. The LRA is a bizarre and brutal rebel group funded by Sudan that, among other atrocities, has forcibly recruited thousands of children as soldiers, often after killing their parents.

From the point of view of the ICC and its supporters, this case of a self-referral posed a number of unexpected problems. One problem was that the arrest warrants issued by the ICC against five leaders of the LRA complicated the peace process within Uganda. In addition, there was the question of who would execute the arrest warrants. Various candidates were named, among them the Ugandan army, which had tried and failed to capture or kill the LRA commanders over many years in spite of its heavy-handed methods, and United Nations peacekeeping troops in Congo and southern Sudan. The French government even suggested that NGOs on the ground should help to hunt down the LRA. So far, none of these proposals has proved satisfactory in practice. States are unwilling or unable to add teeth to the new rules of international criminal justice, while local NGOs are torn between the necessity to appear neutral in order not to jeopardize their presence on the ground and the desire to lobby governments into pursuing justice through the exercise of power.

Also, the referral of the situation in Darfur, Sudan by the Security Council in March 2005 engendered much initial euphoria that did not last long. According to some counts, more than two hundred thousand people have been killed since 2003 in a government-controlled campaign of ethnic cleansing or possibly even genocide against ethnic groups in western Darfur. The ICC prosecutor opened investigations against the government of Sudan but had to rely on evidence existing outside of Sudan because the Sudanese government had no intention in cooperating with external forces seen as a threat to its survival. For the same reason, the Sudanese government objected to the deployment of a UN-mandated peacekeeping force that might one day be authorized to arrest members of the government in Khartoum.[111] Like the ICC itself, NGOs sympathetic to the idea of universal jurisdiction have to face the reality of a sovereignty-based international society in which the independence of an eager prosecutor in a faraway European capital counts for little, as long as he cannot persuade powerful states to assist in bringing criminals to justice.

Thus, the paradox is that in order to challenge sovereign statehood, NGOs and the institutions they have helped to create must think hard about how to strengthen and mobilize it.

The Mine Ban Treaty and the Unassailability of Sovereignty

The Mine Ban Treaty has more of an unambiguously "taming" effect on the exercise of state sovereignty because the countries that ratified the treaty can improve the global situation by beginning *at home* to destroy their stockpiles of landmines and to prohibit the production and transfer of landmines. Also, some of those states that did not join the treaty, notably the United States, still fulfill many of the normative expectations of the treaty by increasing their funds for mine detection and demining and by eliminating most of those landmines from their arsenal that are not self-deactivating ("dumb"). Moreover, the United States has no intention to sabotage the treaty in the same way it has attempted to sabotage the ICC. Yet the case also shows that the NGOs engaged in this campaign both exaggerate their independence from states and downplay the extent to which their influence is limited by state sovereignty. According to its advocates, the entering into force of the Mine Ban Treaty demonstrates that "small and medium-sized states can, in partnership with global civil society, overcome great power opposition: the U.S. does not always have to lead in the new post–Cold War environment."[112] This assertion contains a truth as well as an illusion.

The truth is that the dividing line in both the conflicts over the ICC and the ban on landmines did not run between morally enlightened NGOs and power-hungry governments, but between small and middling powers plus NGOs on the one side, and great powers plus smaller countries in war-prone regions on the other side. If we dig a little deeper, it becomes clear that activist governments were more important in the whole process than NGOs are willing to concede. One of the most remarkable features of the negotiation process was indeed the closeness between the highly centralized ICBL and the Canadian government, which consistently "championed and steered the issue" with much determination.[113] Both sides held joint press conferences; the Canadian government openly referred to NGOs as a source of information and encouraged other governments to include NGOs on delegations to negotiation meetings. For Norway, researchers have described a similar dynamic between activist civil servants and NGOs.[114] At the root of this harmonious relationship is the "high resonance of goals"[115] between some governments and the NGO community. In this sense, NGOs proved to be backers of state sovereignty and partners in the pursuit of medium and small-sized countries to redefine themselves as other-regarding powers.

Far from demonstrating the primacy of global civil society over the world of states, the anti-landmine campaign is also one more showcase example of how a praiseworthy moral effort *runs aground* on powerful states instead of "overcoming" them. China, Russia, India, Pakistan, Israel, and others did not even consider a comprehensive ban on landmines. The United States does not allow foreign powers and moral zealots to decide on its arms arsenal. Another rarely mentioned nonparty to the treaty is Finland, which wants to keep mines to protect its long border with Russia; still, the country has been persuaded into accepting the slow phasing out of the deployment of landmines—which, according to officials, might then be replaced by cluster bombs.

The Biosafety Protocol and the GMO Cold War

As many states have committed themselves to implementing the concept of precaution in trade laws, the Biosafety Protocol to the Convention on Biological Diversity (CBD) has contributed to the taming both of sovereign states and of nonstate actors like multinational corporations. With regard to developing countries, NGOs struggled to enhance state power so that countries would be able to assess possible dangers of new biotechnological applications and protect their people. Broadly speaking, however, NGOs played only a minor role in a global conflict that was likened to a "cold war" between the United States and the European Union over GMOs and agriculture in world trade.[116] This cold war has led to pressures on developing countries to take sides, and NGOs have largely been part of this pressure. Germany, for example, has over many years channeled funds through the Protestant Church Development Service (EED) to Vandana Shiva's anti-biotech NGO, which advocates the wholesale transformation of Indian agriculture by using nothing but "cow dung" as a fertilizer.[117] Many Western NGOs were happy to point to their foreign-funded political clones as voices of the "Global South" and did not spend much time on researching the highly diverse interests of the countries and farmers on whose behalf they were speaking. As NGOs have lobbied for the Biosafety Protocol, which is considered a counterweight against unchecked free trade in a particular category of controversial products, they have contributed to the strengthening of the regulatory powers of nation-states vis-à-vis powerful private actors and the WTO. However, to the extent that the have uncritically supported one side of the GMO cold war, they have also exploited the fact that many developing countries are weak and vulnerable to external pressures.

THE KYOTO PROTOCOL AND THE MORALITY OF GREENHOUSE GAS EMISSIONS

In campaigning for the ICC and the ban on landmines, NGOs formed close professional bonds with officials and experts from some states in order to oppose officials and experts from other states. This contradicts the notion of a global civil society at loggerheads with states as such. Similarly, advocacy in the lead-up to the Kyoto Protocol has once more proven that NGOs entertain close relationships with like-minded states, although they are not handmaidens of the West or an imaginary Empire. After all, climate NGOs endorsed the concept of "common but differentiated" responsibility and had no qualms with *exempting* the G77 and China altogether from any emission reduction targets. Yet from a more regional perspective, it could well be argued that NGOs supported not just a cosmopolitan cause, but also single states and their specific interests. Aynsley Kellow has demonstrated that Greenpeace happens to support the policies of those northern European countries—Germany, the Netherlands, Switzerland, and Britain—whose citizens provide most of the funds for the organization.[118] For example, Greenpeace has uncritically accepted 1990 as the baseline year with which all subsequent emissions levels of countries are compared. Yet the choice of this year was far from arbitrary; it massively advantages Germany, since it coincides with the year of German reunification and hence the beginning of the contraction of industrial activity and energy consumption in the former German Democratic Republic.[119]

More importantly, by throwing their weight behind the Kyoto Protocol as it stands, Greenpeace and other NGOs have *decoupled* causal and moral responsibility for global warming. The Kyoto Protocol is designed to tackle *current* emission levels and does not take into account the carbon dioxide emissions that have been accumulated in the atmosphere *over time* since the beginning of industrialization. A truly cosmopolitan policy would have put the heaviest burden on early industrializers like Germany and Britain, since these countries have contributed more to the cumulative total emissions than late industrializers. But this proposal, which would have narrowed the gap between causal and moral responsibility to the disadvantage of Europe, was not made by Greenpeace, but by official negotiators from Brazil.[120] These observations cast further doubts on the twin claims that NGOs are by their very nature *challengers* of states and that they are always morally *superior* than states or other actors.

The Delhi-based Centre for Science and Environment (CSE), probably the most influential and best-connected environmental NGO in South Asia, has gone one step further by not even pretending to defend cosmopolitanism against the nation-state. As the two directors wrote some time ago, "In a world that is still extremely unequal in terms of power, knowledge and wealth, the framework of nationalism cannot yet be given up in favour of unbridled internationalism."[121] Consequently, CSE did not just set out to strengthen the position of India in international climate negotiations; the organization wanted to bolster India's very claim to autonomy as a sovereign state and its right to development. Of course, as a science-oriented environmental group, CSE has been well aware that greenhouse gas emissions are in all likelihood responsible for harmful climate changes. However, its members developed a discourse that made some emissions appear morally defensible, while others are considered blameworthy. In response to a widely circulated report by the independent World Resources Institute (WRI) in Washington, DC, the Centre strongly objected to the suggestion that all greenhouse emissions were readily comparable across cultures and countries. From a global justice perspective, it would be more reasonable, the CSE argued, to calculate emissions not per country, but on a per capita base. Each human being should have an equal share of the global greenhouse budget. More importantly, the CSE advocated drawing a line between "survival" emissions, which are a by-product of activities like rice cultivation, and "luxury" emissions related to the use of cars or air conditioners.[122]

Leaving aside the question of whether this discourse is entirely plausible, it clearly helped India and other G77 countries to redefine their national interest in the uncharted terrain of international climate negotiations. Indian officials, in particular, read the CSE report as an encouragement to insist on their "right to *increase* greenhouse gas emissions."[123] India and China even excised language from the Kyoto Protocol that would have encouraged voluntary self-commitments to curb emissions. This case is the strongest example I could find for an internationally oriented and financed NGO that has not only strengthened a state, but was instrumental in restructuring the national interest of the state.

Summary

This chapter started by highlighting the pathfinder role of the antislavery movement for contemporary post-traditional civil associations. Activists described the Atlantic slave system as a man-made injustice for which certain categories of people bore responsibility: they assigned moral responsibility for the evil of slavery not only to slaveholders themselves, but also to the public of knowing "spectators" and a broad range of accomplices. Whoever bought sugar "made by slaves" was liable to be blamed for supporting an odious system. The flip side of this critique was a strong concept of common humanity. I have also argued that the abolitionist experience is interesting because the protagonists described and opposed the whole range of forms of misrecognition as they have been conceptualized by modern thinkers like Axel Honneth and others. Apart from the obvious denial of rights, social critics were acutely aware of the neglect of care for black laborers and their families, the denigration of their labor, and the willful disruption of primary relationships by masters and overseers.

Drawing on a distinction introduced by Jeffrey Alexander, I have elaborated on how NGOs, in the footsteps of the abolitionists, are active both in the fields of communicative and in regulative institutions. As communicators they are investing in the creation of new civil discourses that are replacing classical divide between friends and foes with a new divide between victims of harmful actions and agents responsible for these actions. Like traditional political ideologies, these new discourses play an important role in typifying societies, events, and actions in terms of binary codes of good and evil. My thesis is that in many ways, NGOs have overcome the tradition of essentializing an evil Other, which explains harmful actions as the predictable outcome of the nature of groups, classes, and nations. This disincarnation of evil can be read as a symptom of moral progress. Yet, post-traditional associations continue to symbolically divide the world into good and evil, even if they concentrate on actions and events instead of actors and essences. In particular, I provided examples of how environmental NGOs secularized the religious metaphor of pollution by blending it with its literal referent.

In my brief discussion of Western environmentalism, I showed that while environmental NGOs are mindful of the undesirable side effects of modernization processes, their own actions and programs have sometimes produced harmful consequences of their own. Thus, NGO-supported nature conservation efforts have driven countless subsistence farmers and pastoralists off their lands, thereby creating a whole new category of conservation refugees in countries that are already poor and vulnerable; similarly, global anti-hunting campaigns and boycotts have seriously damaged the prospects for survival of indigenous communities in the North America. Ironically, in the case of animal rights campaigns, national governments with indigenous constituencies proved to be more open to the needs of these minorities and were thus morally more advanced than certain NGOs—at least if we concede that under most circumstances, human rights trump the concern for nonhumans.

The examples of environmental activism in India discussed in this chapter are interesting for other reasons. Some influential groups engage in a discourse that is meant to be anticolonial, although a closer reading reveals that it caters to colonial stereotypes, which have returned in a green disguise among Western publics. Much of the discourses I have presented are nationalistic in the full nineteenth-century sense of the term. Yet there is also an undertow of self-criticism, expressed more in personal interviews than on Web sites, that is directed against "wicked officials" and others who are blamed as much or even more so than "wicked" foreigners for damaging societies and environments in the Global South.

Like international organizations, and often in conjunction with them, NGOs go beyond describing and denouncing injustices by lobbying for binding rules designed to prevent harm. More precisely, one of the key activities of all modern NGOs is the struggle for cosmopolitan harm conventions that protect individuals regardless of their belonging to a state or a cultural or religious community. I examined six cases of treaties and other policy measures to show how NGOs advocated different kinds of rules in order to maximize benefits for perceived victims. My point here has been to illustrate that the preferences of different actors—states, international organizations, NGOs—for different types of rules change according to circumstances. NGOs, in particular, have opted for comprehensive, exceptionless rules and global bans in the conflicts over the International Criminal Court, the use of landmines, and the Biosafety Protocol, and for customized rules, differential treatment, and generous exemptions in the fields of climate change policies, global intellectual property protection, and the sanctions policies of great powers.

The last section of this chapter is devoted to the key question about the relationship between states and NGOs. I have made the rather counterintuitive argument that NGOs tend to strengthen states instead of weakening them. Clearly, their overall program is to tame the exercise of sovereign power. Yet, in their search to find agents who can remedy bad situations, NGOs often choose states that are pressured to discharge newly defined obligations, even if those states were not causally and morally responsible for the creation of the bad situation. Essentially, state power is seen as both the problem and the solution. Instead of simply challenging state power in the name of "global civil society," NGOs are caught in a peculiar dialectic of taming and backing sovereignty.

CHAPTER 5

WHERE DO NGOS SEEK INVOLVEMENT?

SHIFTING ISSUE AREAS

The question of *where* NGOs become active requires different answers depending on whether we talk about thematic areas, geographical scales, or physical places that can be located on maps. The Statistics Division of the United Nations (UNSD) looks at the first of these meanings by classifying NGOs according to their main thematic purpose such as "culture and recreation," "education," "health," or "law, policy, and advocacy." Social scientists including political geographers have contributed to our knowledge of how social actors are shifting their involvement from the local to the global and back again, while at the same time manipulating the meanings of these spatial markers. Others have explored the consequences for NGOs of being physically situated in places where they try to lobby power holders (national capitals and UN hubs) or deliver aid (war and disaster zones)—as opposed to the many placeless activities NGOs engage in, such as online information dissemination. This chapter discusses each of these distinct spaces in turn.

When the United Nations was founded, nongovernmental speakers were present right from the beginning; like other war-weary citizens, they were hoping to witness the birth of a neutral world body that would be universally accepted as a common meeting ground. In the same vein, the Universal Declaration of Human Rights was adopted in 1948 as an expression of the belief in the existence and value of a common humanity shared by all people on earth. But human rights soon became a battleground of the Cold War. Communist states claimed to defend economic and social rights, while Western NGOs emphasized political and civil rights, which in turn drew the ire of Soviet spokespersons who flatly called human rights advocates "weeds in the field" to be uprooted.[1] Even after the fall of the Berlin Wall, human rights were far from constituting a neutral frame of reference backed by a global consensus.

Parallel to human rights, development was considered an ideal to be pursued by the allegedly neutral means of science and industry, as President Truman explained in his famous 1949 Four Point Speech. Yet, development also ceased to be a neutral sphere when a new generation of "postdevelopment" NGOs, whose members had lost faith in the superior wisdom of Western models of economic life, began to turn against seemingly neutral projects such as big hydroelectric dams and the unleashing of market forces.

The next area, widely hailed as allowing for the final reconciliation of humankind, was the environment. Before states devised environmental policies, scientists and engaged citizens discovered this apparently neutral field that seemed ideally suited as a way of moving beyond the frozen lines of the Cold War. In the 1960s, the American scientific community made the first steps by laying the groundwork for ecology as part of Big Science in the context of the International Biological Program (IBP) (1968–74), which was massively supported by Congress. For the first time, Americans felt that "[we] will go down in history as an elegant technological society struck down by biological disintegration."[2] Activists, too, saw the environment as an opportunity to dig beneath the surface of global ideological conflicts in order to uncover "the underlying community of the species man."[3]

In brief, human rights, development, and the environment were all promoted as nonideological issue areas outside a dominant pattern of conflict, which promised to broaden the scope of understanding and mutual agreement, before they became themselves battlegrounds. NGOs were always among those who moved from a conflictual sphere to a not yet conflictual sphere as well as among the forces that turned these spheres into arenas of new global conflicts.[4]

This dual movement of neutralization and repoliticization must remain mysterious to observers who see NGOs only as forces of universal reconciliation and peace.[5] One thesis in this book is that NGOs do not struggle against harm as such, but against harms that can be symbolized as evil. In other words, the struggle is not directed against *all* kinds of harm understood as setbacks to interests. Tax hikes are harming the interests of taxpayers; cutting subsidies for European and U.S. farmers spells the end for many of them; the immigration of unskilled workers is hurting the income of workers at the bottom of the economic ladder in host countries. Yet there are no NGOs (as defined in this book) addressing these harms, which are covered by other actors such as political parties and trade unions. NGOs are interested only in harm that can be symbolized as *evil* in the sense that it violates fundamental and "sacred" normative rules and values. For the abolitionists, African slaves working on plantations in America did not just suffer a setback to their interests; they were victims of an injustice of the most profound kind. Antislavery activists targeted the power of the state as a source of harm directed against innocent victims who were fellow humans; they meticulously documented the practices of enslaving, trafficking, and mistreating humans; and they lobbied for the legal prohibition of the entire transatlantic system of slavery. This has become the moral template for many latter-day NGOs.

Interestingly, some currents within the abolitionist movement also planted the first seeds of animal rights movements. The antislavery campaigner William Wilberforce was a co-founder of the first animal rights society in Britain in the 1820s. More than one hundred years later, Hannah Arendt spoke—quite disapprovingly—of the "uncanny similarity" between the language of human rights groups and that of certain "societies for the prevention of cruelty to animals."[6] In many ways, early animal rights groups created a second and often neglected paradigm of NGO activism. Some of them, like the British Union for the Abolition of Vivisection, did not directly target the government, but rather longstanding social customs such as cockfighting or fox hunting as cruel and pointless. Others consciously took aim at modern industry as a source of harm. Thus, Lina Haehnle, the founder of the League for the Protection of Birds in Germany, opposed the fashion industry for persuading people to buy things like hats decorated with birds' feathers. The killing of birds and other animals for fun or fashion was decried as a scandalous practice to be abolished by law.

A third model is exemplified by mid-nineteenth-century associations like the International Committee for the Relief of the Wounded, the predecessor of International Committee of the Red Cross (ICRC) and other humanitarian agencies. These groups differ from antislavery and animal protection societies, first, by looking at war as a distinct source of evil, and second, by demanding not the abolition of war, but its regulation through what became to be known as international humanitarian law. Thus, the Geneva Conventions do not prohibit the killing of soldiers in combat, but the killing of soldiers who have surrendered; they do not prohibit the capturing of combatants, but insist that prisoners of war are entitled to respect for their lives and humanity. They assume the wounding of others in hostilities as inevitable, but condemn the infliction of unnecessary losses and excessive suffering, including the willful neglect of the wounded and sick by any party to the conflict that has the power and the medical equipment to care for them. In brief, the ICRC draws a line between harming and wronging; only beyond a certain legal threshold, the legitimate victors of a conflict turn into perpetrators and the vanquished into victims.

In table 5.1 I have sketched a simple matrix intended to capture the universe of issues that NGOs can possibly create and pursue. Note that the table must be read not as a grid, but as a menu that allows for various combinations of items from the different columns. The first column reminds us that *state power* has never been regarded as the only source of harm. Since men do not necessarily fight each other only in state-run armies, *war* is potentially a source of harm separate from the state. The same is true for *industry*, which in capitalist societies is not run by the state. Are there no more than these three sources of harm? Not in the moral universe of contemporary NGOs. Unlike in much of classical political theory, neither "nature" nor "human nature" figures as a distinct source of human suffering. Neither the argument that man is a wolf to men, nor the view that the world is an inhospitable place governed by random luck is taken into account. Of course, NGOs are prompted into action by extreme weather events, such as hurricanes, that regularly cause enormous damage to life, health, and property. But even relief agencies tend to attribute the suffering of hurricane victims to the prior failure of government agencies to invest in disaster-preparedness and emergency-response systems. Similarly, the AIDS crisis has been framed as being made worse by pharmaceutical corporations and the patent laws protecting them. Like nature and bad luck, "tradition" is also dismissed as a candidate for a source of human suffering. Instead, "tradition" and "religion" are represented as pretexts used by states and corporations not to help vulnerable people.[7] In all these cases, even if they are not considered directly responsibly for the harm suffered by others, states and corporations tend to be judged as at least "passively unjust."[8]

Moving to the second column of table 5.1, we recognize that classical other-regarding associations mostly focused on humans in general as victims of harm. Military commanders, lawmakers, and the public were, in fact, called on to perceive and treat others as fellow humans by *abstracting* from primordial qualities such as skin color, national belonging, or cultural background, either permanently (in the case of slavery) or temporarily (in the case of wounded or captured soldiers and civilians in war). Next to humans, animals, too, were considered potential victims of mistreatment and senseless killing. Yet, animals were defended on the basis of

Table 5.1 Generating issues for NGOs: A menu

Sources of harm	Victims of harm	Acts of harming	Harm conventions
State power	Humans	killing	Prohibition
War	Animals	mistreating	Regulation
Industry	Children	disenfranchising	
	Women	enslaving	
	Minorities	trafficking	
	Ecosystems	damaging	
		raping	
		excluding	
		neglecting	
		stigmatizing	

their unique species-related qualities, not on the basis of an imagined "common animality," analogous to the common humanity of wounded soldiers, prisoners of war, or bonded laborers. Over time, the list of victims "worthy" of advocacy has grown and continues to grow. The third column of the table lists some of the most common harmful activities to which humans and nonhumans can be subjected. These activities can be further broken down into countless other, more specific ways of doing harm. The fourth column illustrates that in light of these harmful activities, activists can either opt for blanket prohibition or for regulatory provisions. This choice depends partly on how radical single groups are and partly on pre-existing norms applicable to the harmful practices in question. It would be ludicrous to call for anything less than the complete prohibition of practices such as slavery; on the other hand, there are no NGOs calling for the prohibition of killing humans and animals under *any* circumstances.

New issues have emerged with the discovery of new victims of harm and new categories or subcategories of acts of harming. An early addition to the issues of slavery and cruelty to animals is, for example, the issue of "children in war," which gave rise to the United Nations Children's Fund (UNICEF) and Save the Children and has since then generated more issues like orphans left behind by victims of war, including refugees or, more recently, child soldiers. Table 5.1 can also be used as a heuristic device: combining key words from the first two columns and running down the list of harmful acts in the third column, we find clues to the range of issues around which campaigns have emerged or might emerge in the future. At the interface of "industry" and "children," for instance, issues like child labor or the abuse of children by the global sex industry have gained prominence. Similarly, the adverse effects of war on women have drawn increasing attention. Thus, "sexual violence in armed conflicts" has become an issue created by women's rights groups and successfully institutionalized by recent war crimes tribunals, which have declared the systematic rape of women as a crime against humanity.[9] Even the effects of war on animals have become an issue with animal rights groups organizing or advocating rescue missions for pets left behind by their owners in war and disaster zones.[10]

The overall trend is that the "issue pool"[11] administered by transnational activists is constantly growing. The explanation is probably to be found on the supply side rather than the demand side. It is not that things are getting always worse, but that our capacity to discover and describe forms of avoidable harming is improving. One could also say that our ability to perceive others as "vulnerable" and "innocent" and hence as potential victims of harm has grown.

The growth and proliferation of many NGOs are additional incentives to take up more issues and to diversify activities and "products." Thus, conservationist NGOs have expanded their agendas from a narrow concern with single endangered species to a concern for entire ecosystems; human rights groups that started as advocates for individual political prisoners have moved on to include issues related to poverty, arms control, and the reform of UN human rights mechanisms. New issues also emerge in the process of monitoring and keeping track of the side effects and ramifications of harmful events or substances. The environmental damage caused by the excessive use of pesticides in agriculture is a famous example. Groups such as the Pesticide Action Network (PAN) have followed the path of the chemicals as they seep into rivers and streams and move up the food chain, where they can cause all kinds of serious health problems for humans. In this way, a single group of chemicals gave rise to a series of agricultural, environmental, and health issues. Similarly, as soon as rape in war became an issue, people began to wonder what happens to the babies who are sometimes born as a result of rape or sexual slavery in armed conflicts. As Charli Carpenter has pointed out, the possible neglect and stigma suffered by these children is indeed something like an issue in the waiting for the international children's rights community.[12]

There are, of course, external limits to the growth of the issue pool, which coincide with the limits to the growth of NGOs themselves. But the generation of issues also hits internal limits. Not every problem or crisis can be transformed into an issue around which activists organize and mobilize. At the beginning of chapter 6, I will return to this question of internal constraints of issue generation, which touches on the range of definitions of what it means for NGOs to be successful.

SHIFTING SCALES

The growth and proliferation of NGOs affect, and are affected by, different geographical scales of activity and identification. Together with multinational corporations, NGOs have challenged the status of the nation-state as the primary scale for public participation and claimsmaking. In positive terms, they have been characterized as brokers between "the local" and "the global."[13] More recently observers have become careful in using such spatial markers, which seem to suggest that some settings are by and in themselves more global than others. Yet United Nations or World Bank headquarters are distinct locales and "small worlds" like any other place on earth; what motivates people to identify these places with the global level is that they are sites where *global* issues are at stake and where the decisions taken are believed to affect potentially everybody.

Seen this way, NGOs have strong incentives to rescale their activities "upward," toward international or regional organizations. The search for funds and reputation further motivates NGOs to seek access to foreign donors and international organizations as well as to celebrate the "global" as the privileged scale for action. In doing so, they have contributed to the "common conflation of global-powerful and local-powerless,"[14] which does not mesh well with the simultaneously invoked mystique of the "grassroots." I have two brief comments on this.

First, broadly speaking, non-Western NGOs are under stronger pressure than their Western counterparts to seek global connections in order to be heard even by their own governments.[15] Second, the conflation of global-powerful and local-powerless is both affirmed and questioned in the context of global summits of political leaders, which have become so important in recent diplomatic history. The moral significance of summits lies in the opportunity offered to NGOs to enact a sense of collective identity between themselves and their supporters.

TAMING OR CANNIBALIZING THE LOCAL?

Mary Kaldor has argued that within global civil society, NGOs represent the "taming" of lower-scale social movements.[16] Returning to the Indian NGOs mentioned in the previous chapter, I want to show that the metaphor of taming is misleading as soon as we adopt a non-Eurocentric perspective. Taming presupposes a close, even intense relationship between two categories of agents. Yet in third world contexts, NGOs are typically parts of the urban elite culture that is largely disconnected from the local realities of the hinterland. Often the decision to set up a foreign-funded NGO is made precisely for the reason that activists do not find a firm basis in whatever social movements may exist in their country. Both Gene Campaign and the Research Foundation (RFSTE) are examples of internationally oriented NGOs that are far from "taming" social movements, either because such movements do not exist or because relationships with those movements are ephemeral.

The intellectual roots of Gene Campaign go back to the opposition against emergency rule under Indira Gandhi in the 1970s when a highly respected representative of the independence movement, Jayaprakash Narayan, called for "total revolution" and the establishment of a "non-party democracy." In the name of moral renewal, this movement was directed against the higher castes whose power was not touched by modernization and who where branded for skimming off the already-modest fruits of industrial progress. Also, the Green Revolution had led to an increase in prosperity and the standing of the lower rural castes, but did not result in greater political participation.

Against this backdrop, both Gene Campaign and the Research Foundation shared their moment in the sun when in the early 1980s new farmers' movements emerged, which appeared to provide an audience for the anti-globalization agendas of the two NGOs.[17] The farmers' movements arose in areas that had benefited from the Green Revolution. Yet, in contrast with earlier movements, they were not taking aim at large landowners but against the liberalization of agriculture and the increasing power of international organizations over domestic affairs. Both Vandana Shiva, director of the Research Foundation, and Suman Sahai, director of Gene Campaign, for a time served as advisors to the leaders of the farmers. These movements reached their zenith in March 1999 with huge rallies in Delhi against transgenic seeds and the early drafts of what was to become the TRIPS Agreement.

However, none of the NGOs could cement relations with the rural masses and their charismatic political leaders who to this day are lovingly revered as "mahatmas" or "great souls." Indeed, cotton farmers successfully struggled for their right to try out new genetically modified seeds, which was bad news especially for Shiva's network. Environics, a Toronto-based public environmental polling firm, found in 1999 that Indians were close to the technophile Americans in accepting biotechnologies in agriculture (76 percent) and medicine (81 percent).[18] In September 1999, at a village gathering in the Alwar district of Rajasthan that I attended together with leaders of Gene Campaign, the NGO representatives encountered great difficulties in committing the farmers to the fight against "patents on life," the "*dadagiri* (bullies) of America," and other symbols of evil located somewhere far off abroad. For many farmers, problems such as a chronic lack of water or the pressure put on prices by the local harvest purchasers were much more urgent than the patent models of international organizations. The Gene Campaigners did not like what they heard and ostensibly looked down on the farmers as country bumpkins and simpletons.[19]

Yet in their external relations with donors, both NGOs were able to pass as somehow close to the Indian countryside. In the eyes of many Westerners, Shiva, in particular, "came to represent Indian farmers, sometimes India itself," as Ronald Herring observed.[20] The carefully crafted memory of the large demonstrations of 1993 and manipulative accounts of her role in earlier protests like the famous tree-hugging Chipko movement in the Himalayas[21] were instrumental in increasing her standing with foreign donor organizations like the Church Development Service in Germany (EED) and others, which lasts to this day. This is a good example of how views held by donors can differ from the views of the supposed beneficiaries of funding programs. Local farmer activists of a Save the Seeds movement, for instance, have accused the Research Foundation of having surreptitiously used the farmers' documented knowledge on traditional seed varieties of rice, beans, and millet for writing glossy reports for the Food and Agriculture Organization (FAO) without giving them any credit.[22]

The case of Gene Campaign is different. The leaders of Gene Campaign decided to settle for the second best and become an NGO, after they realized that their early leftist nationalistic agenda of total revolution was doomed to fail. Although less prominent and less well-connected than the "green" and "feminist" Research Foundation, Gene Campaign was also successful in crafting a favorable public image of itself by capitalizing on its bygone relationships with local farming communities. Both these cases reveal a curious irony: for international donors, being grassroots and close to local communities is a prerequisite for any group that seeks foreign funds; at the same time, these groups apply for funds only because the project of going grassroots and building a basis of supporters in their own country has failed. Instead of taming preexisting social movements in which would-be NGOs are rooted, they are reinterpreting and "cannibalizing" their former relationships with farmers' associations, originally established with more far-reaching intentions in mind, as indicative of the closeness to locals in accordance with the sponsorship guidelines of donor organizations. Not the reality, but the public image of being grassroots is crucial for shifting scales and becoming a globally active NGO.[23]

The Moral Meaning of Global Summits

"Summit" meetings of heads of government have become a stable feature of international society since the 1950s when Winston Churchill first introduced the term into diplomatic and popular usage.[24] Today, high-level meetings organized by governments or international organizations are much more frequent than at Churchill's time, and they are being called for a growing range of purposes beyond the urgent need of crisis management. In particular, the 1990s have seen a series of UN mega-conferences on issues and themes dear to the worldwide NGO community: there were summits on children (New York, 1990), environment and development (Rio de Janeiro, 1992), human rights (Vienna, 1993), population and development (Cairo, 1994), social development (Copenhagen, 1995), women (Beijing, 1995), and racism (Durban, 2001), to name the most prominent. All these summits were accompanied by "parallel summits" for NGOs that thousands of people attended. The 2002 World Summit on Sustainable Development in Johannesburg attracted sixty-five thousand delegates, forty thousand of them from NGOs, while iconoclastic journalists spoiled the fun by figuring out the amount of carbon dioxide produced and the millions of dollars spent by the attendants.[25]

In socio-spatial terms, world summitry allows NGOs, including its many mutant variants, to "jump scales" by turning global events into local venues for activists from all over the world. In the 1970s, European activists discovered through their attendance of summits that the world is no longer "essentially white, Western and Christian."[26] Later on, the experience of summits formed the intuitive background of the idea of a "global" civil society. Large numbers of people began to live as if this idea was real. From the perspective of those participating in the mega-events of international society, global civil society was not so much a set of propositions about reality, but a myth or an imagining that produced real consequences because it motivated real people to act. As a myth many people live by, global civil society has become real in the way of an "imagined community." Imagination, in the sense of the term as it was introduced by Benedict Anderson, is an inexhaustible energy capable of reordering both the reality of social relationships and our feelings toward this reality.[27]

Without stretching the analogy between NGO networks and national imagined communities too far, I would still like to point out two similarities. The emergence of international summitry including the invention of "parallel summits" on the occasion of UN conferences or meetings of the World Trade Organization (WTO) are critical for the emergence of a sense of global togetherness, perhaps as critical as motorized traveling "by huge and variegated crowds"²⁸ has been for the rise of nationalism in the former European colonies. Thus, a positive outcome of the widely denounced 2001 UN World Conference against Racism was that representatives of oppressed and completely neglected minorities like the Dalits in India (who were once known as "untouchables") met likeminded people from other parts of the world. "We are feeling connected. We are not alone," as a Dalit woman put it during the conference.²⁹

Also, global meeting events serve as points of reference for the engineering of a collective memory buttressing the self-description of NGO activists as global civil society. The dramatic protests against the World Trade Organization's Millennium Round of trade negotiations that took place in Seattle, Washington, at the end of 1999 have been enshrined in the memory of millions as an event that bristles with moral significance: the "Battle of Seattle." A young Italian who was killed during demonstrations at the G8 summit in Genoa, Italy, in 2001 was soon after transfigured into the "first martyr"³⁰ of global civil society. Intellectuals thereby invented something like an analogy to the Tomb of the Unknown Soldier famously characterized by Anderson as a major hallmark of the modern imagination of community.³¹

Second, the effect of the physical meeting of people is paralleled and enhanced by the Internet, which creates an unfamiliar sense of global simultaneity. This is similar to the role played by the print media in the nationalist era, which also suffused everyday life with a new sense of belonging and togetherness. Some authors have described the Internet and NGO networks as mutually reinforcing, overlapping, and closely related phenomena.³² Quite tellingly, NGOs are often counting the number of hits on their Web sites, and donor agencies have made the intensity of Web-based communication a benchmark for funding decisions. Allowing for real-time, many-to-many communication, the Internet is even better at generating a sense of global simultaneity than newspapers or other traditional media have ever been, although we do not know yet how the "imagined linkage"³³ between like-minded activists made possible by the Internet will change real people's sense of belonging.

THE HUMANITARIAN PRESENCE

Much neglected spaces of NGO involvement are physical localities such as refugee camps or makeshift hospitals in dangerous world regions. Any discussion of the spatial contexts of the activity of post-traditional civil associations is incomplete without an account of humanitarian field operations that are by definition situated in concrete places. A good starting point is the missionary analogy that has been applied to NGOs by both radical and conservative critics.[34] All things considered, I believe the analogy is largely misleading. Unlike NGO projects, historically, Christian overseas missions were not emergency-oriented, but permanent enterprises based on the sacrifice and the immersion of foreigners into local cultures that, in turn, led to the indigenization of Christianity. Missionaries learned local languages, observed the local customs, and tried to make friends.[35] In contrast, most international humanitarian NGOs have been characterized as professional "interface experts"[36] without any intention of crossing the line and staying in the place of others for good. Moreover, unlike missionaries, they usually do not attempt to persuade ordinary people, but power holders. And most importantly, humanitarian NGOs organize a physical presence on the ground under conditions of a postcolonial international society and norms of territorial control, which are either exercised by sovereign states or by armed nonstate actors such as warlords.

So the only thing present-day humanitarian activists have in common with colonial missionaries is that they, too, put themselves literally "in the place of others," not only by identifying with them, but also by physically moving to where "the others" live. The missionary analogy is also misleading because it obscures changes in territorial practices that are crucial for understanding the ethical dilemmas faced by humanitarian relief agencies since the early days of the International Committee of the Red Cross (ICRC). In order to get close to prisoners of war and other victims in need of assistance and counseling, relief agencies have to cooperate with the authorities in control of the situation. If relief agencies want to remain impartial, they cannot align themselves with those authorities; nor can they afford to antagonize those who control access to the victims by involving the wider public. The compromise that has been institutionalized is that the ICRC exchanges the promise of being discreet about what they see in war zones in return for getting access to prisoners and other victims. The ICRC not only refrains in all but very exceptional cases from public protests against rights-violating governments; it has also made sure that its testimonial privilege (the right not to be called as a witness) has been legally recognized in all countries in which it carries out operations. In the remainder of this chapter, I introduce some basic features of the ICRC—which in chapter 2 I have defined not as an NGO, but as a Quango—before I move on to explore the more recent proliferation of post–Red Cross or "second wave" humanitarian NGOs.[37]

International humanitarian activism started with the ICRC, which linked up with victims, states, and the public in a way that sometimes had a very real impact on the fate of prisoners of war, disaster victims, and other categories of unfortunate people. Furthermore, given its critical role in drafting the Geneva Conventions, the ICRC has actively contributed to the emergence of contemporary international society itself by helping to persuade states to endorse a number of common rules regarding the practice of warfare. At times, the moralists who later founded the International Red Cross and Red Crescent Movement articulated a vision of order in human society as a whole, which clearly went beyond concerns about the order of interstate relations. Thus, in their early days, Henry Dunant and his comrades committed themselves to fight widespread social ills like "ignorance, selfishness, mercenary motives, indifference to the common good, idleness and debauchery, isolation and abandonment."[38] Yet the ICRC was from its infancy constrained by the structure of a political world composed of individual nation-states within which it pursued its goal of protecting the "lives" as well as the "dignity" of victims of war and violence.[39]

The relationship between nation-states and the ICRC has always been strikingly lopsided. This is because the rules of international society are such that states can make the first move and select the preferred course of action, which sometimes is war. Without war, there would be neither humanitarian law nor a humanitarian space to protect. In the light of the choice of war made by states, the Red Cross has no satisfactory option apart from coordinating its own behavior on that same choice. It is interesting to note that ICRC delegates themselves have occasionally described their relationship with foreign states as something close to a "marriage"—a kind of arranged marriage, however, that lacks emotional attachment and is punctuated by periods of "icy formality."[40] In playing a game in which states always have the sovereign right of the first move, with the ICRC left with the only option to join in and to take care of the victims of that first move, humanitarianism had to model itself on what was later criticized as a subaltern service to the prevailing world order.

Now, for a number of reasons, this longstanding constellation has become more complex by the rise of genuine NGOs in the field of humanitarian assistance. What accounts for this rise of a new generation of voluntary humanitarian agencies? Here it is worth recalling the simple deal on which the whole idea of Red Cross humanitarianism is premised. Basically, the smart moral entrepreneurs who founded the Red Cross argued that in the order of things, the assistance given to the wounded, sick, and captured neither affects the outcome of battles nor interferes in any other way with the pursuit of power by states. They suggested taking care of those whose suffering was senseless, even from the point of view of the warring states themselves. Victims should be seen as *neutrals* whose fate does not alter the power equation in the world of states.[41] In Andrew Linklater's terms, the Geneva Conventions are on the borderline between "international" and "cosmopolitan" harm conventions;[42] they are designed to protect human beings as ends in themselves, but they also protect states in their interaction with other states by keeping them from using excessive force against civilians or soldiers *hors de combat* who no longer pose a threat to national security.

Yet, as the Nazi episode in European history has shown, modernity can give rise to states whose servants would not have been impressed at all by such an appeal to rational self-interest. Instead of sparing the weak and the sick, the Nazis took extra care not to let escape the handicapped, the elderly, or even children who were deported and killed by the thousands after the invasion of France and Poland, if they were Jewish. From this we learn that the ICRC cannot work effectively with *any* state, but depends on the existence of an international society whose members feel bound by a basic set of rules regarding the use of violence—rules that the Swiss philanthropists themselves helped to institutionalize. The rethinking of humanitarian action and the role of human rights in it started from a reflection on the structural weaknesses of the ICRC, which became most visible under the extreme circumstances of National Socialism when the European society of states bound by common rules and values ceased to exist. The ICRC has been accused of unduly separating material aid from wider demands for the moral equality of individuals and necessary regime change. Thus, the Swiss responded to the Holocaust by devising a "Concentration Camp Parcels Scheme."[43] They showed such an exaggerated respect for their own principles that it ultimately failed to honor them in light of new, unforeseen circumstances.[44]

THE FRENCH INNOVATION

The French founders of Médicins Sans Frontières (MSF) must be credited with having invented a new concept of professional activism called *sans-frontièrisme*, which is driven by an ethic explicitly directed against the historical failure of the ICRC during the Nazi rule in Europe. Thus, Bernard Kouchner, co-founder of MSF, has named the Swedish diplomat Raoul Wallenberg as his principal hero, the man who put his life on the line to save tens of thousands of Jews during the Second World War.[45] Today, *sans-frontièrisme* is a brand name for a family of organizations including Médicins du Monde/Doctors of the World (MDM) and Action contre la faim/Action Against Hunger (ACF), but also pharmacists, reporters, veterinarians, and other professionals "without borders." The defiance of borders by MSF and like-minded voluntary organizations refers first of all to *international* borders, which are not respected and sometimes actively ignored, especially when political authorities try to stop aid workers from helping people in danger. MSF believes that vulnerable civilian populations have a human right to be assisted regardless of the legal authority structures in the countries where these populations happen to live. Bearing witness to abuses and violations that would otherwise go unreported is thus a central imperative of these organizations.

Another corollary to *sans-frontièrisme* is the "right to intervene," a formula that, from the late 1980s on, inspired a number of UN resolutions.[46] The original term was coined in 1979 by the liberal writer and philosopher Jean-Francois Revel, who at that time urged the Europeans to end the rule of despots like Bokassa in Central Africa or Idi Amin in Uganda. Interventionist rhetoric has another aspect. It is easily overlooked that the "French doctors" not only advocate human rights for others. They also refer to *themselves* as citizens who confidently make use of these rights, in particular the "freedom to cross borders without a visa."[47] These rights—not only of victims, but also of aid agencies—are defined in contrast to state sovereignty and the current rules of international society. According to Jean-Christoph Rufin, former vice-president of MSF, moving beyond borders also means to "transgress the law"[48] in the name of higher standards of legitimacy. This is more than empty talk. In 2001, for example, MSF-Belgium illegally imported life-saving antiretroviral medicines to fight AIDS in South Africa, a practice frowned upon, but ultimately tolerated by the South African government.

Yet, all this does not seem to amount to a policy discourse about goals, obstacles, and strategies of humanitarian action that differs radically and on all counts from that of the ICRC. Like their famous Swiss forerunner, the new organizations want to alleviate and possibly prevent the suffering of innocent victims regardless of their nationality, religion, race, or gender. And like the ICRC, they strongly criticize the misuse not only of humanitarian aid but also of the very rhetoric of humanitarianism, which according to Cornelio Sommaruga, former president of ICRC, has sometimes degenerated into "*un alibi facile*"[49] for power politics. Because of these general family resemblances, MSF and other second-wave humanitarian NGOs have been characterized as still within the fold of the "Dunantist" tradition of independent relief work, named after the founder of the Red Cross Movement.[50] Stronger epistemological and ethical differences emerge only in the field of crucial *secondary* objectives. Thus, in order to achieve the primary goal to avoid extremes of human suffering, the French believe that it is necessary to change the structure of humanitarian activism itself, and more specifically, the structure of the relationship between states and relief agencies, in which humanitarians have so far played the part of an always-too-late "after-sales service of politics."[51] Only in the light of this major secondary objective, new obstacles and adversaries become visible. Unlike the ICRC or the Red Cross Movement in general, MSF as well as Médecins du Monde (MDM) are more like typical NGOs insofar as they identify perpetrators alongside victims. They are outspoken about who are the "bad guys" to be blamed for the continuing suffering of vast populations. As far as the intended beneficiaries of relief are concerned, public and internal documents speak of "the victims"[52] of armed conflicts, "populations facing massive suffering, pain and death,"[53] or just "the people";[54] on the opposite side, those who stand accused are "dictatorships"[55] or simply "the butchers."[56]

Here it is important to emphasize another aspect, apart from the ethics of "speaking up" on behalf of victims, that makes second-wave humanitarians different from both the ICRC and classical human rights NGOs such as Amnesty International. Traditionally, the ICRC and Amnesty have focused mainly on victims who actively incurred certain risks, for example, by their willingness to do what was required of them in the name of the common good (soldiers) or the voice of their conscience (political prisoners). In contrast, MSF and other agencies are taking care of entire populations of civilians who are "innocent" in the sense that they were simply at the wrong place at the wrong time. One of the main concerns of humanitarian activists is actually how to find a way to screen refugee populations so as to make sure that militants are being filtered out and only "passive" victims receive aid.[57] Over time, there has been a shift away from victims motivated by a sense of personal *sacrifice* to passive victims, as well as a shift away from the "Swiss" ethics of discretion to a vaguely revolutionary ethics of public denunciation of alleged perpetrators of evil. Table 5.2 encapsulates this idea.

The shift of focus toward passive victims is accompanied by a certain new emphasis on those who are "passively unjust"[58] by not assisting the victims or fighting the perpetrators. Prominent among the obstacles to a just world society defined by MSF is the "inaction of the international community"[59] in the face of blatant injustice. One of the most surprising and outstanding elements of the French innovation in global humanitarianism is, in fact, the refusal to talk of "humanitarian" crises in situations where the problem is political, not humanitarian. The term "humanitarian" is criticized for turning political responsibilities and sometimes systematic crimes into problems of the logistics of relief operations.[60]

Unlike politicians, who are mostly seen as passively unjust, the moral public is courted as a potential ally. Since states are treated with suspicion

Table 5.2 Types of victims and ways of relating to perpetrators

	Active victims	**Passive victims**
Principled neutrality and confidentiality	ICRC	ICRC and the Red Cross Movement
Public denunciation of alleged perpetrators	Amnesty International	Doctors Without Borders

and since the victims of man-made emergencies cannot by themselves protect those who provide assistance, MSF is seeking "the protection of public opinion."[61] Public indifference as an obstacle to humanitarian action is attributed to failures of the mass media or to flawed information policies, not to the silent workings of a secular theodicy. In the view of the new organizations, we have moved from secular theodicies able to justify massive suffering to the next problem of how to justify the *alleviation* of suffering through intervention from outside, when these interventions happen in some places but not in others. Skeptics have argued that the secular West somehow bears a resemblance to the choosy God of Calvinism whose irresistible grace rescues some sinners while others are doomed to fall into eternal oblivion.[62]

Crucially, MSF not only tries to stay independent from governments, but also declines financial support from private donors such as corporations if their activities are seen to be in conflict with the humanitarian mission.[63] Furthermore, the agency keeps a distance not only toward its own government, but is also critical of *foreign* governments, if they fail, for example, to implement adequate HIV/AIDS policies. MSF's bid for independence from target states is best epitomized by its occasionally bold attempts to operate in countries where political authority is largely exercised by nonstate actors including armed gangs. Whereas the ICRC focused on signatory states of the Geneva Conventions, the new humanitarians try to negotiate access to populations in need with groups who may not even be aware of these conventions and who certainly do not run anything close to a rational state.

American Humanitarianism

During World War II, the anthropologist Margaret Mead declared that "to recognize the *rights* of other peoples" is at the very core of the

"American belief."[64] As long as people feel that this belief is held by everybody including the government, it is morally pointless to be against or autonomous from that government. In fact, private aid agencies in the United States rarely saw a reason to defend or cherish their "independence" in the way Europeans did. Unlike the "Dunantist" European groups, the American counterparts have been described as "Wilsonian," which means more cooperative with governments and also, by and large, more dependent on them.[65]

Accordingly, U.S. humanitarianism did not start as an independent movement trying to constrain state action. Rather, after World War II, agencies like CARE and others believed that the interests of the government and of humanitarians were best served when both sides agreed on a concerted strategy. American humanitarians avoided the neutrality of the ICRC by consciously subscribing to the political ideals of the American Century. If governments and nongovernmental organizations define their relationship in terms of a division of labor to the benefit of a shared goal, we have a structure first described in the parable of the stag hunt in Rousseau's *Discourse on the Origin of Inequality*. In this parable, a mixed group of men sets out to hunt a stag. Given the size of the potential prey, hunting stags is most beneficial for the whole group but requires a lot of trust and cooperation among its members. If individuals get distracted by the sudden chance to shoot a hare, for example, they may obtain a small prey, but at the expense of the rest of the group whose members are now unlikely to catch anything. In Rousseau's reading, the stag hunt fails as long as men have not developed beyond an early stage of cooperation, but it might succeed in higher developed societies.[66]

In light of this parable, major aid groups can be said to have shared with the U.S. government the goal of hunting down the twin "stags" of fascism and communism. CARE started as an agency closely associated with the strategic interests of the United States, which in the immediate aftermath of World War II were often inextricably linked to humanitarian efforts. This link is best epitomized by the Berlin Airlift in 1948–49, in which CARE and its proverbial "packages" played a substantial role. In the beginning, CARE's organizational formula combined three different things: first, a strong needs-oriented moral universalism; second, the sheer industrial power to move tons of standardized relief goods—mostly surplus foods held by the U.S. Department of Agriculture—to any place on earth; and third, the sure feeling to be showered with gratitude.[67] CARE used to be the most American, the most Wilsonian, and the most Fordist player among the big private humanitarian agencies. It has also been a natural ally of the U.S. military until the late 1960s and beyond.

Like other agencies, CARE has become more professional over the last thirty years, creating its own knowledge base and standards of recruitment. This leads to a greater independence from the U.S. government, not necessarily in financial terms, but in terms of policy orientations and agenda setting. As the former advocacy director has told me in an interview, "I do not know to what extent CARE 'endorsed' U.S. intervention in Vietnam, but I think that it is fair to say that we allowed ourselves to be used as 'an instrument of U.S. foreign policy.' In my experience, CARE and the larger NGO community began to examine these issues more carefully in the 1990s, as a result of a whole series of complex emergencies."[68]

Similar changes took place with regard to Catholic Relief Services (CRS). During the early stages of the Vietnam War, when CRS was by far the most resourceful American aid provider in South Vietnam, the agency earned the reputation of being "the most hawkish of the voluntary agencies."[69] At the same time, the agency shared with old-world humanitarianism a decidedly legalistic and state-centric approach. Thus, CRS refused to defy existing laws—like the Trading with the Enemy Act—that hindered relief supplies to North Vietnam, or worse, used these laws as an alibi for not helping "undeserving" civilians in need. There was no vision of a humanitarian universalism liberated from the constraints of international society. Yet, beginning in the late 1960s, the alliance between the U.S. government and voluntary aid agencies—forged to hunt the "stags" of totalitarianism—began to loosen. As Scott Flipse has pointed out, CRS changed their policy around 1967, when the Catholic agency proved to be responsive to the rising anger and frustration about the war in Vietnam within its constituency and the wider American public. The debate triggered by young liberal academics around and within CRS led to the end of an unequal partnership between the U.S. government and the Catholic charity in which the latter increasingly felt it was being misused as an instrument of military pacification experts.[70] From this we learn that the preference rankings and shared definitions of reality on which the humanitarian rulebook followed by states and aid agencies is based are subject to cultural changes that reverberate across society, influencing even the self-description of faith-based agencies.

CARE also has become much more independent and professional, although the organization remains highly resource dependent on government agencies, in some countries like Germany or the Netherlands even more so than in America. Unlike other agencies, CARE also does not focus much on "silent" emergencies in neglected areas but tends to follow the attention given to certain areas by the U.S. foreign policy establishment. Yet, on the other hand, CARE is certainly independent in the sense that it can stick to the problems of one region even when this region has largely dropped from the administration's view. It has also demonstrated that it can lobby both national and international policymakers effectively in order to stop certain emergencies from falling "silent." Unlike digging wells or rehabilitating schools, consistent advocacy is almost by definition based on the moral independence of those who try to push for policy changes. Thus, to the extent that CARE strengthened its human rights–oriented advocacy activities, it also grew more independent from shifting U.S. foreign policy interests.

The Christian charity World Vision is another interesting case of American-inspired humanitarianism. Like others, World Vision had turned a blind eye to the humanitarian consequences of the American war in Southeast Asia in the 1960s and later. But the relationship between the agency and the U.S. government also changed in those troubled years. With hindsight, internal observers see the assistance given to Cambodia after the Vietnamese army had toppled the Khmer Rouge regime in 1979 as a watershed event that marked a clear split from mainstream U.S. foreign policy makers, for whom communist countries were unworthy of any kind of support.[71]

In terms of the stag hunt parable, these were cases of unilateral defection on the part of aid agencies from the joint project of stalking a deer in favor of taking smaller prey. Aid workers began to think of themselves as having had insensibly acquired "some crude idea of mutual commitments"[72] between NGOs and the government, which in retrospect and under the influence of normative changes and new perceptions did not seem worth the effort. These changes also affected the relationship between humanitarians and soldiers in American political culture.

A RETURN TO PURE HUMANITARIANISM?

For CRS, a test case for the new policy was the devastating famine in Ethiopia in 1984 during which the aid group lobbied, energetically and with much success, a conservative U.S. government reluctant to help a Soviet satellite. By that time, CRS no longer tailored charitable objectives with foreign policy goals like it did in Vietnam. Rather, the organization now insisted on the opposite course of radically *separating* aid and politics. Unfortunately, this also did not work out well.

As a matter of fact, the communist government in Addis Abeba used famine assistance as an incentive to speed up a forced resettlement program imposed on peasants who were deliberately starved. Hunger was used as a weapon and foreign food assistance as an incentive for peasants to leave their land. After having escaped the embrace of the U.S. government, CRS was now blamed for being inadvertently instrumental in the wicked designs of a tyrannical *host* government. Faced again with the charge of complicity, CRS officials engaged in angry antipolitics by claiming that "a political agenda is incompatible with the humanitarian principle, which aims at providing assistance to all those in need regardless of race, creed, or politics."[73] They did not realize the paradox that in Ethiopia this very claim, as soon as it was put into practice, produced completely counterintentional results: humanitarianism driven solely by apolitical good intentions is perfectly compatible with the most ruthless power politics as long as humanitarians do not study and evaluate the political context into which they intervene and which shapes the outcomes of their intervention. CRS preferred the "small prey" of giving emergency relief to many individual peasants without addressing the moral hazard created whenever efforts to insure against senseless suffering inadvertently encourage political behavior contributing to this very suffering.

Overall, World Vision and CARE have been more consciously focused on maintaining a certain distance from the U.S. government without being mucked around by oppressive foreign governments, thereby keeping in line with the "American belief" in the rights of others. Both try to strike a balance between the ambition to separate humanitarian concerns from broader U.S. foreign policy goals and the reluctance to return to a pure humanitarianism that ignores the often political causes of senseless suffering.

World Vision can be said to be the relief organization farthest away from European-style Dunantist humanitarianism. No other agency has gone as far as World Vision in combining the redistribution of material goods with an ideology of holistic recognition of individuals, especially children. The agency's mission points far beyond the mundane tasks of assisting people in need by handing out blankets or biscuits. The goal is to transform the sufferer instead of merely alleviating her suffering. Whereas the Red Cross Movement always insisted on the importance of decoupling humanitarian from political and other issues, World Vision has turned the much-denounced *confusion des genres* between aid and politics, religious sentiment and media orientation, into a systematic policy approach.[74] In recent decades, the agency has been undergoing a process of routinization, ideological liberalization, and remarkable economic success.

In the early 1990s, World Vision started to build up an advocacy team centered on a (religiously reinterpreted) human rights agenda with a strong focus on children's rights. With growing concern for human rights and the consolidation of a network of policy experts, the agency also began to advocate humanitarian interventions, starting from the controversial peace enforcement mission in Somalia in 1992 and after, which was later defended against those who gave the impression "that we squandered our blood and treasure with no good results."[75]

CARE has been the aid group that took the lead in reframing conventional relief and development goals in human rights terms. Individual executive-level staff members now openly argue for a "politicized humanitarianism," partly by drawing on the early philosophy of MSF that is played off against more recent attempts of this organization to snatch the clothes of the Red Cross and look more "neutral" again.[76] To some extent, this intriguing reversal of roles between a French and an American agency has been triggered by recent developments in Afghanistan, which have made the distinction between the Dunantist European NGOs and Wilsonian U.S. groups look a bit outdated.

After the fall of the Taliban regime, CARE combined emergency relief and development assistance with lobbying for the "security rights" of the Afghan people. The organization joined the warnings from international organizations as well as from the U.S. military that the victory over the Taliban was far less decisive than the government had portrayed it. Given the specter of a sneaking return of the Islamist extremists in some provinces of Afghanistan and the grim reality of a number of ruthless killings of aid personnel, election registration workers, and others, the agency decided not to stay "neutral" between the formally sovereign Karzai government and its armed opponents. Instead, CARE aimed to highlight what ordinary Afghans actually deserved in terms of human security and to get policy makers from Washington to Brussels to live up to their earlier commitment not to leave this country high and dry again. The expansion of the mandate of the International Security Assistance Force (ISAF) beyond Kabul by the UN Security Council in October 2003 is widely credited to the dogged persistence of NGO advocacy on this issue.

Not only ordinary Afghans but aid agencies as well would have profited from an improved security situation in a country from which MSF withdrew after five of its staff, driving in a clearly marked vehicle, were shot dead in June 2004. As in other cases, MSF reacted by blaming the authorities for not providing enough security while at the time bashing other aid agencies that had openly advocated a tougher mandate for the international armed force. The example illustrates that MSF never solved the dilemma of how to stay politically neutral while at the same time appealing to and depending on sovereign decision making. It always wanted it both ways: taking sides and staying neutral, being political and shrouded in an air of eternal innocence like a modern-day Jeanne d'Arc. Only in most recent times did MSF take the dilemma by its horns and return to a discourse of prepolitical humanitarianism. In Afghanistan, MSF used its favorite policy tool of "speaking out" publicly only to denounce those (like CARE) who spoke out in favor of strengthening security rights. Today, the agency dissociates itself from international reconstruction efforts in Afghanistan and elsewhere—a dissociation that is premised on the ingenious belief that it can control the way it is perceived by local insurgents ready to target aid workers in a very literal sense.

FUTURES OF HUMANITARIAN ACTION

The merits of different models of humanitarian assistance and protection cannot be judged in the abstract, regardless of the host regions where these models are supposed to be put into practice. It is therefore useful to insert a political-geographical perspective into the debate on the viability and future of different strands of humanitarianism. Aid agencies may change their organizational values and perceptions and may favor particular institutions and ways of acting. The intentions of aid agencies are, however, largely irrelevant as particular conflict settings function as powerful selective pressures on those agencies. Three types of conflict that never occur in their pure forms, but that help us to judge the appropriateness of different humanitarian approaches in crisis regions, can be distinguished.

Resource conflicts in "failed" states. Many so-called silent emergencies are the result of highly fragmented armed conflicts dominated by warlords who do not obey higher authorities and who also do not care about world opinion. These conflicts are not politically motivated, and the civilian population caught up in them is, at best, completely neglected. Some aid agencies have occasionally been quite successful in negotiating access to these civilians and to provide minimal assistance. In these most desperate places, the classical values of impartiality, independence, and neutrality are almost self-evident. There is no problem of keeping a distance from the state since the indigenous state is dysfunctional or absent, and the far-away democratic states try everything not to get involved in these seemingly hopeless battles.

"Ethnic" conflicts over state formation. In these conflicts, which have ravaged former Yugoslavia and other regions, it is both very well possible and meaningful to stay neutral and to help people impartially. Usually, belligerents are not completely indifferent to what outsiders and the international community think. Attacks on aid workers are rare, and

political considerations are overriding commercial or criminal intentions, which are also present in some of these situations. In conflict settings from Kosovo to Palestine, aid agencies with a second-wave humanitarian agenda have sometimes gambled away their credit by openly admitting to seeing things "through the eyes"[77] of only one of the conflict parties.

Neo-totalitarian conflicts. In countries like Afghanistan and Iraq, where not even the Red Cross / Red Crescent emblem is bulletproof, humanitarians can either withdraw completely (as has happened in many cases) or engage in another stag-hunt scenario by cooperating closely with members of the host government as well as with foreign powers including the military or private military firms. Deliberate killings of aid workers, kidnappings, and videotaped decapitations have shown that unlike the criminal belligerents in resource conflicts, radical Islamic insurgents are very much interested in projecting a carefully crafted image of barbarism to the global public.[78] Against this background, the apolitical holier-than-thou attitude of some humanitarian agencies that tried to stay aloof from the military and the foreign-backed local state has proved to be simply lethal. At the time of this writing, North Korea and Burma are also countries that are largely given up by NGOs as well as by the ICRC.[79]

The three types of conflicts characterizing much of today's global political landscape require different approaches. Both resource conflicts and ethnic conflicts may often require the development of an extended version of classic humanitarianism taking into consideration (in the case of resource conflicts) the absence of the state that used to provide the orientation for understanding the role of Dunantist relief agencies. Foreign states can sometimes be persuaded by aid agencies and other groups to get involved in these situations without actually fighting other peoples' wars. It should also be noted that in light of many cases of selective aid provision, the ICRC's call for "depoliticizing"[80] humanitarianism still has its merits.

Yet depoliticizing humanitarianism may not be an option in areas like Afghanistan and Iraq. NGOs continue to stay neutral in the sense of not becoming instruments of strategic hearts-and-minds work for short-term military gain. On the other hand, it is seen as problematic to stick to the principles of classic humanitarianism in situations in which these principles are not only ridiculed by local strongmen, but in which Red Cross or MSF workers are deliberately killed. Especially the bombing of the Red Cross headquarters in Baghdad on October 27, 2003, by Islamic militants was widely perceived as an iconic event symbolizing a new global evil.[81] Whereas the separation of military and humanitarian powers is still essential, all sides have begun to contemplate the integration of different mandates and capabilities into a workable regime by balancing separateness with interdependence and reciprocity.

SUMMARY

In this chapter, I have looked at the spatial contexts of NGO activism. The first of these contexts is spatial in a largely metaphorical sense. NGOs have mandates covering certain issue "areas," and sometimes they redefine their mandate to cover adjacent areas. Thus, conservationists moved from wildlife protection to include ecosystems and even agriculture; human rights organizations that for decades worked exclusively on the rights of prisoners of conscience have expanded their mandate to include economic and social rights as well. I have proposed a model that captures the entire range of issues pursued by modern NGOs. The list of victims of injustice and ways of victimizing people has constantly grown over the last decades, unlike the list of perpetrators, which basically comprises only three categories: states, war, and industry (the last one includes harmful applications of technologies). The harmful consequences of other factors such as backward traditions or oppressive religious practices are regularly reduced to the failure of states or corporations to adequately discharge their moral and legal obligations. I have explored some of the limits to the expansion of the issue pool controlled by NGOs and what determines the selection of particular issues.

Next, I have discussed ways in which NGOs are using socio-spatial resources by shifting scales from the "local" to the "global" and back again. Both upward and downward rescaling is subject to strategic decisions, and both the global and the local are important reference points in the rhetoric of NGOs. Paradoxically, the local is often invoked as a privileged geographical scale of identification, although most groups are dying to leave the fold of the local by going global. I have briefly explored the rhetorical uses of the local by globally minded NGOs in India, as well as the peculiar moral meaning of global summits for NGOs.

The remainder of the chapter is devoted to humanitarian organizations, which by their very nature are bound to privilege highly specific face-to-face interactions in often inhospitable or dangerous places. Unlike other NGOs, humanitarian organizations are multilocal actors who literally and physically put themselves in the place of others. I have sought to demonstrate how the ethics and mode of operation of ICRC has been challenged by the rise of new humanitarian models in Europe and the United States. Yet, given the monopoly position of the ICRC in terms of its mandate laid down in the Geneva Conventions and the fact that states control access to territories and hence to victims, the pattern of interaction between sovereign states and humanitarian agencies has not changed fundamentally.

CHAPTER 6

How Do NGOs Succeed (or Fail)?

MEANINGS OF SUCCESS

The literature on NGOs tends to focus on the successes of this new form of moral activism. Yet few authors discuss the multiple meanings of success, and even fewer ask whether we should take the desirability of NGO successes for granted. First of all, it is notoriously difficult to define success in politics. One reason is that successes can be deceptive. Policymakers including activists have all too often celebrated the signing of treaties and protocols as major successes only to find out later that those treaties and protocols did not achieve anything.[1] Conversely, a defeat can turn out to energize a movement and thus increase its power and influence over the long term. Defeats can pave the way for eventual victory. The other reason for the elusiveness of success has to do with the fact that there is always a gap between the ideals we formulate and the progress we can make in realizing those ideals. In war there is "no substitute for victory," as General Douglas MacArthur once famously declared; but in politics, actors are considered pretty successful even if they do not achieve all of their previously articulated policy goals. Furthermore, certain events count as successes only in the light of ideals, which can easily be adjusted so as to make given achievements look better. The undying allure of opportunism has its root in that it allows people to appear always successful and on the winner's side simply by switching goals and commitments.

For NGOs, that is not so easy. Although they are not inherently immune against opportunism and even blatant wrongdoing,[2] NGOs tend to be more serious about their ideals than many conventional politicians. To the extent that they are seriously idealistic, it is important to repeat that they do not struggle for the realization of abstract ideas. One of the innovative features of NGOs is rather that they break down abstract ideas into manageable "issues" that are then pursued in carefully selected social contexts and institutional fora. This makes it easier to assess the successes of post-traditional civil associations.

But who decides about what counts as a success? Given the multi-pronged structure in which NGOs are embedded, there are a several candidates. Donors (private and government) and the public are systematically fed with information that suggests an unrealistically rosy picture of NGO successes, and both donors and the public are most willing to accept this picture.[3] Numerous agencies such as, for example, the United Nations Online Network in Public Administration and Finance (UNPAN) encourage NGOs to share their "success stories" in implementing the universal goals of peace, sustainable development, human rights, and so on ("in three hundred words or less").[4] The Web sites of many NGOs typically provide links where visitors can view "Our successes!" In this way, the entire system is biased toward highlighting successes at the expense of failures and shortcomings. It is thereby also encouraging hypocrisy. Official reports abound with success stories, but anonymous surveys reveal that NGOs in many fields do not think of themselves as very successful.[5]

A second category of people who might have something interesting to say about successes are the supposed beneficiaries of NGO actions. We can assume that political prisoners appreciate the work of Amnesty International and are happy if they are released as a result of orchestrated international pressure. But very few cases are as clear-cut as this one. How can we find out what the much-invoked locals at the receiving end of global aid chains think about the success stories posted on the Internet by groups who claim to act on their behalf? After all, donors are normally not present on the ground to witness what they have paid for. Donors usually cannot communicate with the beneficiaries, but depend on reports submitted by NGOs. These reports are hard to audit, and very few people are in a position to follow the experiences of those on whose behalf NGOs speak.[6] Given the structural unreliability of donor and NGO sources, and the muteness of the recipients of action, we are left with the only option of exploring possible meanings of success from an observer's point of view.

The concept of success needs to be split into two closely interconnected yet distinct types. The first type is the *simple* success that occurs when NGOs prove able to change the observable behavior of an opponent or an ally in line with its professed policy goals. In contrast, a *strategic* success is achieved when many simple successes add up to the establishment of new rules or the amendment of already existing rules for international society. Simple successes have been, for example, the defeat of the plan drawn up in the mid-1970s by the United States and the European Commission to seal radioactive waste in special canisters and sink them into sediment on the ocean floor;[7] Shell's decision in 1995 not to dump the redundant oil storage buoy Brent Spar into the Atlantic and instead pursue only on-shore disposal options;[8] the breakaway in 1997 of the BP Oil Company from the private-sector lobby coalition against binding climate-change rules;[9] or the abolition in 2000 of user fees for primary education and public health services set up by the World Bank in a number of least developed countries.[10] Strategic successes go beyond these limited victories by introducing binding anti-ocean-dumping treaties, new industry-wide standards for emissions control, or structural changes in how the World Bank is run.

Success can be assessed at different levels. One obvious meaning of success refers to real-world achievements of previously articulated goals: rules enacted, prisoners released, emissions cut, toxics banned, or endangered animals saved and protected. But there are two other meanings that often precede any real-world achievements. First, even before having achieved anything in real political terms, NGOs can claim a success if they change what citizens and policymakers *know* about a given issue in their own and other societies. Thanks to networks of NGOs, we know (or can easily find out) how often women are battered by their partners in a given country, what life looks like in areas infested by landmines, or what happens to defenseless villagers who are in the way of Western-financed infrastructure projects in developing countries. Similar to international organizations, NGOs classify and count victims, and they make an effort to measure their misery to provide information to back support for instruments for changing the situation. Sometimes they propose entirely new metrics for measuring harm and well-being that both challenge and mimic official classifications. A good example is the Happy Planet Index (HPI), sponsored by Friends of the Earth, which ranks countries based on average life expectancy, life satisfaction, and resource consumption ("ecological footprint").[11]

Generally speaking, the literature on NGOs has often failed to see their role as producers and brokers of knowledge while overestimating their role as normative innovators. Yet, as Elizabeth Bloodgood has persuasively argued, campaigners against antipersonnel landmines, for instance, "did not need to convince decision-makers that the indiscriminate killing of civilians was immoral (a normative claim), but that landmines killed civilians indiscriminately (an information claim)."[12] Against the background of already established moral and legal norms and of collapsed secular theodicies, the dissemination of knowledge about unacceptable realities is in itself a success. This is somewhat counterintuitive because just to know that things are not right does not *feel* like a success. As Keck and Sikkink have noted, the generation of reliable knowledge about previously unknown situations paradoxically creates a sense that the situation is deteriorating while in reality we only know more about certain incidences of harm to others.[13]

Second, NGOs are successful when they change what citizens and policymakers *want* with regard to a known situation as a result of how this situation is framed. It is plausible to count recent changes in the way in which the World Bank *defines* poverty, for example, by including access to education or women's rights as success, even if this redefinition does not in itself reduce the number of poor people. With the shaping of the background of what we know and want, NGOs prepare the ground for debates about the limits of what states, corporations, consumers, and others are able or willing to do in order to change the situation for the better. The possibility of change in the mind of members of a society already makes a difference. A society in which alternatives to the present state of affairs are absent from the consciousness of the public is different from a society in which alternatives are calmly considered, enthusiastically embraced, or passionately rejected, even before those alternatives are implemented. For this reason, changes in public knowledge or normative preferences are successes if they help to imagine and flesh out new policy goals and ways to realize them.

In the remainder of this chapter, I discuss two key determinants of success, inner and outer limits to the success of NGOs, as well as the question whether from an observer's point of view success is always desirable.

Two Keys to Success

Politicians and business leaders frequently criticize NGOs for scoring successes by stirring public emotions for their causes, thereby rendering any rational dialogue impossible. Sympathetic researchers, on the other hand, depict NGOs as knowledgeable actors who are often successful because of their ability to feed novel information into the political process. My own thesis is that in order to succeed, campaigns have to do both: mobilize targeted information and enlist the public and its passions. The campaign against conflict diamonds is an example of how the combination of knowledge and emotion contributes to political achievements, as I show below.

Mobilizing Information

I have already pointed out that NGOs are avid collectors of information to an extent that sometimes makes them look like the ethical branch of intelligence agencies.[14] Many campaigns are evidence-driven contests about the truth of toxic discharges, refugee crises, or war crimes. In order to identify gradations of good and evil and to galvanize public attention, NGOs often convert available information into rankings. Web sites teach the public about the most underreported humanitarian emergencies, the worst human rights abusers, or about which company shows the strongest commitment to reduce greenhouse gases. All this means that NGOs improve our knowledge about what goes wrong in international society. Information advantages also account for their improved standing with international organizations. As described below, empirical research has shown that in a number of instances and areas, participation rights in international rule-making have been afforded to NGOs on the basis of the information the new actors are presumed to have. This is most obviously the case with the UN human rights treaty bodies, which could not do their job of monitoring country compliance without the information provided by NGOs. During the 1970s, the treaty bodies changed the rules of procedure in such a way as to actively seek information from NGOs both about the human rights situation and about the freedom of operation granted to independent human rights NGOs in specific countries.[15]

In a meticulous study on NGOs in international environmental negotiations, the German political scientist Tanja Brühl has demonstrated that participation rights for NGOs directly correlate with the resources they are expected to bring to bear on the rule-making effort, either during formal negotiations or in advance by informing domestic foreign-policy makers.[16] Using interviews with official delegates to the negotiations of the Biosafety Protocol to the Convention of Biological Diversity (CBD), Brühl substantiates her claim that the needs of state parties to tap into resources provided by NGOs vary with different phases of international negotiations. Three distinct and successive phases can be marked out. Parties seek maximum input from NGOs in the early and middle phases in which the definition of the problem and the search for possible solutions are at stake. Because their input is in high demand, NGOs have been able to secure far-reaching participation rights in these phases. However, the need to consult with NGOs and hence the participation rights afforded to them recede in the third phase of international negotiations when officials discuss specific measures designed to implement envisioned solutions. So what are the resources sought by state delegations and provided by NGOs? To some extent, NGOs are welcomed because they legitimize the outcomes of international negotiations in the eyes of the global public. But more important from the point of view of delegates is the *information* produced and disseminated by NGOs. This information is of different kinds. Sometimes NGOs make up for the lack of technical expertise among state delegations in particular from developing countries. To a lesser extent, NGOs are commended for their local and social knowledge about particular geographical areas or populations.[17]

These findings have been further substantiated by Elizabeth Bloodgood who shows that the success of two major campaigns—the International Campaign to Ban Landmines (ICBL) and the campaign to end the production of ozone-depleting chemicals—can at least partly be attributed to the information mobilized by NGOs.[18] Bloodgood stresses not only the information gaps filled by NGOs but also the fact that often decision making is stymied by information overload. Apart from generating useful information, NGOs are also streamlining and repackaging existing information for political consumption. The ICBL was exceptionally good at drawing on a wide range of sources in order to collect information that was credible, new, and often shocking. The campaign presented reliable data about the number of landmines used, the number and composition of people killed or injured by landmines, and the kind of pain caused by these injuries. Physicians played a key role, but also military professionals who cast doubt on the tactical utility of landmines.

In the anti-ozone campaign, Friends of the Earth (FoE) collected scientific research finding and hired a renowned dermatologist to create an accurate picture of the damage done by man-made chlorofluorocarbons (CFCs) to the ozone layer and the likely effects of ozone depletion on human health. Together with other organizations like Greenpeace and the World Resources Institute (WRI), FoE helped to present science in a way so that ordinary people, including policy makers, could understand it and act on what they were made to know. In both cases, the novelty as well as the credibility of the information transmitted by NGOs in the form of congressional testimonies, press releases, news reports, and other publications were crucial variables in achieving political victories.

This line of research supports the idea brought up in chapter 2 that NGOs function in the way of benign parasites. Like the uninvited dinner guest in ancient Greek comedies, they earn their meal by telling their hosts new, credible, and exciting stories. It is important to note that NGOs use scientific findings as inputs for stories that are not in themselves scientific. Scientists hypothesize about probable connections between events, whereas NGOs present all their information with bullheaded certitude. They are go-betweens who link and "parasitize" science, common sense, and power, while at the same time altering each of these modes of connecting with the world.

ENLISTING PUBLIC PASSIONS

While the focus on targeted information as a key to success is certainly illuminating, it tends to ignore the manner in which NGOs are not only oriented to the mind of policy makers, but also to the sentiments of the public. Post-traditional activism is not only about norms and information, but also about shaping public *responses* to events that are perceived as violating sacred norms and values. The simple reason why NGOs appeal to collective emotions is that they are politically weaker than those political and economic elites whose minds and behavior they want to change; being weak, they must try to widen the scope of conflict by involving more and more people until the balance of power shifts in their favor.[19] This insight has been taken to heart by many founders of post-traditional civil associations. In their early years, Greenpeace activists recorded the plaintive cries of captured orcas and then played the tapes on radio stations in order to win over the sentimental public. Bernard Kouchner of MSF insisted that the first task of advocacy-oriented humanitarian groups was to end the *"indifférence occidentale."*[20]

To turn the public mood around, NGO leaders need to think about how to attract widespread media attention. Overall, I see two broad strategies of molding public emotions: one that is meant to arouse indignation, shock, and anger, and another that is aimed at pleasing and ingratiating people without asking them to act in any effective way. The goal of the first strategy is to encapsulate the otherwise unfathomable enormity of a man-made evil in images or phrases that strongly resonate with the public. Greenpeace has built a Noah's Ark on Mount Ararat in eastern Turkey to alert the public to the mortal dangers caused by global warming. Some years ago, Handicap International, a co-founder of the ICBL, has built a 1.5 ton pyramid of shoes in Trafalgar Square, London, to symbolize the loss of life and limbs from landmines. While less conspicuous, photo essays and videos posted on the Web sites of major human rights groups serve the same purpose of humanizing and adding a face to good and evil. In addition, many groups have a remarkable knack for recycling all the major symbols of evil from recent history. Referring to the forced labor camps in the former Soviet Union, Amnesty International called the Guantanamo Bay Detention and Interrogation Camp set up by the United States in 2002 the "gulag of our time." Anti-biotech groups in Western and non-Western countries used the copious symbolism of "colonial rule" to denounce multinational corporations, free trade, and global patent laws. When some time ago Intel Corp. revealed plans that its new microprocessor chips will contain embedded electronic serial numbers that will allow individual computers to be readily identified, civil liberties groups launched a campaign against the return of "Big Brother." Some years later, Greenpeace Canada likened the unambitious approach of a conservative Canadian government to greenhouse gas emissions to the "appeasement" of Hitler by British Prime Minister Neville Chamberlain in the late 1930s. All these examples are not about informing, but about scaring people into buying the message offered by campaigners—a tactic that has often been successful.[21]

On a different plane, NGOs have tried to go with the mainstream and exploit the celebrity and spin mechanisms of the media to create an undertow of positive emotion. Campaigning is in many ways a profoundly conventional activity, based on a simple toolkit of public relations instruments and the imperative "Go where the cameras are."[22] That is why there is a mutual attraction between high-profile NGO campaigns and celebrities. The attention for the anti-landmine campaign reached its peak when Diana, the former Princess of Wales and the "world's most photographed woman"[23] joined the movement as a goodwill ambassador. Other issues such as "conflict diamonds" sold for funding dirty wars in Africa have been boosted by Hollywood directors (Edward Zwick's *Blood Diamond* or the James Bond movie *Die Another Day*). Animal rights and conservationist groups have gone farthest in adjusting their themes to the trends of capitalist popular culture. People for the Ethical Treatment of Animals (PETA), for example, has launched a campaign under the slogan "I'd rather go naked than wear fur," in which it hired models to pose for the noble cause. Much of the imagery produced by the WWF and Greenpeace—cuddly or imposing animals, orange-clad heroes in rubber dinghies, and so on—is now part of the same popular culture in which *Free Willy* movies, toys and T-shirts, *Super Mario*, and the *Bad Dudes* shape and reflect the desires and fantasies of what has been called the global "kinderculture"[24] that, as a matter of fact, appeals to both children and adults.

Winning Hearts and Minds: The Case against Conflict Diamonds

Neither the mobilization of public emotion nor the command of information is in itself conducive to political success. Even the skillful combination sometimes does not yield tangible results. However, both knowledge and passion are indispensable preconditions for campaigns to succeed. The public must be made to perceive a clear and imminent threat to "sacred" norms; and activists must be able to produce novel and reliable information about the causal chain that leads to the evil and that allows to assign moral and remedial responsibilities. Like a two-component value and the mystique of diamonds, particularly in North America, where diamond rings are a symbol of love and commitment. It is for a reason that the anticonflict diamond campaign was launched on Valentine's Day in 2001. The campaign achieved material results only because of the powerful symbolic and emotional meaning of diamonds and the incalculable losses faced by jewelry stores in the event of a collapse of that meaning. NGOs won because they could credibly threaten to undermine the emotional status of diamonds by changing the ideas people attach to diamonds and hence their consumption preferences. Diamonds symbolize love and romance; but from an activist's point of view, they could as well make us think of war, rape, and slavery.

INNER AND OUTER LIMITS

Winning the hearts and minds of the public and policy makers is a crucial prerequisite of successful campaigns; at the same time, these conditions for success teach us something about the inner limits of the strategies pursued by post-traditional civil associations. These limits are defined by the selective pressure exerted on the surfeit of problems around which policy issues and campaigns can be created and organized. There are numerous instances of injustice and undeserved suffering, but only few of them ever become policy issues, and still fewer become the focus of global campaigns. Keck and Sikkink have argued that in order to become an "issue," a given problem must have certain *attributes* or, at least, must lend itself to be *represented* as having such attributes: injustices "involving physical harm to vulnerable and innocent individuals appear particularly compelling"; next, there must be "a short and clear causal chain" connecting the victims to deliberate actions of identifiable perpetrators; finally, the whole situation must fly in the face of well-established norms of "legal equality of opportunity."[26]

In other words, polarization is crucial for the construction of issues. In addition to victims, NGOs need perpetrators. Both the "we are all to blame" message and references to God or nature as the causes of suffering are useless for constructing an issue. Some issues do emerge, but without blossoming into a successful campaign. Examples are the possible harmful impact of emerging nanotechnologies on marginalized communities worldwide,[27] or the issue of third world farmers' rights, which are invoked to claim exemptions from global intellectual property laws.[28] These issues seem to lack the evocative power of truly global campaign issues that catch the attention of millions: child soldiers, conflict diamonds, and landmines are well-known examples. Campaign issues are explosive, the ideal successful campaign consists of two elements, neither of which is effective in itself, and their right mixture. Perhaps the most striking case that illustrates the appropriateness of this metaphor is the campaign against conflict diamonds (also known as "blood diamonds").

The campaign against conflict diamonds has its roots in investigations around the question of how some wars that occurred in the 1980s and 1990s in parts of Africa continued even when the Cold War came to an end, and the superpowers withdrew support from their former proxies in the region. The answer is that in many countries, rebel movements and governments discovered natural resources as an easy way to fund ongoing conflicts. Around 1996, the British NGO Global Witness began to see a connection between seemingly unstoppable wars in countries such as Angola, the Democratic Republic of Congo, and Sierra Leone and the flow of rough diamonds. Diamonds are small and easy to move and smuggle; neither particular skills nor much infrastructure are needed to harvest them. In those countries, rebels simply press-ganged miners to search for the stones. Yet in order to generate revenues for governments or warlords, diamonds needed to be funneled through middlemen into the legitimate international trade. Global Witness then focused on important players in the international diamond trade (such as De Beers) and branded them as the main accomplices in wars waged by warlords who terrorized and preyed on civilian populations.

Within a few years, conflict diamonds emerged as a popular global "issue" for two reasons: first, because of the polarization between brutalized victims of war on the one hand and ruthless warlords on the other hand; and second, because international companies with well-known brand names could be targeted for alleged collusion in purchasing rough diamonds from criminal and deeply immoral sources. The campaign was notably successful in tainting the image of diamonds and in putting enormous pressure on a sixty-billion-dollar-a-year industry and governments to legitimize the diamond trade. This was achieved through a global regulatory system called the Kimberley Process, which is not a treaty, but an apparently fairly successful certification scheme aimed at preventing trade of conflict diamonds and allowing the UN Security Council to impose commodity-related sanctions.[25]

In short, it was the unique combination of knowledge and public emotion that contributed to a relative success. Groups like Global Witness were immensely successful in presenting a novel and credible causal story linking rough diamonds, local wars, and global markets and pinning moral responsibilities on various intermediary actors along the commodity supply chain. Yet what is equally important is how crucial are the symbolic always about a massive harm inflicted on innocent others—a harm that is perceived as fundamentally evil and threatening to nonnegotiable norms and values.

With this in mind, it is easy to understand why—to give an example—the staggering diffusion of small arms and light weapons across the world and the corresponding need for "microdisarmament" has been described as an issue, but has never really gained much attention. There is no doubt that firearms cause significant bodily harm and that arms dealers can easily be depicted as evil. Activists of the small arms movement who have raised this issue have tried to capitalize on the success of the anti-landmine campaign, but with only meager results.[29] One reason is that it is difficult to arouse public emotion against small arms as such: good guys, it is believed, keep and bear arms as well. The other reason is that the knowledge production encouraged by small arms activists provides a factual basis for reflection that complicates the case against small arms. Thus, the Small Arms Survey 2004 suggests that there is no direct correlation between the availability of firearms and the rate of homicides. Latin America and the Caribbean have only a comparatively small number of weapons in circulation but carry 36 percent of the global total of gun deaths.[30] Whereas the number of active landmines per inhabitant clearly results in corresponding numbers of victims, there is much doubt whether and how gun accessibility affects overall levels of violence.[31] The campaign was a nonstarter because of these combined failures: the failure of linking gun accessibility to emotionally arresting symbols of good and evil, and the failure of bolstering the case against small arms by convincing information.

Let us look at another instance of harming that has not developed into a campaign issue: caste discrimination against India's Dalits (who were called "untouchables" until some time ago). It is not that this issue has not been documented, yet it has never moved to the center of a global campaign. This is all the more surprising since in 2006, even Indian Prime Minister Manmohan Singh acknowledged the parallel between Dalit oppression and the crime of apartheid. The same is true for religious persecution in many countries (which is well documented, for example, by the Christian charity Open Doors) but not an important concern for major international human rights organizations. The reason for this is, I believe, that in the Western public mind, these issues have a "cultural" background that makes it difficult to clearly assign responsibility to identifiable perpetrators. Although the issues are recognized as real, there is reluctance to rally more strongly against what is perceived as other cultures. Pointing to the failure of early campaigns against female circumcision,

Keck and Sikkink have already shown that the harmfulness of certain actions (or the wrongfulness of harmful actions) is sometimes heavily contested: "One person's harm is another's rite de passage."[32] In other words, the shortness of causal relations may be debatable, and "cultural" perceptions can make a causal chain look much more convoluted than it is.

While the importance of choosing polarizing issues is an inner limit to the form of media-oriented politics pursued by most NGOs, there are also considerable outer limits to their success. The first external limiting factor that often impedes the emergence of a campaign issue is the impossibility to change the behavior of actors who are causing harm to vulnerable individuals, but who cannot be *shamed* into changing their ways. Attempts to shame the government of the People's Republic of China into respecting human rights have been ineffective or even counterproductive.[33] A more extreme example is Islamic terrorism. During the first years of the new millennium, jihadists have deliberately flown airplanes into skyscrapers during working hours; bombed United Nations buildings; and slaughtered captured soldiers, aid workers, and journalists on tape—practices that caused "physical harm" and were incompatible with the norm of "legal equality of opportunity," to repeat the words of Keck and Sikkink.[34] Yet these groups cannot be shamed into accepting human rights standards, because they consider these standards as being themselves evil. Unlike high-ranking officials in the West who have been complicit in illegal abuses, they are not preoccupied with the construction of "deniability." It would therefore be silly and pointless to suggest a campaign under the heading "Stop videotaped decapitations" or "Stop blowing up subway stations," whereas it makes a lot of sense, on the other hand, to call for the closure of secret detention centers for terrorist suspects run by intelligence agencies of the United States. The difference is that the United States is not impervious to attempts of shaming; perhaps some officials are, but certainly not the entire judicial system or the general public.

There are three points I want to make in this context. First, *shameability* is a precondition not only for the success of campaigns but often also for the very rise to prominence of an NGO-driven issue. If this is the case, and if NGOs want to win and appear successful, they have a reason to focus on situations where perpetrators or accomplices can be shamed into better behavior, regardless of whether other situations might deserve more attention. In other words, NGOs might be tempted to pick lowlying fruit where more ambitious goals appear to be out of reach. Is it more comfortable to stock the showcase of despicability with evildoers who can be shamed rather than with evildoers who could not care less about what the public thinks of them. To give an example: The fact that human rights organizations seem to be obsessed with violations committed by Israel may have its reason not only in an anti-Israel bias, but also in the perceived chance of embarrassing officials and the public in that country and thus of achieving tangible results—something that is unlikely to happen in many other countries with incomparably worse human rights records.

Second, shameability is not a character trait or a stable feature that some states and corporations exhibit while others do not. Substantial public attention on multinational corporations seems to have an influence on their behavior and the choice of investment locations.[35] On the other hand, for the sake of sovereignty and national defense, even democratic nations may consciously decide to act in way that invites shaming by others. In short, the power of shaming is context dependent.

Third, the immunity to shaming tactics is by no means confined to fanatics. This is the reason why NGOs are searching for accomplices who are links in the causal chain leading to unjust suffering and who can be pried away from that chain through moral pressure. We know that already the slaveholders in prerevolutionary America did not lose any sleep over the deteriorating image others had of them.[36] Slavery came to an end not because Southern planters changed their minds, but because abolitionists were able to shame a range of knowing and unknowing accomplices, from British civil servants to ordinary consumers, who at some point stopped supporting slavery.

Sovereign statehood itself is an outer limit to the success of NGOs; although, as we have seen, sovereignty is Janus-faced because it also works in favor of NGOs. Sovereignty is a limit because no combination of polarization, knowledge, and public sentiment can defeat it from outside. In August 2001, a researcher at the head office of MSF in Paris wrote the following sentence about North Korea: "Kim Jong-Il, the north Korean leader, bought £300m worth of weapons from Russia at the weekend. Meanwhile at home, millions of his people are starving to death."[37] Here we have a maximum of bodily harm, a short causal chain leading from deliberate choices to countable deaths, and a clear antagonism between good and evil—but no hope to change the situation. Regime change is not on the agenda of any NGO, and if there is a universal right to be governed democratically, NGOs have no way of implementing it.[38] But NGOs even fail to achieve much more modest goals. The experiences of relief agencies in the last three decades have taught them that it is not up to them to dictate the terms of cooperation with foreign states. Therefore, the strategy of activists to radicalize the agenda of the Red Cross Movement has achieved only moderate successes. While many activists deplored the humanitarian situation in Saddam Hussein's Iraq under the UN-imposed embargo, various sections of MSF proposed six or seven projects in poor neighborhoods in Baghdad and elsewhere to improve the health situation. But the group was only welcome to donate money to the Ministry of Health, not to enter the country.[39] Similar situations occurred in North Korea, Somalia, Ethiopia, Afghanistan, and other countries where governments or local strongmen did not like the idea of politicized liberal NGOs operating on their turf. Consequently, as long as states control territories and thus access to victims, the low-key, publicity-shy approach favored by the ICRC in its dealings with foreign governments is not so much an expression of peculiar Swiss cultural preferences, but rather the result of "functional necessity."[40]

Furthermore, there are scale-related limits. States regulate access to "the global" as an important site of visibility for good causes. In particular, state representatives in UN commissions can block or reverse the quasi-diplomatic status of NGOs. In 2003, Libya and Cuba rallied a number of like-minded states to cancel the consultative status held by the Paris-based group Reporters Without Borders with the UN Commission on Human Rights. In 2007, Muslim countries led the opposition to the bid by Gay and Lesbian Coalition of Québec (CGLQ) for observer status at the UN, arguing that discrimination against gays and lesbians is not a global problem, since there is no homosexuality in Muslim countries.[41] Arguably more important are cases where groups attempt to circumvent the outer limits of sovereign decision making by deliberately choosing the path of downward rescaling. Here feminist groups have often been trailblazers, but also environmental organizations, which increasingly focus on municipalities as a privileged site of action below national sovereignty.[42]

The ultimate external limiting factor is, of course, the lack of resources and personnel. Money is probably not even the biggest concern. Global capitalism makes more and more people seriously rich, and recent studies show that many of these nouveaux riches are no less other-regarding in their ethical outlook than many ordinary citizens. The problem here, as elsewhere, is that those who put money into foundations and NGOs usually also want to take control in ways that threaten the moral credentials of post-traditional civil associations.[43] Not only rich people, but NGOs themselves occasionally suffer from the condition of pulling in more money than they can digest. During the Indian Ocean tsunami in late 2004, MSF called on the public to stop donating money because nongovernmental structures were simply not adept at spending the money wisely.[44] This may have been an extreme step, but it sheds light on the structural problem that the capacity for helping disaster victims, reporting on human rights violations, or lobbying governments does not depend on funding alone. For humanitarian organizations, in particular, a more serious concern appears to be the recruitment crunch they find themselves in. There is a mismatch between the high number of sympathetic spectators and the tiny number of people who are willing to take personal risks by working in one of the crisis zones of the world.

SHOULD WE WISH THEM SUCCESS?

For the purpose of the present work, I have used a normative definition of what constitutes a "nongovernmental organization." This definition differs from the more relaxed way in which the United Nations applies the term as an abbreviatory notation for groups that are granted consultative status. In order not be misguided by how international organizations like the UN apply a self-created classificatory scheme, I have created my own definition that characterizes that NGOs as moral universalists that advocate for those who are deprived and misrecognized in some way. NGOs are one of the political expressions of powerful other-regarding moral orientations that have come to transform much of the landscape of contemporary Western politics. This sounds as if NGOs are by definition "good." But if that is the case, what is the point of asking whether we should wish them success?

Before I make an attempt to answer this seemingly tautological question of whether it is good to side with the good guys, let me summarize four general reasons why I believe that NGOs do indeed contribute to moral progress. There may be more reasons, but these are the ones I find most significant.

Pursuing a politics of inclusivity. NGOs are part of a broader movement to transnationalize struggles against denying recognition to others. The three dominant forms of abuse targeted by NGOs are physical maltreatment, the denial of basic rights, and the cultural degradation of ways of life. Individuals and groups who are subjected to these forms of disrespect do not suffer simply a setback to their interests, but a more fundamental kind of harm that entails the threat to their very sense of self.[45] One could say that NGOs are a down-to-earth version of Immanuel Kant's ideal of a "transnational elite of enlightened *philosophes* who would seek to improve international society by bringing violations of human rights anywhere to the attention of the world"[46]—except that the agenda of NGOs goes beyond human rights.

Promoting Western self-criticism. Many prominent NGOs emerged amid the Culture Wars in the West. The Culture Wars did not invent, but further reinforced and institutionalized self-monitoring and self-criticism in Western and Western-style societies. They also laid to rest the myth of a civilizing mission of the West while at the same time encouraging substantial numbers of citizens to seek new forms of political engagement. These new forms of engagement were meant to harness the power of the United States and other democratic nations that are called on to tame global anarchy by enacting and enforcing cosmopolitan harm conventions. Many non-Western NGOs emerged when Western cosmopolitanism bumped up against different standards in particular regions, and donor agencies decided to fund external critics of Western models of development and human rights.

Rationalizing blame. Unlike many journalists, politicians, and bloggers, NGOs typically make a serious effort to identify unjust acts of harming accurately and to reconstruct the chain of events that leads from the actions of one group of people to the suffering of another group of people. They also specify the norms that are violated in particular acts of harming. Thus, both causal and moral responsibilities are largely distributed on the basis of evidence. While NGOs still occasionally give in to the human urge to blame evil events on evil people, they usually do not accuse others of things that cannot be proven. As a result, they lift themselves out of the morass of sanctimonious moralism and conspiracy thinking in which many of those who use "the power of the pen" find themselves in today.[47] The moral idea of degrees of complicity has also contributed to a policy style that no longer collects and focuses all negative energies of exclusion and repression toward one single culprit.

Problematizing consumer goods. Following up on early anti-toxics movements and the critique of consumerism in the 1960s, NGOs have contributed to a different semiotics of seemingly harmless consumer goods. Diamonds have been redescribed as the shiny product of dark microhistories of enslavement, racketeering, and war; toys, paper, dresses, and tampons have been tainted as sources of carcinogenic or otherwise harmful poisons; rugs and furniture are perceived as parts of a commodity chain that often entails the forced labor of children and the destruction of rainforests; eggs, dairy, meat, or poultry products look suspicious; in cold countries like Sweden, greenhouse tomatoes now stand trial for using too much energy and thus "killing the planet." This trend represents moral progress insofar as individuals learn to see themselves as links in chains of causes and consequences that may entail considerable harm to others.

Occasionally, all these worthy approaches show signs of disintegration. Environmentalism has been criticized for degenerating into just another special interest.[48] The longstanding pattern of Western self-criticism is weakened by a revival of the equally longstanding tendency among Europeans to project all the downsides of the Western modernity on "America."[49] Human rights groups have sometimes distributed causal and moral responsibilities without corroborating their charges or without fully clarifying the norms they refer to.[50] Ethical consumerism, finally, can easily collapse into a practice that is grounded in the desire to express values and to appear "different" rather than to change the world.[51]

Yet, some critics have argued that the problem with NGOs lies not in their occasional straying from the path of virtue, but rather in their conspicuous goodness itself. David Chandler, for example, sees much of the contemporary transnational activism as a force within a larger movement that dismisses interest-based in favor of value-based international policies.[52] The pervasive rhetoric of values no longer conceals the true, self-regarding intentions of elites, but indicates a fundamental uncertainty among Western leaders and publics about the ends for which political power should be mobilized. Unsure of their interests, both nonstate actors and established political parties prefer the narcissism of expressing the "right" values over engaging with the real world. The result is a widespread "flight into idealism" and the "avoidance of political responsibility."[53] This language recalls Weber's distinction between *two ways of being good*. In his famous speech on the "vocation of politics" he explained,

> Ethically oriented activity can follow two fundamentally different, irreconcilably opposed maxims. It can follow the "ethic of principled conviction" (*Gesinnung*) or the "ethic of responsibility." It is not that the ethic of conviction is identical with irresponsibility, nor that the ethic of responsibility means the absence of principled conviction—there is of course no question of that. But there is a profound opposition between acting by the maxim of the ethic of conviction (putting it in religious terms: "The Christian does what is right and places the outcome in God's hands"), and acting by the maxim of the ethic of responsibility, which means that one must answer for the (foreseeable) *consequences* of one's actions.[54]

This distinction is relevant to our discussion of why we might have reasons to qualify our support for NGOs. We may suspect that NGOs are above all "conviction-moralists"[55] who wish to be judged by the staunchness of their faith and not so much by what they achieve. There is, in fact, evidence that the struggle against the harmful consequences of certain acts or conditions masks a more urgent struggle for recognition by unrelenting defenders of sacred norms and values. Most of the time, NGOs insist that no beneficial consequence can ever justify the crossing of the red lines that keep humans from doing certain things to other humans and the environment. As I have pointed out in chapter 4, transnational moral activism is about defining profane and sacred things as well as about the "interdictions" that "protect and isolate" the latter from the former.[56] Whales are declared sacred, no matter what indigenous hunting communities or democratic nations like Iceland, Norway, or Japan have to say. Transgenic seeds are evil, regardless what farmers think. These are cases where NGOs define success in terms of values expressed and upheld, while important consequences flowing from the realization of these values are ignored. In another example, according to many observers, the proposal advanced by Western and Indian NGOs to completely convert the agriculture in South Asia to "traditional" and "organic" farming would reap disastrous results. In light of the foreseeable consequences, we should *not* wish the NGOs success, even less so since they do not have to bear the consequences of whatever decision is taken.

A more complicated case is the anti-landmine campaign, which does not lend itself to the charge of blindly defending convictions with little regard for outcomes. To the contrary, the campaigners were the first who actually studied some of the horrific effects of using antipersonnel landmines and deserve praise for having made others aware of these hitherto neglected consequences. Yet there was also an element of bracketing out certain inconvenient consequences that would have resulted from a truly universal ban on landmines. As is well known, the U.S. government refused to sign the Mine Ban Treaty because it would have forced the military to remove more than one million landmines buried along the border between North and South Korea. The crucial detail that has regularly been glossed over by the NGOs involved in the campaign is that there are credible assessments predicting that in the event of a conflict on the Korean Peninsula, the absence of landmines would result in a dramatic increase in American combat losses.[57] If these assessments are correct and if NGOs were interested in producing the best overall outcome, as judged from an impartial viewpoint, the NGOs would have advocated either (1) a customized treaty granting some countries a narrowly circumscribed exemption from the general prohibition of landmines or (2) a burden-sharing scheme that would have required the signatories of the treaty to commit soldiers to missions deemed necessary by the international community. Instead, the NGO community supported Canada and other states that saw the landmine issue as an opportunity to grandstand at the expense of America and to garner some moral prestige without paying a price.[58]

Still a different picture emerges the more we move toward groups that are active in the fields of international trade, foreign aid, environment, and development. Here we often find a reversal of roles, with NGOs taking a consequentialist stand, and World Bank and IMF officials espousing an "absolute ethics"[59] that seeks to apply ready-made blueprints to highly diverse situations across the world with little regard to the wider consequences.[60] By contrast, NGOs in these fields are pioneers of an ethic of responsibility who highlight the full spectrum of impacts resulting, for example, from the introduction of patent laws that may harm HIV/AIDS patients in poor countries, or from World Bank projects such as large hydroelectric dams that have forced millions of people from their homes and lands with impacts including economic hardship, community disintegration, and an increase in mental and physical health problems. Humanitarian groups and "aid-watch" NGOs, too, have contributed to a better understanding of the harm to others that can result from well-intentioned, but poorly thought out foreign aid.[61] At the end of this spectrum, we find environmental groups that sometimes hardly show any deep convictions at all, as they seem to be looking only to short-term policy payoff and simple technical solutions to complex political problems.[62]

In short, NGOs, being a diverse lot, cannot be simply assigned to either of the two ethical approaches sketched out by Weber. The staff of some organizations are clearly motivated by an ethic of conviction that tells them to do the "right" thing regardless of the wider consequences and ramifications of their actions; other activists, by contrast, think almost like social engineers whose only concern is the achievement of good ends. This ethical diversity makes NGOs a fascinating site where the the conflict between Weber's two ways of being good is played out in the most exemplary manner.

SUMMARY

In this chapter, I have introduced a range of distinctions in order to make the unwieldy topic of political "success" amenable to further exploration. Apart from the ultimate impact of political achievements, there are two lesser forms of success worth considering. With regard to global public policy, NGOs influence both what we know and how we frame our preferences. To make people aware of a calamity or to make them willing to act on their awareness can be a success in itself.

Unlike previous contributors to the NGO literature, I believe that the role of NGOs as normative innovators has been overestimated. Crucial for their success at different levels are rather the specific information and the public emotion they are able to generate around certain issues. The campaign against conflict diamonds from West Africa is a success story because NGOs succeeded in combining accurate information with popular imaginations about the meaning of diamonds in a way that alerted and changed the behavior of large firms, states, and international organizations. It would be nice if similar successes could be repeated endlessly, or if money and goodwill would be enough to take on all the other injustices in the world. Unfortunately, due to a number of structural limits, that is not possible. Some of these limits are inherent to the very organizational form of NGOs. Thus, real-world problems need to be transformed into "issues," and not every problem fits into the required format. The diffusion of small arms and light weapons throughout the world, for instance, is a problem causing a lot of harm, but it has never become a successful campaign issue, mostly because victims and perpetrators cannot be unambiguously identified. Western perceptions and prejudices about alien "cultures" can also hamper the rise of an issue, as I have shown referring to the case of the oppression of Dalits in India.

Among the outer limits to the success of NGOs I have stressed the role of shame on the part of those who are accused by activists of doing harm or of not preventing others from doing harm. In my mind, this point is critical for understanding the limited role played by NGOs in international society. For NGOs to achieve their ends, evildoers need to be in touch with an internalized "other" who evaluates and sometimes rejects their actions, which is the same as to say that they must be able to feel shame. If the perpetrators can not be shamed (because there is no overlap between their own and their critics' moral and legal standards, or because they are fanatics or plain criminals), there must be some key accomplices who can be shamed. In some cases, if, for example, a company depends on the reputation of its brand, activists can harm the reputation of this brand. In any case, shameability is another limiting factor that restricts what NGOs can achieve.

Having delineated the boundaries of the possible within which NGOs have to work, I conclude by asking whether success is always desirable. Here the key point is that as *members of the critical public*, we should develop criteria for success that differ from those of the organizations themselves. There is no way to rule out a priori that some campaigns bring incidental gain while at the same time producing significant losses for others. Following Weber, I contend that there are at least two ways of being good, depending on whether we follow the inner voice of our "convictions" or the lessons learned from constantly following up on the "consequences" of our actions. Both paths have been taken by NGOs, and both are lined with obstacles that are difficult to anticipate.

CHAPTER 7

Conclusion
Paradoxes of Organized Goodness

Over the course of the preceding chapters, I have combined theoretical arguments and empirical material to support the following three claims. First, NGOs have to be understood as forces that foster the international society of states instead of transcending it; this is true, even though activists tend to treat states and the membership of individuals in states as harmful abstractions and as barriers to genuine solidarity across borders. NGOs may think of themselves as harbingers of a post-sovereign "global civil society," but that is at best a necessary illusion. Second, although NGOs are an offshoot of the moral climate and the resources of liberal-capitalist societies, they are not a tool of Western elites attempting to remodel the whole world in their image. Instead, I have preferred to describe them metaphorically as active intermediaries and "benign parasites" in private and public networks of power into which they slip information and legitimacy in exchange for reputation, funds, and social contacts. What makes them different from mere tools is that they alter the behavior of those to whom they are attached. Third, the common theme underlying the various streams of organized moral activism is the struggle for recognition on behalf of individuals and groups who are perceived as victims of harm and injustice. The advantage of the vocabulary of recognition is that it encompasses both law-based and law-transcending forms of mutual respect: recognition of basic rights, but also "love" and "care" as well as social esteem and just rewarding for contributions made to the reproduction of society. NGOs are following what Charles Taylor called the "imperative of benevolence," which goes beyond the invocation of rights.[1]

Moreover, NGOs do not only struggle *for* the recognition of others, but also *over* principles of recognition that can be applied to situations of injustice across the globe. In constitutional democracies, these principles of recognition, which define what people can reasonably expect from each other and the community in terms of rights, love, and solidarity, have taken on a robust institutionalized form. In international society, by contrast, principles of recognition are by no means well established, but in flux and heavily contested. The global world is Babel-like with widely differing value systems and standards of judgment merely coexisting, often without mediation. People do not agree on what their fellow humans deserve, on how to define and prioritize human rights, or on what should count as a valuable contribution to the reproduction of global society. "Our Babel is not one of tongues," as John Dewey noted, "but of the signs and symbols without which shared experience is impossible."[2]

Most advanced groups describe themselves as opposing certain actions by states or multinational corporations without turning these entities into perennial enemies.[3] NGOs are not made for a world neatly divided between friends and foes, or between victors and vanquished. Their struggles are centered on the question not of *who* wins, but of *how* political power is exercised. The structural dualism of friends and foes is replaced by the situational dualism of victims and perpetrators. Accordingly, the concept of evil is relative and contextual rather than essentialist. Both the strengths and the weaknesses of post-traditional ways of doing politics must be understood against this background.

In this concluding chapter, I present a brief reflective survey of the manner in which NGOs combine strengths and weaknesses. Downsides of "being good" can be summarized under six headings: empiricism and wishful thinking, end of radicalism, empathy and misanthropy, contestation without representation, the paradox of clean hands, and mobilization and expropriation of moral outrage.

Empiricism and wishful thinking. Post-traditional civil associations are empirically minded agents that invest large amounts of money, time, and energy into investigating situations in which innocent people, environments, and nonhuman beings are harmed. This openness toward changing empirical realities makes them different from religious sects and traditional political parties. Two elements of their worldview are particularly striking.

First, a common assumption is that there is a preordained harmony between different social goods that can all be pursued simultaneously without significant trade-offs. Human rights groups, for instance, do not only claim that women's rights, the rule of law, and the prevention of torture are worthy goals in themselves, but also that the realization of these goals has a positive impact on other, more mundane goals like wealth creation or national security. Contra Hedley Bull and much of classical political science, post-traditional civil associations gloss over tensions between "justice" and "order."[4] In their view, it pays to be good: War crime tribunals prevent war; the humane treatment of terrorist suspects softens them and produces useful information; women's rights are good for economic growth; and ending the occupation of the West Bank would improve Israel's security.[5] At the heart of these tacitly assumed causal links is a managerialist liberalism that portrays reality as a series of iterative win-win situations. Without further reasoning, contemporary NGOs exclude the possibility that human goods are often incommensurable and cannot be pursued successfully at the same time.

Second, many NGOs behave as if in order to get rid of a particular evil, it is enough to inject moral "values" into politics. This is wrong on two counts. For one, it is wrong to believe that evil persists only as long as it is impossible to shake people out of their indifference. The new civil associations tend to ignore that both the public and those who are morally responsible for a bad situation may have their own values that radically differ from those held dear by liberal activists. As Jeffrey Alexander has argued, an iconic megacrime like the Holocaust did not happen because people were forgetful of moral values. Rather, this event was itself value driven: "It was an evil event motivated not by the absence of values . . . but by the presence of heinous values."[6] A certain kind of righteousness can also be wrong for another reason. There is evidence that the focus on values and symbolism has sometimes stifled badly needed discussions about adequate policy tools in situations in which the right values alone did not achieve much on the ground.[7]

End of radicalism. The implicit political theory of NGOs has no place for the classical concept of a state of emergency requiring the temporary suspension of moral and legal norms; yet, in a different sense, the entire worldview and mode of operation of post-traditional associations are centered on a culture of emergency. Emergencies are the results of sudden changes and thus a magnet for attention, which in turn is a prerequisite for NGO action. Also, emergencies usually lay bare the elementary structure of victimization. At a deeper level, the focus on humanitarian or environmental emergencies is an expression of what Judith Shklar called "the end of radicalism"—her shorthand for the steady decline of enlightenment, rationalism, and the optimistic belief in the possibility of changing the world for the better.[8] Without referring to Shklar's early work, the French political scientist Zaki Laïdi has made a similar argument: "The end of utopia has brought the sanctification of emergency, elevating it to a central political category."[9] Since we have lost faith in the future, we have become absorbed by emergencies that are seized as opportunities to display our moral "awareness." The implication is that virtues mobilized to help distant victims in emergencies are weak and shallow because they are disconnected from any shared project of social transformation.

Empathy and misanthropy. Michael Ignatieff has gone one step further by uncovering a streak of misanthropy in the Western obsession with global victims. As he puts it, "the twentieth-century inflection of moral universalism has taken the form of an anti-ideological and anti-political ethic of siding with the victim; the moral risk entailed by this ethic is misanthropy."[10] The paradox is that moral activists risk "misanthropy" because they see little that is positive in the societies in which they work—only passive victims and their abusers. In particular, contemporary cosmopolitan activists tend to single out "poverty" as the sole cue for thinking about entire continents such as Africa, not realizing that Africans may interpret this compassionate representation as a form of denigration. Referring to certain antipoverty campaigns in Britain, a well-known South African businessman recently made the point that "Africa does not exist simply to make people in this country [that is, Britain] or anywhere else in the developed world feel good about themselves.... In a continent of nearly 700 million people, 50 different countries and hundreds of different languages, there is another Africa, vibrant and full of potential that also demands recognition."[11]

Contestation without representation. Like doctors or teachers, NGOs serve their target groups without representing them. Representation would entail that the activities of NGOs could somehow be ascribed to those on whose behalf they are acting. Because this is not the case, NGOs cannot be expected to contribute to transnational forms of democracy.[12] Post-traditional associations are run by restricted circles of unelected professionals and are externally funded through private donations or public sponsorship. The trend toward bypassing broader constituencies has obvious strategic advantages in terms of flexibility and networking capacity. Yet these tactical advantages come with a price. As sociologist Theda Skocpol has pointed out, the new organizations that are so well adapted to the environments of international policy deliberations are unable to channel the aspirations of ordinary citizens who want to get involved in political life. Citizens may sometimes still be able to follow some of the debates being kicked off by advocacy groups; yet it is difficult for them to relate these debates to the problems of their own lives.[13] The paradox here is that NGOs expand their reach to faraway locations and audiences all over the world, while their domestic reach remains restricted and their roots do not run deep into society.[14] It is fair to say that in this respect, NGOs deviate from the historical model of abolitionism that was still based on intense "public debate and popular participation."[15]

The staff-heavy, top-down structure of modern NGOs ties in with a managerialist approach to problem solving. This approach is, first of all, predicated on the understanding that it is "up to us" to fix the problems of global poverty, environmental degradation, and political tyranny, because in one way or another we are ultimately responsible for the current state of affairs. This implies the belief that citizens directly affected by these problems can do little to change their situation. Another aspect of managerialism is to redefine the problems in such a way as to make them amenable to the means already available to NGOs and international organizations. For example, some NGOs frame the HIV/AIDS crisis as if internationally imposed patents on new medicines were the single biggest cause of the easily avoidable misery of millions of patients. This ignores the sociocultural conditions of harm and misrecognition in the countries most affected by the epidemic, from quackery and governmental indifference to the social exclusion and stigmatization of AIDS victims. NGOs have a tendency to treat causal factors as negligable if they have no way to address them effectively.[16]

The structural shortcomings of advocacy groups are compounded by asymmetrical donor-NGO relationships, which are fraught with paradoxes. Thus, in order to become eligible for funding, groups in less developed countries are required to be grassroots—yet foreign funding frequently contributes to establishing "civic oligarchies," as Sarah Henderson has shown in her research on Russian civic groups funded by American donors.[17] Groups are also required to cooperate with like-minded groups to build civil society structures—yet the injection of foreign money typically enhances competition between groups and reinforces inequalities. Even from the perspective of program officers with Western donor agencies, the ambition of externally promoting civil society by propping up NGOs is often felt to be "hopeless."[18]

The paradox of clean hands. Humanitarian organizations like Doctors Without Borders (MSF) were among the first to reflect on the many ways in which the other-regarding ethic of sections of the global public has been exploited by ruthless regimes and militias. No longer do warring parties want to intimidate enemies and bystanders by appearing invulnerable and victorious; they rather prefer to manipulate the public by parading their own pain and misery. This has often prompted the morally sensitive to support distant sufferers who were held hostage by their rulers. Seizing an opportunity, rogue regimes have starved their own populations in order to pull in foreign money.[19] In other contexts, war criminals and *génocidaires* have posed as victims, using foreign aid to retool their war-fighting capabilities.[20] Such cases have led to vigorous debates about the circumstances under which the *withdrawal of aid* from a troubled region becomes a morally defensible option.

Perversely, universal benevolence can directly play into the hands of power politics. A liberal state that feels under intense threat may have an interest in projecting a ferocious image of itself in order to deter its enemies. After 9/11, for example, the United States was keen to teach the world that the country, "when severely antagonized, is to be feared; that it grinds its mortal enemies to powder as it did sixty years ago."[21] One could probably make the case that this intention was to some extent well served by the tactic of human rights organizations that compared the Guantanamo detention center to Soviet forced labor camps ("gulag of our time"), to name the most drastic example of NGO rhetoric during the "global war on terror."

Another paradoxical consequence of the clean-hands approach of NGOs is that it leaves responsible politicians to ponder ways to dodge moral criticism by taking hitherto unthinkable measures. Consider the following two examples. Comprehensive sanctions and embargoes were introduced as alternatives to war, but were later denounced to have extremely harmful consequences for innocent civilians, including women and children in target countries. There is some evidence that by tainting this tool as immoral, activists have perversely reestablished war as a comparatively attractive option. For example, Claire Short, a former member of the government of Tony Blair in Britain, justified her support for the Iraq war by pointing to the need of ending the *suffering* of the Iraqi people caused by the sanctions regime.[22]

The second example concerns the relationship between peacekeeping forces and their host governments. In early 2007, Amnesty International Canada legally challenged the transfer of prisoners made by Canadian forces in Afghanistan after it was learned that the Afghan authorities had mistreated prisoners who were handed over to them. While this charge was empirically accurate and morally well founded, Amnesty was vague about what to do in a situation in which the foreign troops in Afghanistan were expected to transfer sovereignty to the authorities on whose behalf they claimed to use force. One proposal was that Canada or other democratic nations should build their own prison camps.[23] However, Amnesty did not spell out the consequences of such a scenario; if Western powers establish or take over law enforcement institutions in foreign countries, they begin to directly run these countries, which would then be reduced to colonies.

Mobilization and expropriation of moral outrage. This book is not only about activists, but about activists who are smart and skilled. NGOs think a lot before acting, but they do not necessarily make other people think. Much of their public rhetoric is geared toward the arousal of moral outrage against the violation of sacred norms and values. It has not become a practice of global NGOs to give reasons for their positions, which are regularly presented as self-evident. While I do not wish to challenge the acceptability of many of the norms and values defended by NGOs, I do believe that their nonargumentative rhetoric poses a problem because it hinders the development of a more deliberative democracy. There are, for example, many valid arguments for the abolition of the death penalty; yet, one can still agree with Amy Gutmann and Dennis Thompson that defending capital punishment within the rule of law is a "position that merits respect,"[24] like various positions one can hold with regard to abortion rights and similar issues.

By removing too much from public debate, NGOs have occasionally themselves become icons of civil religion. An opinion poll in Germany recently revealed that 50 percent of the German population thinks it "should not be allowed" to state that "environmental organizations such as Friends of the Earth, Greenpeace and others do not really care about the environment, but are mainly interested in projecting a favorable image of themselves."[25] In Germany, at least, NGOs are almost worshipped as revelations of "the good" by some sections of the population. The same reason that makes NGOs poor deliberative democrats also makes them ill equipped to mediate between different value systems in international society.

Let me end this discussion by recalling an observation made many years ago by the great American social historian Barrington Moore, who was worried about the trend in contemporary Western societies toward the "expropriation of moral outrage."[26] Writing in a neo-Marxist spirit, he compared this process to the expropriation of the means of production in capitalism. From this perspective, professional organizations are channeling our moral feelings about an ever-growing catalog of injustices that are being presented to us in easily consumable media stories:

> Sorting through the day's mail one can decide whether or not to express moral outrage about political prisoners in Chile or the Soviet Union, black or Spanish-speaking victims of racial injustice in American cities, the plight of farm laborers in California or that of whales in the Pacific Ocean. It is even possible to gauge very nicely the intensity of one's moral outrage by the size of the check. . . . The system allocates society's store of moral outrage in exactly the same way as the market allocates the supply of fruit juices or canned potatoes.[27]

In their own ways, modern NGOs have made this market-like "system" of processing moral feelings more fine tuned and efficient than ever. Moore's observation may have been overly pessimistic (and in some of its political conclusions, wrong headed), but the historian was certainly correct in pointing to the paradox of the creation of a moral public of spectators that is more interested in the display of moral excellence than in political effectiveness. NGOs in international society have often proved to be brilliant, Hermes-like players who move ably between places and geographical scales to dispatch their messages. But they are not good at involving the public in more than superficial ways. Only within much broader alliances of democratic states and social forces can they contribute to "strengthening international order by confirming a new degree of moral solidarity in international society."[28]

Notes

Chapter 1

1. Bill Clinton, speech delivered at a banquet given by RehabCare, Dublin, Ireland, May 23, 2005, http://www.rehab.ie/press/ClintonAddress.pdf (accessed February 1, 2007).
2. Much of this millenarian rhetoric can be found, for example, in Ulrich Beck, *What is Globalization?* trans. Patrick Camiller (Cambridge: Polity, 1999).
3. *Economist*, "The Non-Governmental Order," December 11, 1999, pp. 18–19.
4. Lester M. Salamon et al., *Global Civil Society: Dimensions of the Nonprofit Sector* (Baltimore: Johns Hopkins Institute for Policy Studies, 1999).
5. Peter J. Spiro, "New Global Potentates: Nongovernmental Organizations and the 'Unregulated' Marketplace," *Cardozo Law Review* 18 (1996): 957–69.
6. Quoted in Nicola Short, "The Role of NGOs in the Ottawa Process to Ban Landmines," *International Negotiation* 4 (1999): 481.
7. Max Weber, *The Essential Weber: A Reader*, ed. Sam Whimster (London and New York: Routledge, 2004), 347.
8. Ibid., 132, my italics.
9. I do not want to rule out that some local groups recognized as NGOs, particularly in developing countries, are focussed on the promotion of their members' rights. My inquiry is limited to international and internationally oriented NGOs.
10. See Charles Taylor, *Sources of the Self: The Making of the Modern Identity* (Cambridge, MA: Harvard University Press, 1989), 410–13.
11. See Beck, *What is Globalization?*
12. Mary Kaldor, *Global Civil Society: An Answer to War* (Cambridge: Polity, 2003), 2. Both the term "global civil society" and its close connection to the NGO phenomenon can be traced back to the classic article by Ronnie D. Lipschutz, "Reconstructing World Politics: The Emergence of Global Civil Society," *Millennium: Journal of International Studies* 21, no. 3 (1992): 389–420.
13. See Kaldor, *Global Civil Society*, 46; and John Keane, *Global Civil Society?* (Cambridge: Cambridge University Press, 2003), 18.

14. Amy Gutmann and Dennis Thompson, *Why Deliberative Democracy?* (Princeton, NJ: Princeton University Press, 2004), 39.
15. On international organizations as bureaucracies, see Michael Barnett and Martha Finnemore, *Rules for the World: International Organizations in Global Politics* (Ithaca, NY: Cornell University Press, 2004).
16. See Robert Blood, "Should NGOs be Viewed as 'Political Corporations'?" *Journal of Communication Management* 9, no. 2 (2004): 120–33.
17. See Martha Finnemore and Kathryn Sikkink, "International Norm Dynamics and Political Change," *International Organization* 52, no. 4 (1998): 896–99.
18. See Jan W. van Deth, "Interesting but Irrelevant: Social Capital and the Saliency of Politics in Western Europe," *European Journal of Political Research* 37 (2000): 115–47.
19. See, for example, the recommendations given by the Action Center of People for Ethical Treatment of Animals (PETA), http://www.peta.org/actioncenter/act.asp (accessed February 1, 2007).
20. Michael Hardt and Antonio Negri, *Empire* (Cambridge: Cambridge University Press, 2000), 36. It is interesting to note that Hardt and Negri draw on the work of Michel Foucault, although Foucault himself was a staunch defender of the medical and human rights NGOs of his time. In 1984, for example, he publicly sided with private international efforts to act in support of Vietnamese refugees, defending the right of citizens "to effectively intervene in the sphere of international policy and strategy." See Michel Foucault, "Confronting Governments: Human Rights," in *Power: Essential Works of Foucault 1954–1984*, vol. 3, ed. James D. Faubion, trans. Robert Hurley et al. (New York: The New Press, 2001), 475.
21. Niall Ferguson, *Colossus: The Price of America's Empire* (New York: Penguin, 2004), 11.
22. See Sarah K. Lischer, "Military Intervention and the Humanitarian 'Force Multiplier,'" *Global Governance* 13 (2007): 99–118.
23. For an excellent empirical rebuttal to the "imperialist criticism," see Nanette Funk, "Women's NGOs in Central and Eastern Europe and the Former Soviet Union: The Imperialist Criticism," in *Women and Citizenship in Central and Eastern Europe*, ed. Jasmina Lukic, Joanna Regulska, and Darja Zavirsek (Aldershot, UK: Ashgate, 2006).
24. A good example for this neo-Marxist line of thought is Joachim Hirsch, "The State's New Clothes: NGOs and the Internationalization of States," *Rethinking Marxism* 15, no. 2 (2003): 237–62.
25. To my knowledge, this label was first used by a critic who gave the school a boost by calling for its closure. See Roy E. Jones, "The English School of International Relations: A Case for Closure," *Review of International Studies* 7, no. 1 (1981): 1–13.
26. See Hedley Bull, *The Anarchical Society: A Study of Order in World Politics*, 3rd ed. (New York: Columbia University Press, 2002).

27. See Andrew Linklater and Hidemi Suganami, *The English School of International Relations: A Contemporary Reassessment* (Cambridge: Cambridge University Press, 2006), 44–47.
28. Bull, *The Anarchical Society*, 21.
29. See Linklater and Suganami, *The English School of International Relations*, ch. 5–7.
30. Bull, *The Anarchical Society*, 305.
31. Ibid.
32. See Linklater and Suganami, *The English School of International Relations*, 223–24; and Axel Honneth, "Critical Theory," in *The Fragmented World of the Social: Essays in Social and Political Philosophy*, trans. Charles W. Wright (Albany, NY: State University of New York Press, 1995), 77–78.
33. See Andrew Linklater, "The Transformation of Political Community: E. H. Carr, Critical Theory and International Relations," *Review of International Studies* 23 (1997): 321–38.
34. See, for example, Hartmut Elsenhans, "Marginality, Rent and the Non-Governmental Organisations," in *Non-Governmental Organisations in Development: Theory and Practice*, ed. Noorjahan Bava (New Delhi: Kanishka, 1997).
35. For more on this tripartite scheme, see Axel Honneth, *The Struggle for Recognition: The Moral Grammar of Social Conflicts*, trans. Joel Anderson (Cambridge: Polity, 1995). For a useful introduction to the theme of "recognition," see Simon Thompson, *The Political Theory of Recognition: A Critical Introduction* (Cambridge: Polity, 2006) as well as Jean-Philippe Deranty and Emmanuel Renault, "Politicizing Honneth's Ethics of Recognition," *Thesis Eleven* 88 (2007): 92–111.
36. See Volker Heins, *Der Neue Transnationalismus: Nichtregierungsorganisationen und Firmen im Konflikt um die Rohstoffe der Biotechnologie* (Frankfurt: Campus, 2001). For a short English summary, see Volker Heins, "From New Political Organizations to Changing Moral Geographies: Unpacking Global Civil Society," *Geojournal* 52, no. 1 (2000): 37–44.

Chapter 2

1. See Barnett and Finnemore, *Rules for the World*, 31–33.
2. For details, see Kerstin Martens, *NGOs and the United Nations: Institutionalization, Professionalization and Adaptation* (Basingstoke, UK: Palgrave Macmillan, 2006).
3. Lyman C. White, *The Structure of Private International Organizations* (Philadelphia: George S. Ferguson, 1933); John Dewey, *The Public and Its Problems* (New York: Henry Holt, 1927), 70. A good source on the predecessors of NGOs is William Korey, *NGOs and the Universal Declaration of Human Rights: "A Curious Grapevine"* (New York: St. Martin's, 1998).

4. See the list, "NGOs not in Consultative Status with the Economic and Social Council that have been accredited to the World Conference against Racism, Racial Discrimination, Xenophobia and Related Intolerance," http://www.unhchr.ch/html/racism/05-ngolist.html.
5. Raymond L. Bryant, *Nongovernmental Organizations in Environmental Struggles: Politics and the Making of Moral Capital in the Philippines* (New Haven, CT: Yale University Press, 2005).
6. On NGOs as "civil society organizations," see Ronnie D. Lipschutz, "Power, Politics and Global Civil Society," *Millennium: Journal of International Studies* 33, no. 3 (2005): 747–69; on NGOs as "advocacy networks," see Margaret E. Keck and Kathryn Sikkink, *Activists Beyond Borders: Advocacy Networks in International Politics* (Ithaca, NY: Cornell University Press, 1998).
7. For more on ideal types, see Weber, *The Essential Weber*, 387–99.
8. Ibid., 354.
9. See Jeffrey C. Alexander, *The Civil Sphere* (New York: Oxford University Press, 2006), 92–105.
10. Pascal Dauvin and Johanna Siméant, *Le Travail humanitaire: Les acteurs des ONG, du siege au terrain* (Paris: Presses de Sciences Po, 2002), 52.
11. See Stephen Hopgood, *Keepers of the Flame: Understanding Amnesty International* (Ithaca, NY: Cornell University Press, 2006), 211.
12. Chris Rose, "Dangerous Illusions: Criticism of United Kingdom Environmental Policy," *New Statesman & Society*, January 5, 1996, p. 31. Rose was deputy executive and program director of Greenpeace UK.
13. Susan Dicklitch and Doreen Lwanga, "The Politics of Being Non-Political: Human Rights Organizations and the Creation of a Positive Human Rights Culture in Uganda," *Human Rights Quarterly* 25 (2003): 482–509.
14. Jean-Hervé Bradol, "How Images of Adversity Affect the Quality of Aid," in *Civilians Under Fire: Humanitarian Practices in the Congo Republic, 1998–2000*, ed. Marc Le Pape and Pierre Salignon (New York: Doctors Without Borders, n.d.), 22.
15. See Michael Walzer, "Political Action: The Problem of Dirty Hands," *Philosophy and Public Affairs* 2, no. 2 (1973): 160–80.
16. As one group declares, "We respect one another. We are very different . . . liberals and not so liberals; atheists, agnostics and believers; democrats, anarchists, and monarchists" ("Who and What is Memorial?" http://www.memo.ru/eng/about/whowe.htm).
17. See Andrew Bounds, "EU's Grim Climate Change Warming," *Financial Times*, January 6, 2007, p. 3.
18. Note that the otherness of those on whose behalf NGOs are speaking and acting is not only *situational*. Refugees who raise funds in a host country for their oppressed brethren back home are not other-regarding in the way I use the term in this book.
19. Weber suggested defining the state by its ability to "exercise a monopoly of legitimate physical force" (*The Essential Weber*, 356).

20. Rony Brauman, "Préface," in Abdel-Rahman Ghandour, *Jihad Humanitaire: Enquete sur les ONG islamiques* (Paris: Flammarion, 2002), 16.
21. See Upendra Baxi, *The Future of Human Rights*, 2nd ed. (New York: Oxford University Press, 2006), 76–80.
22. I am paraphrasing E. E. Schattschneider, *The Semisovereign People: A Realist's View of Democracy in America* (New York: Holt, Rinehart and Winston, 1960), 27.
23. Weber, *The Essential Weber*, 195.
24. Ibid.
25. Montesquieu, *The Spirit of the Laws*, ed. Anne M. Cohler et al. (Cambridge: Cambridge University Press, 1989), 21 (book 3, ch. 1).
26. See Max Horkheimer, "Egoism and the Freedom Movement: On the Anthropology of the Bourgeois Era," in *Between Philosophy and Social Science: Selected Early Writings*, trans. G. F. Hunter et al. (Cambridge, MA: MIT Press, 1993). It is interesting to note that the shift from a model of emancipatory and self-regarding politics to a model of ethical and other-regarding engagement can be reconstructed within the intellectual history of the Frankfurt School itself. Thus, already in the 1940s, Adorno saw "true distinction" only in "the virtue of giving" ("A Word for Morality," in *Minima Moralia: Reflections from Damaged Life*, trans. E. Jephcott [London: Verso, 1978], 97). At the same time, self-regarding class struggles were described as degenerating into turf battles among conspiratorial "rackets." See, for example, Otto Kirchheimer, "In Quest of Sovereignty," *Journal of Politics* 6, no. 2 (1944): 139–76, as well as Volker Heins, "Critical Theory and the Traps of Conspiracy Thinking," *Philosophy and Social Criticism* 33, no. 7 (2007): 787–801.
27. It is undeniable that in the real world other-regarding actions often shade into self-interested behaviors. Checkbook contributions to a charity, for example, can generate and might also be motivated by the pursuit of a "warm glow of self-satisfaction" or even feelings of "recreational grief." For this line of sarcastic criticism, see Patrick West, *Conspicuous Compassion: Why Sometimes it Really is Cruel to be Kind* (London: Civitas, 2004), 37, 11.
28. Joel Feinberg, *Harm to Others* (New York: Oxford University Press, 1984), 74.
29. Ibid., 73, 76.
30. See Theda Skocpol, *Diminished Democracy: From Membership to Management in American Civic Life* (Norman: University of Oklahoma Press, 2003).
31. Weber, *The Essential Weber*, 348. For the analogy between NGOs and "mendicant orders," see also Hardt and Negri, *Empire*, 36.
32. Among other things, NGOs differ from the revolutionary "politics of pity" criticized by Hannah Arendt in that they focus on *specific and empirically identifiable* groups of victims, not on amorphous masses. See Hannah Arendt, *On Revolution* (London: Penguin, 1990); and Volker Heins,

"Reasons of the Heart: Weber and Arendt on Emotion in Politics," *The European Legacy* 12, no. 6 (2007): 715–28.

33. See the analysis in Patrice Palmer, "Race and Representation: The Impact of Constructed Images of People in the 'Third World,'" (master's thesis, Department of Sociology and Equity Studies in Education, University of Toronto, 2003), 51–52.
34. See the "Political Apologies and Reparations," Web site at Wilfrid Laurier University in Waterloo, Ontario, Canada, http://political-apologies.wlu.ca/about.php.
35. See Michal Ben-Josef Hirsch, "Agents of Truth and Justice: Truth Commissions and the Transitional Justice Epistemic Community," in *Rethinking Ethical Foreign Policy: Pitfalls, Possibilities and Paradoxes*, ed. David Chandler and Volker Heins (London and New York: Routledge, 2007), 197–99.
36. See the mission statement of Memorial: "Perpetuating the Memory of the Victims of Repression," http://www.memo.ru/eng/memory/intro.htm.
37. Judith N. Shklar, "Putting Cruelty First," in Judith N. Shklar, *Ordinary Vices* (Cambridge, MA: Harvard University Press, 1984), 17.
38. This point has been made by Hanna Fenichel Pitkin, *The Concept of Representation* (Berkeley: University of California Press, 1967), 139.
39. Ibid.
40. See Raymond L. Bryant, "False Prophets? Mutant NGOs and Philippine Environmentalism," *Society and Natural Resources* 15 (2002): 629–39.
41. Stephen Jackson, "'The State Didn't Even Exist': Non-Governmentality in Kivu, Eastern DR Congo," in *Between a Rock and a Hard Place: African NGOs, Donors and the State*, ed. Jim Igoe and Tim Kelsall (Durham, NC: Carolina Academic Press, 2005), 178–80.
42. For a nuanced view on environmental Gongos in China, see, for example, Fenshi Wu, "New Partners or Old Brothers? GONGOs in Transnational Environmental Advocacy in China," *China Environmental Series* 5 (2002): 45–58.
43. Carsten Greve, Matthew Flinders, and Sandra van Thiel, "Quangos: What's in a Name?" *Governance* 12, no. 2 (1999): 130.
44. This distinction is often used for statistical purposes. See, for example, the data and classifications in London School of Economics and Political Science (LSE), ed., *Global Civil Society Yearbook*, http://www.lse.ac.uk/Depts/global/yearbook.htm.
45. Baxi, *The Future of Human Rights*, 220.
46. Here I happen to agree with David Korten's otherwise overly linear four-generation model, which characterizes the provision of relief and welfare services as the very first stage of NGO development. See David C. Korten, *Getting to the Twenty-First Century: Voluntary Action and the Global Agenda* (West Hartford, CT: Kumarian, 1990), 113.
47. See Sidney Tarrow, *The New Transnational Activism* (Cambridge: Cambridge University Press, 2005). For the widely held view that the

"NGOization" of social movements is a symptom of decay, see, for example, Sabine Lang, "The NGOization of Feminism: Institutionalization and Institution Building within the German Women's Movements," in *Global Feminisms since 1945*, ed. Bonnie G. Smith (New York and London: Routledge 2000).
48. See the *Handbook on Non-Profit Institutions in the System of National Accounts* (New York: United Nations Statistics Division, 2003), http://unstats.un.org/unsd/publication/SeriesF/SeriesF_91E.pdf. UNSD also publishes a specialized *Classification Newsletter* that once in a while adds or redefines a group or a subgroup.
49. This aspect has been highlighted by Paul Wapner, *Environmental Activism and World Civic Politics* (Albany, NY: State University of New York Press, 1996).
50. See Feinberg, *Harm to Others*, ch. 3.
51. Ibid., 106.
52. Honneth, *The Struggle for Recognition*, 158.
53. See Michael Flitner and Volker Heins, "Modernity and Life Politics: Conceptualizing the Biodiversity Crisis," *Political Geography* 21 (2002): 319–40.
54. See Honneth, *The Struggle for Recognition*, ch. 5 and 6.
55. On this sense of recognition as "acknowledgement," see Stanley Cohen, *States of Denial: Knowing about Atrocities and Suffering* (Cambridge: Polity, 2001), ch. 9.
56. Thomas Hobbes, *Leviathan*, ed. C.B. Macpherson (London: Penguin Classics, 1985), 185.
57. See Feinberg, *Harm to Others*, 225–32.
58. Axel Honneth, "Redistribution as Recognition: A Response to Nancy Fraser," in Nancy Fraser and Axel Honneth, *Redistribution or Recognition? A Political-Philosophical Exchange*, trans. J. Golb, J. Ingram, and C. Wilke (London: Verso, 2003), 157; my italics.
59. James Tully, "Recognition and Dialogue: The Emergence of a New Field," *Critical Review of International Social and Political Philosophy* 7, no. 3 (2004): 86.
60. For an elaboration of this theme, see Volker Heins, "Realizing Honneth: Redistribution, Recognition, and Global Justice," *Journal of Global Ethics* (forthcoming); on manifesto rights, see Joel Feinberg, "The Nature and Value of Rights," in Joel Feinberg, *Rights, Justice, and the Bonds of Liberty: Essays in Social Philosophy* (Princeton, NJ: Princeton University Press, 1980).
61. Honneth, "Redistribution as Recognition," 135; see also Honneth, *The Struggle for Recognition*, ch. 8.
62. See Hopgood, *Keepers of the Flame*, 35.
63. See, for example, Hagai Katz, "Gramsci, Hegemony, and Global Civil Society Networks," *Voluntas* 17 (2006): 332–47; Ole Jacob Sending and Iver B. Neumann, "Governance to Governmentality: Analyzing NGOs,

States, and Power," *International Studies Quarterly* 50 (2006): 651–72; Alnoor Ebrahim, *NGOs and Organizational Change: Discourse, Reporting, and Learning* (Cambridge: Cambridge University Press, 2003), ch. 1.
64. Honneth, "Redistribution as Recognition," 151.
65. Ken Booth, "Security in Anarchy: Utopian Realism in Theory and Practice," *International Affairs* 67 (1991): 542.
66. Keane, *Global Civil Society?*, 18.
67. Kaldor, *Global Civil Society?*, 46.
68. Martin Shaw, *Global Society and International Relations* (Cambridge: Polity, 1994), 11.
69. See Moses Naim, "From the Vatican to Baghdad, the Little Guy is Calling the Shots," *Financial Times*, June 13, 2006.
70. Robert Rohrschneider and Russell J. Dalton, "A Global Network? Transnational Cooperation among Environmental Groups," *The Journal of Politics* 64, no. 2 (2002): 529.
71. See Sarah L. Henderson, *Building Democracy in Contemporary Russia: Western Support for Grassroots Organizations* (Ithaca, NY: Cornell University Press, 2003), ch. 3.
72. See Kenneth W. Foster, "Associations in the Embrace of an Authoritarian State: State Domination of Society?" *Studies in Comparative International Development* 35, no. 4 (2001): 84–109.
73. Alexander Cooley and James Ron, "The NGO Scramble: Organizational Insecurity and the Political Economy of Transnational Action," *International Security* 27, no. 1 (2002): 5–39.
74. See ibid., 31–36.
75. See David A. Lake and Wendy Wong, "The Politics of Networks: Interests, Power, and Human Rights Norms," working paper, version 6.0, Department of Political Science, University of California, San Diego, 2006.
76. See Paul Brown, "Japanese Branch Outrages WWF with Whaling Plea," *Guardian*, April 2, 2002.
77. See Benchmark Environmental Consulting, *Democratic Global Governance: Report of the 1995 Benchmark Survey of NGOs* (Oslo: Royal Ministry of Foreign Affairs, 1996).
78. Following the early Chicago sociologist Herbert Blumer, I suggest that global problems "should be seen as introducing *situations* that are the occasions for people to develop their activity, their relations, and their institutions. People meet the situations with varying *schemes of interpretation* and sets of expectations, inside a framework of traditional and contemporary pressures. . . . Since people may bring to the situation different perspectives and be led to define the situation differently, the activity they fashion in the situation may differ considerably" (Herbert Blumer, *Industrialization as an Agent of Social Change: A Critical Analysis*, ed. David R. Maines and Thomas J. Morrione [New York: Aldine de Gruyter, 1990], 150, my italics).
79. See Sheri Berman, "Civil Society and the Collapse of the Weimar Republic," *World Politics* 49 (1997): 401–29.

80. Rohrschneider and Dalton, "A Global Network?" 529.
81. See Linklater and Suganami, *The English School of International Relations*, 152.
82. William F. Fisher, "Doing Good? The Politics and Antipolitics of NGO Practices," *Annual Review of Anthropology* 26 (1997): 450.
83. Bryant, *Nongovernmental Organizations*, 120.
84. Kim D. Reimann, "A View from the Top: International Politics, Norms and the Worldwide Growth of NGOs," *International Studies Quarterly* 50 (2006): 63–65.
85. See Michel Serres, *The Parasite*, trans. Lawrence R. Schehr (Baltimore: Johns Hopkins University Press, 1982). For a useful capsule analysis, see Steven D. Brown, "Michel Serres: Science, Translation and the Logic of the Parasite," *Theory, Culture & Society* 19, no. 3 (2002): 1–27.
86. Marc Williams, "The World Bank, the World Trade Organization and the Environmental Social Movement," in *Non-State Actors and Authority in the Global System*, ed. Richard A. Higgott, Geoffrey R. D. Underhill, and Andreas Bieler (London and New York: Routledge, 2000); Jan Aart Scholte, "'In the Foothills': Relations Between the IMF and Civil Society," in *Non-State Actors and Authority in the Global System*, ed. Richard A. Higgott, Geoffrey R. D. Underhill, and Andreas Bieler (London and New York: Routledge, 2000); Marina Ottaway, "Corporatism Goes Global: International Organizations, Nongovernmental Organization Networks, and Transnational Business," *Global Governance* 7 (2001): 265–92; Jonathan P. Doh and Terrence R. Guay, "Corporate Social Responsibility, Public Policy, and NGO Activism in Europe and the United States: An Institutional-Stakeholder Perspective," *Journal of Management Studies* 43, no. 1 (2006): 47–73; Daniel L. Byman, "Uncertain Partners: NGOs and the Military," *Survival* 43, no. 2 (2001): 97–114.
87. See Hendrik Spruyt, *The Sovereign State and Its Competitors* (Princeton, NJ: Princeton University Press, 1994).
88. See Tom J. Farer, "New Players in the Old Game," *American Behavioral Scientist* 38 (1995): 842–66.
89. See the conclusion in Andrew F. Cooper and Brian Hocking, "Governments, Non-Governmental Organisations, and the Recalibration of Diplomacy," *Global Society* 14 (2000): 376.
90. Serres, *The Parasite*, 224.
91. See Susan K. Sell and Aseem Prakash, "Using Ideas Strategically: The Contest Between Business and NGO Networks in Intellectual Property Rights," *International Studies Quarterly* 48 (2004): 143–75.

Chapter 3

1. Interview by the author with Hope Shand, Rural Advancement Foundation International (RAFI), February 1999.
2. See Taylor, *Sources of the Self*, part III.

3. Ibid., 255 et passim.
4. Ibid., 214.
5. Arthur Koestler, "Introduction: The Lion and the Ostrich," in *Suicide of a Nation? An Enquiry into the State of Britain*, ed. A. Koestler (London: Vintage, 1963), 7.
6. Raymond Aron, *L'Opium des Intellectuals* (Paris: Calmann-Lévy, 1955), 64.
7. See Cohen, *States of Denial*, 69, 73.
8. See Max Weber, *Ancient Judaism*, trans. H. H. Gerth and D. Martindale (New York: Free Press, 1952), 375–76.
9. Arthur J. Vidich and Stanford M. Lyman, *American Sociology: Worldly Rejections of Religion and Their Directions* (New Haven, CT: Yale University Press, 1985), 281.
10. Karl Marx, "The British Rule in India," *New York Herald Tribune*, June 25, 1853, http://www.marxists.org/archive/marx/works/1853/06/25.htm.
11. See David C. Engerman, "Modernization from the Other Shore: American Observers and the Costs of Soviet Economic Development," *American Historical Review* 105 (2000): 383–416.
12. I admit that at the margins of the political spectrum we still find people like the right-wing Christian fundamentalist Jerry Falwell, who described the 9/11 attacks as a divine punishment for the presumed moral decadence of present-day Americans—a modern equivalent for the biblical plague of crop-eating locusts. But this and similar statements were later "clarified" and "put back into context," which are indications for the lack of legitimacy of warmed-over theodicies.
13. On the "greening" of modernization, see Michael Goldman, *Imperial Nature: The World Bank and Struggles for Social Justice in the Age of Globalization* (New Haven, CT: Yale University Press, 2005); on the "softening" of Malthusianism, see Flitner and Heins, "Modernity and Life Politics."
14. See Bernard Kouchner, *Le Malheur des autres* (Paris: Odile Jacob, 1991), 114 et passim; and Dauvin and Siméant, *Le Travail humanitaire*, ch. 1.
15. See Sylvie Brunel, *Famines et politique* (Paris: Presses de Sciences Po, 2002).
16. See Anil Agarwal and Sunita Narain, "A New Morality," *Illustrated Weekly of India*, December 24, 1989, pp. 84–87.
17. See, for example, Daniel Levy and Natan Sznaider, "Memory Unbound: The Holocaust and the Formation of Cosmopolitan Memory," *European Journal of Social Theory* 5, no. 1 (2002): 87–106. Levy and Sznaider are drawing a direct line from the global decontextualization of the Holocaust memory to the emergence of a more ethical foreign policy that accepts human rights as "the new measure for a global politics" (p. 100).
18. Taylor, *Sources of the Self*, 396.
19. Cohen, *States of Denial*, 196.
20. Zaki Laïdi, *A World Without Meaning: The Crisis of Meaning in International Politics*, trans. June Burnham and Jenny Coulon (London: Routledge, 1998), 11.

21. See David Chandler, "The Other-Regarding Ethics of the 'Empire in Denial,'" in *Rethinking Ethical Foreign Policy: Pitfalls, Possibilities and Paradoxes*, ed. David Chandler and Volker Heins (London and New York: Routledge, 2007), 162–65.
22. David Chandler, *Constructing Global Civil Society: Morality and Power in International Relations* (Basingstoke, UK: Palgrave Macmillan, 2004), 57.
23. Tony Blair, "Comments at Launch of Stern Review," October 30, 2006, http://www.pm.gov.uk/output/Page10300.asp (accessed April 1, 2007).
24. See Chandler, *Constructing Global Civil Society*, 66–71.
25. See Frank Zelko, *"Make It a Green Peace": The History of an International Environmental Organization* (PhD diss., Department of History, University of Kansas, 2003), ch. 1 and 2.
26. Quoted in ibid., 108.
27. Judith N. Shklar, *After Utopia: The Decline of Political Faith* (Princeton, NJ: Princeton University Press, 1957), 146, 151.
28. Dauvin and Siméant, *Le Travail humanitaire*, 37.
29. Shklar, *After Utopia*, 146.
30. Agarwal and Narain, "A New Morality," 87.
31. See van Deth, "Interesting but Irrelevant."
32. Honneth, *The Struggle for Recognition*, 95. Note that the "fear for the Other" is by no means merely a symptom of idiosyncrasies confined to particular strata. This can be seen from global surveys that show that a majority of the global public today considers the need to "reduce the gap between the Rich and the Poor" to be the most pressing of all issues. See Gallup International, *Voice of the People 2006: What the World Thinks on Today's Global Issues* (Montreal: Transcontinental Books, 2006), ch. 1.
33. Michael Ignatieff, *The Warrior's Honor: Ethnic War and the Modern Conscience* (London: Chatto & Windus, 1998), 23.
34. In this respect, the students' revolt of 1968, in particular its French variant, represented not a new beginning but an end point of history. See the examples of rhetoric given in Andrew Feenberg and Jim Freedman, *When Poetry Ruled the Streets: The French May Events of 1968* (Albany, NY: SUNY Press, 2001), 123–45.
35. Ignatieff, *The Warrior's Honor*, 23.
36. Pier-Paolo Pasqualoni and Alan Scott, "Capitalism and the Spirit of Critique: Activism and Professional Fate in a Contemporary Social Movement/NGO," *Max Weber Studies* 6, no. 1, (2006), 152.
37. Christiane Frantz, *Karriere in NGOs: Politik als Beruf jenseits der Parteien* (Wiesbaden, Germany: VS Verlag für Sozialwissenschaften, 2005), 227.
38. See Pierre Bourdieu, *Homo Academicus*, trans. Peter Collier (Cambridge: Polity, 1988), 179–80.
39. Dauvin and Siméant, *Le Travail humanitaire*, ch. 4 ("Se réaliser en faisant de sa vie un roman.").
40. See the data compiled and regularly updated in London School of Economics and Political Science (LSE), ed., *Global Civil Society Yearbook*,

http://www.lse.ac.uk/Depts/global/yearbook.htm. The Foundation Center in New York estimates that the combined assets of all grant-making bodies in the United States grew from $30 billion in 1975 to $227 billion in 1995 and about $525 billion in 2005. All U.S. foundations gave away more than $33 billion in 2005, which is twice as much in real terms as what they gave only a decade earlier.

41. See Kim D. Reimann, "A View from the Top."
42. Ibid., 55–58.
43. Feinberg, *Harm to Others*, 126–30.
44. Ibid., ch. 4.
45. See Jean-Francois Bayart, Stephen Ellis, and Béatrice Hibou, *The Criminalization of the State in Africa* (Oxford: International African Institute, 1999).
46. Jackson, "The State Didn't Even Exist," 169.
47. See Sending and Neumann, "Governance to Governmentality," 658–63.
48. See Martens, *NGOs and the United Nations*.
49. Felice D. Gaer, "Reality Check: Human Rights NGOs Confront Governments at the UN," in *NGOs, the UN, and Global Governance*, ed. Thomas G. Weiss and Leon Gordenker (Boulder, CO: Lynne Rienner, 1996), 54.
50. See, for example, Roland Vaubel, "Principal-Agent Problems in International Organizations," *Review of International Organizations* 1, no. 2 (2006): 125–38; Gutmann and Thompson, *Why Deliberative Democracy?* 62.
51. See Barnett and Finnemore, *Rules for the World*, 28.
52. See Martens, *NGOs and the United Nations*, 73.
53. Here I am paraphrasing from Filipe Rufino, "Lobby Control Gets Lobbyists on the Move," *EUobserver.com*, April 6, 2005.
54. See John Aglionby, "NGOs boycott World Bank meetings," *Guardian*, September 14, 2006.
55. See Barnett and Finnemore, *Rules for the World*, 23–29.
56. Ibid., 34–41.
57. See *What Global Leaders Want. Report of the Third Survey of the 2020 Global Stakeholder Panel*, February 2005, http://www.2020fund.org/downloads/GSP_3_report.pdf, p. 40.
58. See Elizabeth Anne Bloodgood, *Influential Information: Nongovernmental Organizations' Role in Foreign Policy-Making and International Regime Formation* (PhD diss., Department of Politics, Princeton University, 2002).
59. See William E. DeMars, "Hazardous Partnership: NGOs and United States Intelligence in Small Wars," *International Journal of Intelligence and CounterIntelligence* 14, no. 2 (2001): 193–222.
60. See Vaubel, "Principal-Agent Problems in International Organizations," 128.
61. Quoted in Sending and Neumann, "Governance to Governmentality," 665.

62. Chadwick F. Alger, "Evolving Roles of NGOs in Member State Decision-Making in the UN System," *Journal of Human Rights* 2, no. 3 (2003): 421.
63. See William G. Ouchi, "Markets, Bureaucracies, and Clans," *Administrative Science Quarterly* 25 (1980): 129–41. See also the self-portrait of the Russian group Memorial: "What unites us? First, we are friends," http://www.memo.ru/eng/ about/whowe.htm.
64. Dauvin and Siméant, *Le Travail humanitaire*, 49.
65. Quoted in Zelko, *"Make It a Green Peace,"* 303.
66. See Johanna Siméant, "What is Going Global? The Internationalization of French NGOs 'Without Borders,'" *Review of International Political Economy* 12 (2005): 851–83.
67. See Hopgood, *Keepers of the Flame*, 35–51; Dauvin and Siméant, *Le Travail humanitaire*, 150–52.
68. Frantz, *Karriere in NGOs*, 292.
69. Ibid., 296.
70. See Felice D. Gaer, "Implementing International Human Rights Norms: UN Human Rights Treaty Bodies and NGOs," *Journal of Human Rights* 2, no. 3 (2003): 343.
71. See Ebrahim, *NGOs and Organizational Change*, 99–100.

Chapter 4

1. On non-Western slavery, see William Gervase Clarence-Smith, *Islam and the Abolition of Slavery* (New York: Oxford University Press, 2006).
2. See Martha Finnemore, *The Purpose of Intervention: Changing Beliefs about the Use of Force* (Ithaca, NY: Cornell University Press, 2003), 68–69.
3. Keck and Sikkink, *Activists Beyond Borders*, 41. Charles Taylor also links abolitionism to the theme of universal benevolence and sees this movement as signaling "something unprecedented in history" (*Sources of the Self*, 396).
4. See Christopher Leslie Brown, *Moral Capital: Foundations of British Abolitionism* (Chapel Hill: University of North Carolina Press, 2006), ch. 1.
5. Quoted in ibid., 401.
6. See Honneth, *The Struggle for Recognition*, ch. 8; and Honneth, "Redistribution as Recognition," 131.
7. See David Brion Davis, *Inhuman Bondage: The Rise and Fall of Slavery in the New World* (New York: Oxford University Press, 2006), 330–31.
8. Ibid., 331.
9. See Honneth, *The Struggle for Recognition*, ch. 5 and 6; and Honneth, "Redistribution as Recognition," 138–50.
10. Theodore Dwight Weld, *American Slavery As It Is: Testimony of a Thousand Witnesses* (New York: American Anti-Slavery Society, 1839), quoted from the 2000 electronic edition prepared by the University of North Carolina at Chapel Hill, http://docsouth.unc.edu/neh/weld/weld.html, pp. 56–57. The language of "breeding" is quoted on p. 15.
11. Davis, *Inhuman Bondage*, 248.

12. Keck and Sikkink, *Activists Beyond Borders*, 45.
13. John Wesley, quoted in Brown, *Moral Capital*, 210.
14. Morgan Godwin, quoted in Brown, *Moral Capital*, 71.
15. Brown, *Moral Capital*, 152.
16. See ibid., 152–53.
17. See Davis, *Inhuman Bondage*, 239.
18. See Brown, *Moral Capital*, 14.
19. For this distinction, see Alexander, *The Civil Sphere*, part II.
20. Finnemore, *The Purpose of Intervention*, 158.
21. See ibid., ch. 4.
22. For more on these binaries, see Alexander, *The Civil Sphere*, 57–59.
23. See Rachel Schurman and William Munro, "Ideas, Thinkers, and Social Networks: The Process of Grievance Construction in the Anti-Genetic Engineering Movement," *Theory and Society* 35 (2006): 6–10 (including the references).
24. Emile Durkheim, *The Elementary Forms of Religious Life*, trans. Joseph W. Swain (London: Allen & Unwin, 1915), 40–41.
25. For other attempts to conceptualize NGOs in religious terms, broadly defined, see Hopgood, *Keepers of the Flame*, as well as André Beteille, "Government and NGOs: Similar Goals but Contrasting Styles," *Times of India*, March 10, 1999. Unlike Hopgood, who refers to Durkheim, Beteille draws on Weber and claims that NGOs are to the modern state what sects are to the church.
26. See the cover of the brochure by Transparency International, *Teaching Integrity to Youth: Examples from 11 Countries*.
27. See Schurman and Munro, "Ideas, Thinkers, and Social Networks."
28. See William Cronon, "The Trouble with Wilderness; or, Getting Back to the Wrong Nature," in *Uncommon Ground: Toward Reinventing Nature*, ed. William Cronon (New York: W. W. Norton, 1995), 81–82.
29. Quoted in David Takacs, *The Idea of Biodiversity: Philosophies of Paradise* (Baltimore: Johns Hopkins University Press, 1996), 153–54.
30. See Taylor, *Sources of the Self*, part IV ("The Voice of Nature").
31. Bob Hunter, quoted in Zelko, *"Make It a Green Peace,"* 334.
32. Greenpeace UK, "Are You a Best-of-Breed Company Executive?" June 19, 2002, http://www.greenpeace.org.uk.
33. Ibid.
34. Frantz, *Karriere in NGOs*, 296.
35. Jeffrey C. Alexander, "Towards a Sociology of Evil: Getting beyond Modernist Common Sense about the Alternative to 'the Good,'" in *Rethinking Evil: Contemporary Perspectives*, ed. Maria Pia Lara (Berkeley: University of California Press, 2001), 163.
36. Ibid.
37. For references, see Flitner and Heins, "Modernity and Life Politics," 330–31.

38. See Richard H. Grove, *Ecology, Climate and Empire: The Indian Legacy in Global Environmental History, 1400–1940* (Delhi: Oxford University Press, 1998), ch. 2.
39. See Goldman, *Imperial Nature*, 176–79, 190–200.
40. Charles Geisler, "A New Kind of Trouble: Evictions in Eden," *International Social Science Journal* 55, no. 175 (2003): 70.
41. See ibid.
42. As a senior conservationist explained to me some time ago, in an "African village" people don't understand the ethical orientation toward future generations or the world at large: "They just don't dig it." Interview by the author. WWF-Germany, Frankfurt, December 1999.
43. See IUCN and UNEP World Conservation Monitoring Centre, ed., *2003 United Nations List of Protected Areas*, http://www.unep.org/PDF/Un-list protected-areas.pdf, p. 26.
44. Geisler, "A New Kind of Trouble," 71.
45. Ibid., 74. See also the map "Protecting the Future of Nature" at http://www.worldwildlife.org/wildplaces/.
46. Bob Hunter, quoted in Zelko, *"Make It a Green Peace,"* 423.
47. Paul Spong, quoted Zelko, *"Make It a Green Peace,"* 443.
48. Hugh Brody, *Living Arctic: Hunters of the Canadian North* (London and Boston: Faber and Faber, 1987), 85.
49. Quoted in Robert Sullivan, "Permission Granted to Kill a Whale. Now What?" *New York Times*, August 9, 1998, p. 30.
50. See Alison Brysk, *From Tribal Village to Global Village: Indian Rights and International Relations in Latin America* (Stanford, CA: Stanford University Press, 2000), 230–31.
51. See, for example, Michael Goldman, ed., *Privatizing Nature: Political Struggles for the Global Commons* (London: Pluto, 1998).
52. For an overview on the structure and history of this multilayered conflict, see Flitner and Heins, "Modernity and Life Politics."
53. See *Filartiga v. Pena-Irala*, 630 F.2d 876, 2d Circuit, June 30, 1980.
54. Claude Alvares, "The Great Gene Robbery," *Illustrated Weekly of India*, March 23, 1986, pp. 6–17.
55. See M. S. Swaminathan, "No Robbery: Saving and Sharing of Genetic Resources," *Illustrated Weekly of India*, March 23, 1986, pp. 50–53.
56. Vandana Shiva, *Staying Alive: Women, Ecology and Development* (London: Zed Books, 1989), 2, 11; and Vandana Shiva, *The Violence of the Green Revolution* (London: Zed Books, 1991), 14, 29.
57. *Times of India*, October 29, 1995.
58. Vandana Shiva, "Monocultures, Monopolies, Myths and the Masculinization of Agriculture," *Development* 42, no. 2 (1999): 36.
59. Tewolde Egziabher and Vandana Shiva, *What Are We Doing with Plant Genetic Resources for Food and Agriculture?* (Penang, Malaysia: TWN, 1996), 4.

60. Third World Network, *Earth Summit Briefings* (Penang, Malaysia: TWN, 1992), 34, 47, my italics.
61. See Thomas R. Metcalf, *Ideologies of the Raj* (Cambridge: Cambridge University Press, 1995), 163, 184.
62. Quoted in ibid., 184.
63. See Shiva, "Monocultures, Monopolies, Myths," 36.
64. Personal communication, Protestant Association for Co-operation in Development (EZE), South Asia Desk, Bonn, Germany, September 1999.
65. Interviews by the author with S. K. Sinha, Indian Agricultural Research Institute (IARI), Delhi, October 1999, and with Biswajit Dhar, Research and Information System for the Non-Aligned and Other Developing Countries (RIS), Delhi, October 1999.
66. See Suman Sahai, "Bogus Debate on Bioethics," *Economic and Political Weekly* 31 (1996): 3231–32.
67. Ibid.
68. See Volker Heins, "From New Political Organizations to Changing Moral Geographies."
69. Interview by the author with Suman Sahai, Gene Campaign, Delhi, December 1998.
70. Interview by the author with Anil Agarwal, Centre for Science and Environment (CSE), Delhi, December 1998.
71. Ramachandra Guha, *The Unquiet Woods: Ecological Change and Peasant Resistance in the Himalaya* (Delhi: Oxford University Press, 1991), 65–67.
72. See Alexander, *The Civil Sphere*, 196–99.
73. Even human rights organizations focus a lot on the United States and other democratic countries with pretty good records because they are seen as "models" for the world. See James Ron, Howard Ramos, and Kathleen Rodgers, "Transnational Information Politics: NGO Human Rights Reporting, 1986–2000," *International Studies Quarterly* 49 (2005): 571. Key agencies of U.S. power, on the other hand, cooperate with their critics by periodically declassifying embarrassing documents about past abuses. See, for example, *BBC News*, "CIA Details Cold War Skullduggery," June 26, 2007, http://news.bbc.co.uk/2/hi/americas/6242182.stm.
74. See Alexander, *The Civil Sphere*, 165; see also Catherine Lu, "Agents, Structures and Evil in World Politics," *International Relations* 18, no. 4 (2004): 498–509.
75. See Paul Slovic, "'If I Look at the Mass I Will Never Act': Psychic Numbing and Genocide," *Judgment and Decision Making* 2, no. 2 (2007): 79–95.
76. Judith N. Shklar, *The Faces of Injustice* (New Haven, CT: Yale University Press, 1990), 36.
77. For more on these twin evils, see Volker Heins, "Civil Society's Barbarisms," *European Journal of Social Theory* 7, no. 4 (2004): 499–517.
78. Linklater and Suganami, *The English School of International Relations*, 179.
79. In this sense, there is a connection between cosmopolitanism and what has been called the "privatization" of international politics. See Tanja Brühl,

"The Privatization of Governance Systems: On the Legitimacy of International Environmental Policy," in *Governance and Democracy: Comparing National, European and International Experiences*, ed. Arthur Benz and Yannis Papadopoulos (London and New York: Routledge, 2006).
80. Barnett and Finnemore, *Rules for the World*, 39.
81. See M. Cherif Bassiouni, "Negotiating the Treaty of Rome on the Establishment of an International Criminal Court," *Cornell International Law Journal* 32, no. 3 (1999): 455; Johan D. van der Vyver, "Civil Society and the International Criminal Court," *Journal of Human Rights* 2, no. 3 (2003): 425.
82. See Bassiouni, "Negotiating the Treaty of Rome," 461–62.
83. Quoted in van der Vyver, "Civil Society and the International Criminal Court," 432.
84. On the difference between having rights and being loved or cared for, see Honneth, *The Struggle for Recognition*, ch. 5 and 6.
85. See Short, "The Role of NGOs," 483.
86. On the context of the CBD, see Flitner and Heins, "Modernity and Life Politics."
87. On this distinction, see Feinberg, *Harm to Others*, 227–32.
88. For an overview, see Robert Falkner, "Regulating Biotech Trade: The Cartagena Protocol on Biosafety," *International Affairs* 76 (2000): 299–313.
89. Ibid., 308–9.
90. Sheila Watt-Cloutier, "The Arctic and Climate Change: Inuit Defend Our Right to Be Cold," Stegner Center Eleventh Annual Symposium, University of Utah, S. J. Quinney College of Law, Salt Lake City, Utah, March 4, 2006.
91. See, for example, the Resolutions 2000/7 and 2001/21 of the UN Sub-Commission for the Promotion and Protection of Human Rights; and *The Impact of the Agreement on Trade-Related Aspects of Intellectual Property Rights on Human Rights*, Report of the High Commissioner for Human Rights, UNHCR, Geneva, E/CN.4/Sub.2/2001/13, June 27, 2001.
92. See Steven Robins, "'Long Live Zackie, Long Live': AIDS Activism, Science and Citizenship after Apartheid," *Journal of Southern African Studies* 30, no. 3 (2004): 651–72; and Volker Heins, "Human Rights, Intellectual Property, and Struggles for Recognition," *Human Rights Review* 9, no. 2 (2008) (forthcoming).
93. "Entretien avec Zackie Achmat, président de l'ONG sud-africaine Treatment Action Campaign," *Le Monde*, March 6, 2001. I should add that, in light of the moral geographies explicated above (see Table 4.1), Achmat locates evildoers not only abroad, but also in his own post-apartheid government.
94. See Joint United Nations Programme on HIV/AIDS (UNAIDS), *2006 Report on the Global AIDS Epidemic*, 151–58.

95. See Graham Dutfield, "Indigenous Peoples and Traditional Resource Rights," in *Rights and Liberties in the Biotech Age: Why We Need a Genetic Bill of Rights*, ed. Sheldon Krimsky and Peter Shorett, 107–13 (Lanham, MD: Rowan & Littlefield, 2005).
96. See Francois Jean, ed., *Life, Death and Aid: The Médecins Sans Frontières Report on World Crisis Intervention* (London and New York: Routledge, 1993), 55.
97. See Ariel Colonomos, "Civil Norms and 'Unjust' Embargoes," *Journal of Human Rights* 3, no. 2 (2004): 189–201.
98. Keane, *Global Civil Society?*, 104.
99. See K. J. Holsti, *Taming the Sovereigns: Institutional Change in International Politics* (Cambridge: Cambridge University Press, 2004), ch. 3 and 4.
100. For this distinction, see David Miller, "Distributing Responsibilities," in *Global Responsibilities: Who Must Deliver on Human Rights?* ed. Andrew Kuper (London and New York: Routledge, 2005), 97–98.
101. Ibid., 96.
102. See ibid., 108.
103. See Hopgood, *Keepers of the Flame*, 211; Ralph B. Levering, "Brokering the Law of the Sea Treaty: The Neptune Group," in *Transnational Social Movements and Global Politics: Solidarity Beyond the State*, ed. Jackie Smith, Charles Chatfield, and Ron Pagnucco (Syracuse, NY: Syracuse University Press, 1997), 228.
104. See Jon Western, "Sources of Humanitarian Intervention: Beliefs, Information, and Advocacy in the U.S. Decisions on Somalia and Bosnia," *International Security* 26, no. 4 (2002): 112–42; see also, in general, Finnemore, *The Purpose of Intervention*.
105. Ourdan Remy, "MSF dénounce 'la neutralité face à un genocide,'" *Le Monde*, June 4, 1998.
106. Jean-Hervé Bradol, "Une commission d'enquête sur Srebrenica!" *Le Monde*, July 13, 2000.
107. See the story on Brazil in *Greenpeace International Annual Report 2006*, 8.
108. See Redress Trust and International Federation for Human Rights (FIDH), "Call to End European Safe Havens for Rwandan Perpetrators," press statement, Brussels, April 3, 2007.
109. See, for example, Christien van den Anker, "Trafficking and Women's Rights: Beyond the Sex Industry to 'Other Industries,'" in Rebecca Shah and Audrey Guichon, eds., "Women's Rights in Europe," Special Issue of *Journal of Global Ethics* 3, no. 1 (2006): 161–180, as well as the *Trafficking in Persons Report* (Washington, DC: U.S. Department of State, 2007), which is partly based on information submitted by NGOs.
110. On "forward-looking," as opposed to "backward-looking," theories of allocating remedial responsibility, see Miller, "Distributing Responsibilities."
111. See Stephen Rademaker, "Unwitting Party to Genocide. The International Criminal Court Is Complicating Efforts to Save Darfur," *Washington Post*, January 11, 2007, p. A25.

112. Maxwell A. Cameron, Robert J. Lawson, and Brian W. Tomlin, "To Walk without Fear," in *To Walk without Fear: The Global Movement to Ban Landmines*, ed. Maxwell A. Cameron, Robert J. Lawson, and Brian W. Tomlin (Toronto: Oxford University Press, 1998), 13.
113. Christopher Kirkey, "Washington's Response to the Ottawa Land Mines Process," *Canadian-American Public Policy* 46 (August 2001): 3.
114. See Sending and Neumann, "Governance to Governmentality," 664–68.
115. Short, "The Role of NGOs," 491–92.
116. See Ernestine Meijer and Richard Stewart, "The GM Cold War: How Developing Countries Can Go from Being Dominos to Being Players," *Review of European Community and International Environmental Law* 13, no. 3 (2004): 247–62.
117. See Vandana Shiva, "In Praise of Cowdung," *ZNet: Daily Commentaries*, November 12, 2002, http://www.zmag.org/sustainers/content/2002-11/12shiva.cfm.
118. See Aynsley Kellow, "Norms, Interests and Environmental NGOs: The Limits of Cosmopolitanism," *Environmental Politics* 9, no. 3 (2000): 1–22.
119. See ibid., 10.
120. See ibid., 14.
121. Agarwal and Narain, "A New Morality," 87.
122. See Anil Agarwal and Sunita Narain, *Global Warming in an Unequal World* (Delhi: CSE, 1991). The authors certainly have a point in differentiating between basic and other needs. The question, however, is whether these types of needs neatly correspond to distinct countries or even social classes. The following observation made in the slums of Bombay might give us pause: "The notion of what is a luxury and what is a basic need has been upended in Bombay. Every slum I see in Jogeshwari has a television; antennas sprout in silver branches above the shanties. Many in the middle-class slum have motorcycles, even cars" (Seketu Mehta, *Maximum City: Bombay Lost and Found* [New York: Vintage Books, 2004], 124–25).
123. Mukund Govind Rajan, *Global Environmental Politics: India and the North-South Politics of Global Environmental Issues* (Delhi: Oxford University Press, 1997), 114, my italics. For more evidence on how India reformulated her national interest in climate change negotiations in light of the CSE report, see Susanne Jacobsen, "India's Position on Climate Change from Rio to Kyoto," Centre for Development Research Working Paper 98.11 (Copenhagen, Denmark: CDR, 1998).

Chapter 5

1. Quoted in Korey, *NGOs and the Universal Declaration of Human Rights*, 77.
2. David Gates, IBP hearings before Congress, 1967, quoted in Chunglin Kwa, "Representations of Nature Mediating between Ecology and Science Policy: The Case of the International Biological Programme," *Social Studies of Science* 17 (1987): 423.

3. Barbara Ward and René Dubos, *Only One Earth: The Care and Maintenance of a Small Planet* (London: Norton, 1972), 208.
4. Note that states can also be found both among the neutralizers and the politicizers. For example, during the landmark UN Conference on the Human Environment in Stockholm 1972, a Swedish delegate coined the term "ecocide" as a polemical charge against environmental evildoers, while the head of the U.S. delegation insisted to remain "an environmentalist and not a politician." See Wade Rowland, *The Plot to Save the World: The Life and Times of the Stockholm Conference on the Human Environment* (Toronto: Clarke, Irwin & Co., 1973), 118.
5. See also the observation made by the controversial German jurist Carl Schmitt in the 1920s: "Europeans always have wandered from a conflictual to a neutral sphere, and always the newly won neutral sphere has become immediately another arena of struggle, once again necessitating the search for a new neutral sphere." See Carl Schmitt, "The Age of Neutralizations and Depoliticizations (1929)," *Telos* 96 (1993): 138.
6. Hannah Arendt, *The Origins of Totalitarianism* (New York: Harcourt, Brace, 1951), 289.
7. See, for example, Amnesty International, "Stop Violence Against Women," http://web.amnesty.org/actforwomen/index-eng (accessed June 1, 2007).
8. Shklar, *Faces of Injustice*, 56.
9. See Doris Buss, "Prosecuting Mass Rape: Prosecutor v. Dragoljub Kunarac, Radomir Kovac and Zoran Vukovic," *Feminist Legal Studies* 10, no. 1 (2002): 91–99.
10. In October 2006, groups such as the Humane Society of the United States and others airlifted hundreds of animals from Beirut to Utah. The animals had been left behind by their owners during the short war with Israel in the summer of that year. The Humane Society has also lobbied for legislation that would require state governments in the United States to include pets in disaster plans.
11. Charli Carpenter, "Setting the Advocacy Agenda: Theorizing Issue Emergence and Nonemergence in Transnational Advocacy Networks," *International Studies Quarterly* 51 (2007): 101.
12. Ibid.
13. See Thomas Princen and Matthias Finger, *Environmental NGOs in World Politics: Linking the Local and the Global* (London and New York: Routledge, 1994).
14. Thomas Perreault, "Changing Places: Transnational Networks, Ethnic Politics, and Community Development in the Ecuadorian Amazon," *Political Geography* 22 (2003): 65.
15. Referring to his groundbreaking report *Global Warming in an Unequal World*, Anil Agarwal, the former director of the Delhi-based Centre for Science and Environment (CSE), explained to me, "Who is going to listen to some idiot sitting in New Delhi? We had to make sure was that this message was for New York and London and *everywhere else*. We had to make

sure it's plugged in." Interview by the author with Anil Agarwal, Centre for Science and Environment (CSE), Delhi, December 1998.
16. See Kaldor, *Global Civil Society*, 86.
17. See Tom Brass, ed., *New Farmers' Movements in India* (Ilford, Essex: Frank Cass, 1995).
18. See Ronald J. Herring, "Miracle Seeds, Suicide Seeds, and the Poor: GMOs, NGOs, Farmers, and the State," in *Social Movements in India: Poverty, Power, and Politics*, ed. Raka Ray and Mary Katzenstein (Lanham, MD: Rowman and Littlefield, 2005), 217.
19. Here I am drawing on an unpublished evaluation report I wrote in early 2000 on Gene Campaign for one its donor organizations, the Protestant Church Development Service, Germany (EED).
20. Herring, "Miracle Seeds, Suicide Seeds, and the Poor," 217.
21. On the real Chipko movement and its intentional misreading by Shiva's network, see Jayanta Bandyopadhyay, "Chipko Movement: Of Floated Myths and Flouted Realities," *Economic and Political Weekly* 34 (1999): 880–82.
22. Interview by the author with representatives of Beej Bachao Andolan, Delhi, March 1998. See also Indira Khurana, "The Seed Supremo," *Down To Earth* (Delhi), December 31, 1998, pp. 42–43.
23. For acute observations on the "impression management" of third-world NGOs, see Bryant, *Nongovernmental Organizations*, ch. 2.
24. See David H. Dunn, ed., *Diplomacy at the Highest Level: The Evolution of International Summitry* (Basingstoke UK: Macmillan, 1996).
25. See Paul Brown, "Lobbying Galore," *Guardian*, August 21, 2002.
26. Marc Nerfin, "The Future of the United Nations System: Some Questions on the Occasion of an Anniversary," *Development Dialogue* 1 (1985): 7.
27. Benedict Anderson, *Imagined Communities: Reflections on the Origin and Spread of Nationalism*, 2nd rev. ed. (London: Verso, 1991).
28. Ibid., 115.
29. Rachel L. Swarns, "After the Race Conference: Relief, and Doubt Over Whether It Will Matter," *New York Times*, September 10, 2001, p. 10. See also Tom Lantos, "The Durban Debacle: An Insider's View of the UN World Conference Against Racism," *Fletcher Forum of World Affairs* 26, no. 1 (2002): 31–52.
30. Kaldor, *Global Civil Society*, 103.
31. See Anderson, *Imagined Communities*, 9–10.
32. See Craig Warkentin, *Reshaping World Politics: NGOs, the Internet, and Global Civil Society* (Lanham, MD: Rowman & Littlefield, 2001), 32–33.
33. Anderson, *Imagined Communities*, 33–36.
34. See, for example, Hardt and Negri, *Empire*, 36; *Economist*, "Sins of the Secular Missionaries," January 29, 2000, pp. 25–28.
35. See, for example, Peter Pels, *A Politics of Presence: Contacts between Missionaries and Waluguru in Late Colonial Tanganyika* (Amsterdam: Harwood Academic, 1999).

36. Dorothea Hilhorst, *The Real World of NGOs: Discourses, Diversity and Development* (London: Zed Books, 2003). As interface experts with sometimes-considerable local knowledge, NGOs have attracted both the interest of intelligence agencies and of international business companies looking for local buyers or suppliers. See, for example, DeMars, "Hazardous Partnership"; and Sabine Trannin, *Les ONG occidentales au Cambodge: La réalité derrière le mythe* (Paris: L'Harmattan, 2005), 232.
37. See also Volker Heins, "Democratic States, Aid Agencies, and World Society: What's the Name of the Game?" *Global Society* 9, no. 4 (2005): 361–84.
38. Quoted in Caroline Moorehead, *Dunant's Dream: War, Switzerland and the History of the Red Cross* (London: HarperCollins, 1998), 127.
39. See International Committee of the Red Cross, "The ICRC—its ambitions and its will to act," http://www.icrc.org/Web/Eng/siteeng0.nsf/html/5ZQDFR.
40. Quoted in Moorehead, *Dunant's Dream*, 637–38.
41. On the history of the idea that injured soldiers and other victims of war are "neutrals," see Andrea Russo, "Ferdinando Palasciano et la neutralité des blesses de guerre," in *Préludes et pionniers: Les précurseurs de la Croix-Rouge, 1840–1860*, ed. Roger Durand and Jacques Meurant (Geneva: Société Henry Dunant, 1991).
42. Linklater and Suganami, *The English School of International Relations*, ch. 5.
43. See Jean-Claude Favez, *The Red Cross and the Holocaust* (Cambridge: Cambridge University Press, 1999), 94–99.
44. See ibid., 282.
45. Bernard Kouchner, *Ce que je crois* (Paris: Grasset 1995), 107–8.
46. For an overview, see Noëlle Quénivet, "Humanitarian Assistance: A Right or a Policy?" *Journal of Humanitarian Assistance*, January 1999, http://www.jha.ac/articles/a030.htm.
47. Alain Dubos, MSF-France, public talk and question-and-answer session at the French Library in Boston, February 18, 2004.
48. Jean-Christoph Rufin, "La fin de l'exception humanitaire française," *Le Monde*, January 29, 1995.
49. Massimo Lorenzi, *Entretiens avec Cornelio Sommaruga, Président du CICR* (Lausanne: Favre, 1998), 55.
50. See the typology of secular NGO traditions in Abby Stoddard, "Humanitarian NGOs: Challenges and Trends," in *Humanitarian Action and the "Global War on Terror": A Review of Trends and Issues*, ed. Joanna Macrae and Adele Harmer, HPG Report No. 14, July 2003.
51. Kouchner, *Ce que je crois*, 103.
52. Lesnes Corine et al., "MSF: Les défis d'une génération," *Le Monde*, October 17, 1999.
53. MSF-Holland, "Medium Term Policy 2003–2005," Amsterdam: MSF, p. 8.

54. *Populations Affected by War in the Mano River Region of West Africa: Issues of Protection*, Médecins Sans Frontières Report (New York: MSF, 2002), 30.
55. Philippe Biberson and Rony Brauman, "Le 'droit d'ingérence' est un slogan trompeur," *Le Monde*, October 23, 1999.
56. Bernard Kouchner, "Vive la vie!" *Le Monde*, December 11, 1999.
57. See Sarah Kenyon Lischer, *Dangerous Sanctuaries: Refugee Camps, Civil War, and the Dilemmas of Humanitarian Aid* (Ithaca, NY: Cornell University Press, 2005), 146–49.
58. Shklar, *Faces of Injustice*, 56.
59. Mamou Jacky, "L'urgence est à l'utopie," *Le Monde*, January 5, 2000.
60. See Fiona Terry, *The Paradox of Humanitarian Action: Condemned to Repeat?* (Ithaca, NY: Cornell University Press, 2002), 13.
61. Rufin, "La fin de l'exception humanitaire française."
62. This analogy is used Biberson and Brauman, "Le 'droit d'ingérence' est un slogan trompeur."
63. See Stephanie Strom, "Nonprofit Groups Draw a Line at Some Donors," *New York Times*, January 28, 2007, p. 17.
64. Margaret Mead, *And Keep Your Powder Dry: An Anthropologist Looks At America* (New York: William Morrow & Co., 1942), 220.
65. See Stoddard, "Humanitarian NGOs: Challenges and Trends."
66. Jean-Jacques Rousseau, "Discourse on the Origin of Inequality," in *The Basic Political Writings*, trans. Donald A. Cress (Indianapolis, IN: Hackett, 1987), 62.
67. See Wallace J. Campbell, *The History of CARE: A Personal Account* (Westport, CT: Praeger, 1990).
68. Kevin Henry, CARE-USA, personal communication, March 11, 2004.
69. Michael Novak, quoted in Scott Flipse, "The Latest Casualty of War: Catholic Relief Services, Humanitarianism, and the War in Vietnam, 1967–1968," *Peace & Change* 27 (2002): 257.
70. See ibid.
71. See Alan Whaites, "Pursuing Partnership: World Vision and the Ideology of Development," *Development in Practice* 9 (1999): 410–23.
72. Rousseau, "Discourse on the Origin of Inequality," 62.
73. Lawrence A. Pezzullo, "Catholic Relief Services in Ethiopia: A Case Study," in *The Moral Nation: Humanitarianism and U.S. Foreign Policy Today*, ed. Bruce Nichols and Gil Loescher (Notre Dame, IN: University of Notre Dame Press, 1989), 225.
74. "Confusion des genres" is a typical formula used by ICRC intellectuals both in criticisms of other humanitarian organizations and in self-criticisms. See, for example, Jean-Francois Berger, *The Humanitarian Diplomacy of the ICRC and the Conflict in Croatia, 1991–1992* (Geneva: ICRC, 1995), 22; and Jean-Francois Fayet and Peter Huber, "La mission Wehrlin du CICR en Union soviétique (1920–1938)," *International Review of the Red Cross* 85, no. 846 (2003): 95–117.

75. Andrew Natsios, "Did we make a difference in Somalia?" *World Vision Magazine*, April/May 1995, p. 12.
76. Paul O'Brien, "Politicized Humanitarianism: A Response to Nicholas de Torrente," *Harvard Human Rights Journal* 17 (2004): 31–39.
77. MSF-France, *Palestinian Chronicles*, July 2002, p. 13, http://www.msf.fr/documents/Palestinian_chronicles_EN.pdf.
78. See Michael Ignatieff, "The Terrorist as Auteur," *New York Times Magazine*, November 14, 2004.
79. Since the 1994 Rwanda genocide, Burma is actually the first country that has been publicly denounced by the ICRC for using thousands of detainees, including children, as army porters and for depriving people living along the Thai border of food. See Imogen Foulkes, "Red Cross condemns Burma 'abuses,'" *BBC News*, June 29, 2007, http://news.bbc.co.uk/2/hi/asia-pacific/6252024.stm. On North Korea, see the comment by the MSF researcher Fiona Terry, "Feeding the dictator," *Guardian*, August 6, 2001.
80. Lorenzi, *Entretiens avec Cornelio Sommaruga*, 159.
81. See Kenneth Anderson, "Humanitarian Inviolability in Crisis: The Meaning of Impartiality and Neutrality for U.N. and NGO Agencies Following the 2003–2004 Afghanistan and Iraq Conflicts," *Harvard Human Rights Journal* 17 (2004): 41–74.

Chapter 6

1. The most drastic recent example of a much-touted treaty that has not delivered any results is the Kyoto Protocol. See Gwyn Prins and Steve Rayner, "Time to Ditch Kyoto," *Nature* 449 (2007): 973–75.
2. See Margaret Gibelman and Sheldon R. Gelman, "A Loss of Credibility: Patterns of Wrongdoing among Nongovernmental Organizations," *Voluntas* 15, no. 4 (2004): 355–81.
3. See Ebrahim, *NGOs and Organizational Change*, 101.
4. See NGOs' Success Stories in Implementing the Millennium Development Goals (MDGs), http://www.unpan.org/NGO-MDGs.asp.
5. Regarding the anti-poverty Millennium Development Goals of the UN, see *What Global Leaders Want. Report of the Third Survey of the 2020 Global Stakeholder Panel*, February 2005, p. 15, http://www.2020fund.org/downloads/GSP_3_report.pdf.
6. Two remarkable attempts to capture the perspective of the recipients of international aid are Isabelle Delpla, "Moral Judgments on International Interventions: A Bosnian Perspective," in *Rethinking Ethical Foreign Policy: Pitfalls, Possibilities and Paradoxes*, ed. David Chandler and Volker Heins (London and New York: Routledge, 2007); and Hakan Seckinelgin, "Who Can Help People With HIV/AIDS in Africa? Governance of HIV/AIDS and Civil Society," *Voluntas* 15, no. 3 (2004): 287–304.
7. Kevin Stairs and Peter Taylor, "Non-Governmental Organizations and the Legal Protection of the Oceans: A Case Study," in *The International Politics*

of the Environment: Actors, Interests, and Institutions, ed. Andrew Hurrell and Benedict Kingsbury (Oxford: Oxford University Press, 1992).
8. See Grant Jordan, *Shell, Greenpeace, and the Brent Spar* (New York: Palgrave, 2001).
9. See Environmental Defense, "British Petroleum Announces Plan to Measure and Report Greenhouse Gas Emissions; to Set Targets; and to Practice Emissions Trading," press release, September 30, 1997.
10. See Ralf Bläser, *Gut situiert: Bankwatch-NGOs in Washington, DC*, Kölner Geographische Arbeiten, No. 86 (Cologne University, Department of Geography, 2005), 138–43.
11. See Friends of the Earth and New Economics Foundation (NEF), "The Happy Planet Index," http://www.happyplanetindex.org/.
12. Bloodgood, *Influential Information*, 132.
13. Keck and Sikkink, *Activists Beyond Borders*, 194–95.
14. See DeMars, "Hazardous Partnership"; Western, "Sources of Humanitarian Intervention," 131. On a few occasions, NGOs have engaged in espionage, breaking into industrial labs or nuclear bases to get information about suspicious or illegal activities (see Bloodgood, *Influential Information*, 30).
15. Gaer, "Implementing International Human Rights Norms."
16. See Tanja Brühl, *Nichtregierungsorganisationen als Akteure internationaler Umweltverhandlungen* (Frankfurt: Campus, 2003).
17. Ibid., 320–33.
18. See Bloodgood, *Influential Information*, ch. 4 and 6.
19. The origin of this idea is Schattschneider, *The Semisovereign People*, 39–40.
20. Kouchner, *Le Malheur des autres*, 114.
21. On the subordinate role of expertise and the primacy of "scaring people," see the case study by Jordan, *Shell, Greenpeace, and the Brent Spar*, ch. 6.
22. This was the motto of the former Canadian Greenpeace campaigner Gord Perks.
23. Iain Hollingshead, "Loose Ends: Whatever Happened to Diana's Landmine Fight?" *Guardian*, October 8, 2005, p. 26.
24. Shirley R. Steinberg and Joe L. Kincheloe, eds., *Kinderculture: The Corporate Construction of Childhood* (Boulder, CO: Westview, 1997).
25. See the overview in Ingrid J. Tamm, "Dangerous Appetites: Human Rights Activism and Conflict Commodities," *Human Rights Quarterly* 26, no. 3 (2004): 687–704.
26. Keck and Sikkink, *Activists Beyond Borders*, 27.
27. This a field worked on by the Ottawa-based ETC group, which is the successor of the better-known RAFI.
28. See Heins, "Human Rights, Intellectual Property, and Struggles for Recognition."
29. See Suzette Grillot, Craig Stapley, and Molly Hanna, "Assessing the Small Arms Movement: The Trials and Tribulations of a Transnational Network," *Contemporary Security Policy* 27, no. 1 (2006): 60–84.

30. *Small Arms Survey 2004* (Oxford: Oxford University Press, 2004), 175.
31. Ibid., 199.
32. Keck and Sikkink, *Activists Beyond Borders*, 27.
33. See Alan M. Wachman, "Does the Diplomacy of Shame Promote Human Rights in China?" *Third World Quarterly* 22, no. 2 (2001): 257–81.
34. Keck and Sikkink, *Activists Beyond Borders*, 27.
35. See, for example, Matthias Busse, "Democracy and FDI," *HWWA Discussion Paper 220* (Hamburg: HWWA, 2003).
36. See Brown, *Moral Capital*, 75.
37. Terry, "Feeding the Dictator."
38. See Thomas Franck, "The Emerging Right to Democratic Governance," *American Journal of International Law* 86 (1992): 46–91.
39. Wouter Kok, MSF-Holland, email message to the author, June 25, 2003.
40. David P. Forsythe, "Naming and Shaming: The Ethics of ICRC Discretion," *Millennium: Journal of International Studies* 34, no. 2 (2005): 467.
41. See Steven Edwards, "Canada Protests UN Rejection of Gay Group," *National Post* (Canada), February 2, 2007, p. 1.
42. See, for example, Dominique Masson, "Constructing Scale/Contesting Scale: Women's Movement and Rescaling Politics in Québec," *Social Politics: International Studies in Gender, State and Society* 13, no. 4 (2006): 462–86; and *The Municipal Powers Report* (Vancouver: Sierra Legal, 2007).
43. See Stein Ringen, "Give but Don't Give Up," *Times Literary Supplement*, February 16, 2007, p. 28.
44. See Aisling Irwin, "'Don't Ask, Don't Give': Disaster Appeals do More Harm Than Good, Says MSF," *Reuters AlertNet*, October 6, 2006.
45. See Honneth, *The Struggle for Recognition*, ch. 6.
46. Linklater and Suganami, *The English School of International Relations*, 162.
47. See Heins, "Critical Theory and the Traps of Conspiracy Thinking."
48. See Kellow, "Norms, Interests and Environmental NGOs"; Michael Shellenberger and Ted Nordhaus, *Break Through: From the Death of Environmentalism to the Politics of Possibility* (Boston, MA: Houghton Mifflin, 2007).
49. See Andrei S. Markovits, *Uncouth Nation: Why Europe Dislikes America* (Princeton, NJ: Princeton University Press, 2007); Volker Heins, "Orientalising America? Continental Intellectuals and the Search for Europe's Identity," *Millennium: Journal of International Studies* 34, no. 2 (2005): 433–48.
50. See, for example, "Amnesty's Moral Blindness," *Jerusalem Post*, May 24, 2007.
51. See Chandler, *Constructing Global Civil Society*, ch. 6.
52. David Chandler, "Hollow Hegemony: Theorising the Shift from Interest-Based to Values-Based International Policy-Making," *Millennium: Journal of International Studies* 35, no. 3 (2007): 703–23.
53. Ibid., 719.

54. Weber, *The Essential Weber*, 261–62.
55. Ibid., 267.
56. See Durkheim, *The Elementary Forms of Religious Life*, 40–41.
57. See Kirkey, "Washington's Response to the Ottawa Land Mines Process," 24–25 (including footnotes).
58. For a discussion on the "moral snobbery" of medium-sized powers in contemporary international society, see Volker Heins, "Crusaders and Snobs: Moralizing Foreign Policy in Britain and Germany, 1999–2005," in *Rethinking Ethical Foreign Policy: Pitfalls, Possibilities and Paradoxes*, ed. David Chandler and Volker Heins (London and New York: Routledge, 2007).
59. Weber, *The Essential Weber*, 260.
60. For examples of environmental assessments by the World Bank, see Goldman, *Imperial Nature*, ch. 3 and 4; on the IMF, see Barnett and Finnemore, *Rules for the World*, ch. 3.
61. See, in particular, Lischer, *Dangerous Sanctuaries*.
62. See the critique in Shellenberger and Nordhaus, *Break Through*.

Chapter 7

1. Taylor, *Sources of the Self*, 396.
2. Dewey, *The Public and Its Problems*, 142.
3. See the section on "symbolic labor" in chapter 4 of this book.
4. See Bull, *The Anarchical Society*, 83–89.
5. See, for example, Amnesty International, "Israel/OPT: Forty Years of Occupation—No Security without Basic Rights," press release, June 4, 2007.
6. Alexander, "Towards a Sociology of Evil," 161.
7. Again, the best example is the Kyoto Protocol, whose failure has been analyzed in Prins and Rayner, "Time to Ditch Kyoto."
8. Shklar, *After Utopia*, ch. 6. For Shklar, President Woodrow Wilson's "Fourteen Points" speech of January 1918 was "the last great document" (Shklar, *After Utopia*, 218) testifying to a radical belief in global enlightenment values.
9. Laïdi, *A World Without Meaning*, 11.
10. Ignatieff, *The Warrior's Honor*, 25
11. Nicky Oppenheimer, quoted in Terry Macalister, "I am an African," *Guardian*, July 2, 2005.
12. See Michael T. Greven, "The Informalization of Transnational Governance: A Threat to Democratic Government," in *Complex Sovereignty: Reconstituting Political Authority in the 21st Century*, ed. Edgar Grande and Louis W. Pauly (Toronto: Toronto University Press, 2005).
13. See Skocpol, *Diminished Democracy*, 128, 226.
14. See ibid., 224 ("Associations with Restricted Reach").
15. Brown, *Moral Capital*, 111.

16. See Seckinelgin, "Who Can Help People With HIV/AIDS in Africa?"; Heins, "Human Rights, Intellectual Property, and Struggles for Recognition."
17. Henderson, *Building Democracy in Contemporary Russia*, ch. 6.
18. Quoted in ibid., 174.
19. See, for example, Terry, "Feeding the Dictator."
20. See Lischer, *Dangerous Sanctuaries*.
21. Conrad Black, "What Victory Means," *National Interest*, Winter 2001/02, p. 156.
22. "I can't claim to be a responsible member of the UK government," Short argued, "if we're willing to see the UN endlessly humiliated and the people of Iraq endlessly suffer" (quoted in *The Independent*, February 23, 2003. See also Heins, "Crusaders and Snobs"; and, in particular, Colonomos, "Civil Norms and 'Unjust' Embargoes."
23. See Mike Blanchfield and Andrew Maveda, "Police Beat Detainee, Canadian Officer Says," *Gazette* (Montreal), May 4, 2007.
24. Gutmann and Thompson, *Why Deliberative Democracy?*, 77. See also the interesting article by Charles Lane, "The Paradoxes of a Death Penalty Stance," *Washington Post*, June 4, 2005.
25. Elisabeth Noelle and Thomas Petersen, "Optimistisch und intolerant," *Frankfurter Allgemeine Zeitung*, March 21, 2007. The authors summarize the findings of a study published in March 2007 by the Allensbach Institute for Opinion Polling.
26. See Barrington Moore, *Injustice: The Social Bases of Obedience and Revolt* (White Plains, NY: M. E. Sharpe, 1978), 500–505.
27. Ibid., 501–2.
28. Bull, *The Anarchical Society*, 92.

Selected Bibliography

Agarwal, Anil, and Sunita Narain. "A New Morality." *Illustrated Weekly of India*, December 24, 1989.
———. *Global Warming in an Unequal World*. Delhi: CSE, 1991.
Alexander, Jeffrey C. "Towards a Sociology of Evil: Getting beyond Modernist Common Sense about the Alternative to 'the Good.'" In *Rethinking Evil: Contemporary Perspectives*, edited by Maria Pia Lara, 153–72. Berkeley: University of California Press, 2001.
———. *The Civil Sphere*. New York: Oxford University Press, 2006.
Anderson, Benedict. *Imagined Communities: Reflections on the Origin and Spread of Nationalism*. 2nd rev. ed. London: Verso, 1991.
Arendt, Hannah. *On Revolution*. London: Penguin, 1990.
Arts, Bas. *Political Influence of Global NGOs: Case Studies on the Climate and Biodiversity Conventions*. Utrecht: International Books, 1998.
Bandyopadhyay, Jayanta. "Chipko Movement: Of Floated Myths and Flouted Realities." *Economic and Political Weekly* 34 (1999): 880–82.
Barnett, Michael, and Martha Finnemore. *Rules for the World: International Organizations in Global Politics*. Ithaca, NY: Cornell University Press, 2004.
Baxi, Upendra. *The Future of Human Rights*. 2nd ed. New York: Oxford University Press, 2006.
Beteille, André. "Government and NGOs: Similar Goals but Contrasting Styles." *Times of India*, March 10, 1999.
Bläser, Ralf. "Gut situiert: Bankwatch-NGOs in Washington, DC" Kölner Geographische Arbeiten, No. 86. Cologne University, Department of Geography, 2005.
Blood, Robert. "Should NGOs be Viewed as 'Political Corporations'?" *Journal of Communication Management* 9, no. 2 (2004): 120–33.
Bloodgood, Elizabeth Anne. *Influential Information: Nongovernmental Organizations' Role in Foreign Policy-Making and International Regime Formation*. PhD diss., Department of Politics, Princeton University, 2002.
Brody, Hugh. *Living Arctic: Hunters of the Canadian North*. London and Boston: Faber and Faber, 1987.
Brown, Christopher Leslie. *Moral Capital: Foundations of British Abolitionism*. Chapel Hill: University of North Carolina Press, 2006.

Brühl, Tanja. *Nichtregierungsorganisationen als Akteure internationaler Umweltverhandlungen.* Frankfurt: Campus, 2003.

———. "The Privatization of Governance Systems: On the Legitimacy of International Environmental Policy." In *Governance and Democracy: Comparing National, European and International Experiences,* edited by Arthur Benz and Yannis Papadopoulos, 228–51. London and New York: Routledge, 2006.

Bryant, Raymond L. "False Prophets? Mutant NGOs and Philippine Environmentalism." *Society and Natural Resources* 15 (2002): 629–39.

———. *Nongovernmental Organizations in Environmental Struggles: Politics and the Making of Moral Capital in the Philippines.* New Haven, CT: Yale University Press, 2005.

Brysk, Alison. *From Tribal Village to Global Village: Indian Rights and International Relations in Latin America.* Stanford, CA: Stanford University Press, 2000.

Bull, Hedley. *The Anarchical Society: A Study of Order in World Politics.* 3rd ed. New York: Columbia University Press, 2002.

Byman, Daniel L. "Uncertain Partners: NGOs and the Military." *Survival* 43, no. 2 (2001): 97–114.

Carpenter, R. Charli. "Setting the Advocacy Agenda: Theorizing Issue Emergence and Nonemergence in Transnational Advocacy Networks." *International Studies Quarterly* 51 (2007): 99–120.

Chandler, David. *Constructing Global Civil Society: Morality and Power in International Relations.* Basingstoke, UK: Palgrave Macmillan, 2004.

———. "Hollow Hegemony: Theorising the Shift from Interest-Based to Value-Based International Policy-Making." *Millennium: Journal of International Studies* 35, no. 3 (2007): 703–23.

———. "The Other-Regarding Ethics of the 'Empire in Denial.'" In *Rethinking Ethical Foreign Policy: Pitfalls, Possibilities and Paradoxes,* edited by David Chandler and Volker Heins, 161–83. London and New York: Routledge, 2007.

Chandler, David, and Volker Heins, eds. *Rethinking Ethical Foreign Policy: Pitfalls, Possibilities and Paradoxes.* London and New York: Routledge, 2007.

Cohen, Stanley. *States of Denial: Knowing about Atrocities and Suffering.* Cambridge: Polity, 2001.

Colonomos, Ariel. "Civil Norms and 'Unjust' Embargoes." *Journal of Human Rights* 3, no. 2 (2004): 189–201.

Cooper, Andrew F., and Brian Hocking. "Governments, Non-Governmental Organisations, and the Recalibration of Diplomacy." *Global Society* 14 (2000): 361–76.

Dauvin, Pascal, and Johanna Siméant. *Le Travail humanitaire: Les acteurs des ONG, du siège au terrain.* Paris: Presses de Sciences Po, 2002.

Davis, David Brion. *Inhuman Bondage: The Rise and Fall of Slavery in the New World.* New York: Oxford University Press, 2006.

Delpla, Isabelle. "Moral Judgments on International Interventions: A Bosnian Perspective." In *Rethinking Ethical Foreign Policy: Pitfalls, Possibilities and Paradoxes*, edited by David Chandler and Volker Heins, 137–57. London and New York: Routledge, 2007.

DeMars, William E. "Hazardous Partnership: NGOs and United States Intelligence in Small Wars." *International Journal of Intelligence and CounterIntelligence* 14, no. 2 (2001): 193–222.

Deranty, Jean-Philippe, and Emmanuel Renault. "Politicizing Honneth's Ethics of Recognition." *Thesis Eleven* 88 (2007): 92–111.

Dewey, John. *The Public and Its Problems*. New York: Henry Holt, 1927.

Durkheim, Emile. *The Elementary Forms of Religious Life*. Translated by Joseph W. Swain. London: Allen & Unwin, 1915.

Ebrahim, Alnoor. *NGOs and Organizational Change: Discourse, Reporting, and Learning*. Cambridge: Cambridge University Press, 2003.

Elsenhans, Hartmut. "Marginality, Rent and the Non-Governmental Organisations." In *Non-Governmental Organisations in Development: Theory and Practice*, edited by Noorjahan Bava, 21–50. New Delhi: Kanishka, 1997.

Falkner, Robert. "Regulating Biotech Trade: The Cartagena Protocol on Biosafety." *International Affairs* 76 (2000): 299–313.

Favez, Jean-Claude. *The Red Cross and the Holocaust*. Cambridge: Cambridge University Press, 1999.

Feinberg, Joel. "The Nature and Value of Rights." In *Rights, Justice, and the Bonds of Liberty: Essays in Social Philosophy*, edited by Joel Feinberg, 143–58. Princeton, NJ: Princeton University Press, 1980.

———. *Harm to Others*. New York: Oxford University Press, 1984.

Finnemore, Martha. *The Purpose of Intervention: Changing Beliefs about the Use of Force*. Ithaca, NY: Cornell University Press, 2003.

Finnemore, Martha, and Kathryn Sikkink. "International Norm Dynamics and Political Change." *International Organization* 52, no. 4 (1998): 887–917.

Fisher, William F. "Doing Good? The Politics and Antipolitics of NGO Practices." *Annual Review of Anthropology* 26 (1997): 439–64.

Flitner, Michael, and Volker Heins. "Modernity and Life Politics: Conceptualizing the Biodiversity Crisis." *Political Geography* 21 (2002): 319–40.

Forsythe, David P. "Naming and Shaming: The Ethics of ICRC Discretion." *Millennium: Journal of International Studies* 34, no. 2 (2005): 461–74.

Foster, Kenneth W. "Associations in the Embrace of an Authoritarian State: State Domination of Society?" *Studies in Comparative International Development* 35, no. 4 (2001): 84–109.

Franck, Thomas. "The Emerging Right to Democratic Governance." *American Journal of International Law* 86 (1992): 46–91.

Frantz, Christiane. *Karriere in NGOs: Politik als Beruf jenseits der Parteien*. Wiesbaden, Germany: VS Verlag für Sozialwissenschaften, 2005.

Fraser, Nancy, and Axel Honneth. *Redistribution or Recognition? A Political-Philosophical Exchange*. New York: Verso, 2003.

Funk, Nanette. "Women's NGOs in Central and Eastern Europe and the Former Soviet Union: The Imperialist Criticism." In *Women and Citizenship in Central and Eastern Europe*, edited by Jasmina Lukic, Joanna Regulska, and Darja Zavirsek, 265–86. Aldershot, UK: Ashgate, 2006.

Gaer, Felice D. "Reality Check: Human Rights NGOs Confront Governments at the UN." In *NGOs, the UN, and Global Governance*, edited by Thomas G. Weiss and Leon Gordenker, 51–66. Boulder, CO: Lynne Rienner, 1996.

———. "Implementing International Human Rights Norms: UN Human Rights Treaty Bodies and NGOs." *Journal of Human Rights* 2, no. 3 (2003): 339–57.

Geisler, Charles. "A New Kind of Trouble: Evictions in Eden." *International Social Science Journal* 55, no. 175 (2003): 69–78.

Gibelman, Margaret, and Sheldon R. Gelman. "A Loss of Credibility: Patterns of Wrongdoing Among Nongovernmental Organizations." *Voluntas* 15, no. 4 (2004): 355–81.

Goldman, Michael. *Imperial Nature: The World Bank and Struggles for Social Justice in the Age of Globalization*. New Haven, CT: Yale University Press, 2005.

Greven, Michael T. "The Informalization of Transnational Governance: A Threat to Democratic Government." In *Complex Sovereignty: Reconstituting Political Authority in the 21st Century*, edited by Edgar Grande and Louis W. Pauly, 261–84. Toronto: Toronto University Press, 2005.

Grillot, Suzette, Craig Stapley, and Molly Hanna. "Assessing the Small Arms Movement: The Trials and Tribulations of a Transnational Network." *Contemporary Security Policy* 27, no. 1 (2006): 60–84.

Grove, Richard H. *Ecology, Climate and Empire: The Indian Legacy in Global Environmental History, 1400–1940*. Delhi: Oxford University Press, 1998.

Guha, Ramachandra. *The Unquiet Woods: Ecological Change and Peasant Resistance in the Himalaya*. Delhi: Oxford University Press, 1991.

Gutmann, Amy, and Dennis Thompson. *Why Deliberative Democracy?* Princeton, NJ: Princeton University Press, 2004.

Hardt, Michael, and Antonio Negri. *Empire*. Cambridge, MA: Harvard University Press, 2000.

Heins, Volker. "From New Political Organizations to Changing Moral Geographies: Unpacking Global Civil Society." *Geojournal* 52, no. 1 (2000): 37–44.

———. *Der Neue Transnationalismus: Nichtregierungsorganisationen und Firmen im Konflikt um die Rohstoffe der Biotechnologie*. Frankfurt: Campus, 2001.

———. "Civil Society's Barbarisms." *European Journal of Social Theory* 7, no. 4 (2004): 499–517.

———. "Democratic States, Aid Agencies, and World Society: What's the Name of the Game?" *Global Society* 9, no. 4 (2005): 361–84.

———. "Orientalising America? Continental Intellectuals and the Search for Europe's Identity." *Millennium: Journal of International Studies* 34, no. 2 (2005): 433–48.
———. "Crusaders and Snobs: Moralizing Foreign Policy in Britain and Germany, 1999–2005." In *Rethinking Ethical Foreign Policy: Pitfalls, Possibilities and Paradoxes*, edited by David Chandler and Volker Heins, 50–69. London and New York: Routledge, 2007.
———. "Reasons of the Heart: Weber and Arendt on Emotion in Politics." *The European Legacy* 12, no. 6 (2007): 715–28.
———. "Critical Theory and the Traps of Conspiracy Thinking." *Philosophy & Social Criticism* 33, no. 7 (2007): 787–801.
———. "Human Rights, Intellectual Property, and Struggles for Recognition." *Human Rights Review* 9, no. 2 (2008) (forthcoming).
———. "Realizing Honneth: Redistribution, Recognition, and Global Justice." *Journal of Global Ethics* (2008).
Henderson, Sarah L. *Building Democracy in Contemporary Russia: Western Support for Grassroots Organizations*. Ithaca, NY: Cornell University Press, 2003.
Herring, Ronald J. "Miracle Seeds, Suicide Seeds, and the Poor: GMOs, NGOs, Farmers, and the State." In *Social Movements in India: Poverty, Power, and Politics*, edited by Raka Ray and Mary Katzenstein, 203–32. Lanham, MD: Rowman and Littlefield, 2005.
Higgott, Richard A., Geoffrey R. D. Underhill, and Andreas Bieler, eds. *Non-State Actors and Authority in the Global System*. London and New York: Routledge, 2000.
Hilhorst, Dorothea. *The Real World of NGOs: Discourses, Diversity and Development*. London: Zed Books, 2003.
Holsti, K. J. *Taming the Sovereigns: Institutional Change in International Politics*. Cambridge: Cambridge University Press, 2004.
Honneth, Axel. *The Struggle for Recognition: The Moral Grammar of Social Conflicts*. Translated by Joel Anderson. Cambridge: Polity, 1995.
———. "Redistribution as Recognition: A Response to Nancy Fraser." In Nancy Fraser and Axel Honneth, *Redistribution or Recognition? A Political-Philosophical Exchange*, translated by J. Golb, J. Ingram, and C. Wilke, 110–97. London: Verso, 2003.
Hopgood, Stephen. *Keepers of the Flame: Understanding Amnesty International*. Ithaca, NY: Cornell University Press, 2006.
Ignatieff, Michael. *The Warrior's Honor: Ethnic War and the Modern Conscience*. London: Chatto & Windus, 1998.
Jackson, Stephen. "'The State Didn't Even Exist': Non-Governmentality in Kivu, Eastern DR Congo." In *Between a Rock and a Hard Place: African NGOs, Donors and the State*, edited by Jim Igoe and Tim Kelsall, 165–96. Durham, NC: Carolina Academic Press, 2005.
Jordan, Grant. *Shell, Greenpeace, and the Brent Spar*. New York: Palgrave, 2001.
Kaldor, Mary. *Global Civil Society: An Answer to War*. Cambridge: Polity, 2003.

Katz, Hagai. "Gramsci, Hegemony, and Global Civil Society Networks." *Voluntas* 17 (2006): 332–47.

Keane, John. *Global Civil Society?* Cambridge: Cambridge University Press, 2003.

Keck, Margaret E., and Kathryn Sikkink. *Activists Beyond Borders: Advocacy Networks in International Politics.* Ithaca, NY: Cornell University Press, 1998.

Kellow, Aynsley. "Norms, Interests and Environmental NGOs: The Limits of Cosmopolitanism." *Environmental Politics* 9, no. 3 (2000): 1–22.

Kirkey, Christopher. "Washington's Response to the Ottawa Land Mines Process." *Canadian-American Public Policy* 46 (August 2001): 1–45.

Korey, William. *NGOs and the Universal Declaration of Human Rights: "A Curious Grapevine."* New York: St. Martin's, 1998.

Kouchner, Bernard. *Le Malheur des autres.* Paris: Odile Jacob, 1991.

———. *Ce que je crois.* Paris: Grasset, 1995.

Laïdi, Zaki. *A World Without Meaning: The Crisis of Meaning in International Politics.* Translated by June Burnham and Jenny Coulon. London: Routledge, 1998.

Lake, David A., and Wendy Wong. "The Politics of Networks: Interests, Power, and Human Rights Norms." Working Paper, Version 6.0, Department of Political Science, University of California, San Diego, 2006.

Lang, Sabine. "The NGOization of Feminism: Institutionalization and Institution Building within the German Women's Movements." In *Global Feminisms since 1945*, edited by Bonnie G. Smith, 290–304. New York and London: Routledge 2000.

Lantos, Tom. "The Durban Debacle: An Insider's View of the UN World Conference Against Racism." *The Fletcher Forum of World Affairs* 26, no. 1 (2002): 31–52.

Levering, Ralph B. "Brokering the Law of the Sea Treaty: The Neptune Group." In *Transnational Social Movements and Global Politics: Solidarity Beyond the State*, edited by Jackie Smith, Charles Chatfield, and Ron Pagnucco, 225–42. Syracuse, NY: Syracuse University Press, 1997.

Linklater, Andrew. "The Transformation of Political Community: E. H. Carr, Critical Theory and International Relations." *Review of International Studies* 23 (1997): 321–38.

Linklater, Andrew, and Hidemi Suganami. *The English School of International Relations: A Contemporary Reassessment.* Cambridge: Cambridge University Press, 2006.

Lipschutz, Ronnie D. "Reconstructing World Politics: The Emergence of Global Civil Society." *Millennium: Journal of International Studies* 21, no. 3 (1992): 389–420.

———. "Power, Politics and Global Civil Society." *Millennium: Journal of International Studies* 33, no. 3 (2005): 747–69.

Lischer, Sarah Kenyon. *Dangerous Sanctuaries: Refugee Camps, Civil War, and the Dilemmas of Humanitarian Aid*. Ithaca, NY: Cornell University Press, 2005.

———. "Military Intervention and the Humanitarian 'Force Multiplier.'" *Global Governance* 13 (2007): 99–118.

Lu, Catherine. "Agents, Structures and Evil in World Politics." *International Relations* 18, no. 4 (2004): 498–509.

Markovits, Andrei S. *Uncouth Nation: Why Europe Dislikes America*. Princeton, NJ: Princeton University Press, 2007.

Martens, Kerstin. *NGOs and the United Nations: Institutionalization, Professionalization and Adaptation*. Basingstoke, UK: Palgrave Macmillan, 2006.

Masson, Dominique. "Constructing Scale/Contesting Scale: Women's Movement and Rescaling Politics in Québec." *Social Politics: International Studies in Gender, State and Society* 13, no. 4 (2006): 462–86.

Metcalf, Thomas R. *Ideologies of the Raj*. Cambridge: Cambridge University Press, 1995.

Miller, David. "Distributing Responsibilities." In *Global Responsibilities: Who Must Deliver on Human Rights?* edited by Andrew Kuper, 95–115. London and New York: Routledge, 2005.

Moore, Barrington. *Injustice: The Social Bases of Obedience and Revolt*. White Plains, NY: M. E. Sharpe, 1978.

Ottaway, Marina. "Corporatism Goes Global: International Organizations, Nongovernmental Organization Networks, and Transnational Business." *Global Governance* 7 (2001): 265–92.

Pasqualoni, Pier-Paolo, and Alan Scott. "Capitalism and the Spirit of Critique: Activism and Professional Fate in a Contemporary Social Movement/NGO." *Max Weber Studies* 6, no. 1 (2006): 147–69.

Princen, Thomas, and Matthias Finger. *Environmental NGOs in World Politics: Linking the Local and the Global*. London and New York: Routledge, 1994.

Prins, Gwyn, and Steve Rayner. "Time to Ditch Kyoto." *Nature* 449 (2007): 973–75.

Rajan, Mukund Govind. *Global Environmental Politics: India and the North-South Politics of Global Environmental Issues*. Delhi: Oxford University Press, 1997.

Reimann, Kim D. "A View from the Top: International Politics, Norms and the Worldwide Growth of NGOs." *International Studies Quarterly* 50 (2006): 45–67.

Robins, Steven. "'Long Live Zackie, Long Live': AIDS Activism, Science and Citizenship after Apartheid." *Journal of Southern African Studies* 30, no. 3 (2004): 651–72.

Ron, James, Howard Ramos, and Kathleen Rodgers. "Transnational Information Politics: NGO Human Rights Reporting, 1986–2000." *International Studies Quarterly* 49 (2005): 557–87.

Rowland, Wade. *The Plot to Save the World: The Life and Times of the Stockholm Conference on the Human Environment.* Toronto: Clarke, Irwin & Co., 1973.

Schattschneider, E. E. *The Semisovereign People: A Realist's View of Democracy in America.* New York: Holt, Rinehart and Winston, 1960.

Schurman, Rachel, and William Munro. "Ideas, Thinkers, and Social Networks: The Process of Grievance Construction in the Anti-Genetic Engineering Movement." *Theory and Society* 35 (2006): 1–38.

Seckinelgin, Hakan. "Who Can Help People with HIV/AIDS in Africa? Governance of HIV/AIDS and Civil Society." *Voluntas* 15, no. 3 (2004): 287–304.

Sell, Susan K., and Aseem Prakash. "Using Ideas Strategically: The Contest Between Business and NGO Networks in Intellectual Property Rights." *International Studies Quarterly* 48 (2004): 143–75.

Sending, Ole Jacob, and Iver B. Neumann. "Governance to Governmentality: Analyzing NGOs, States, and Power." *International Studies Quarterly* 50 (2006): 651–72.

Serres, Michel. *The Parasite.* Translated by Lawrence R. Schehr. Baltimore: Johns Hopkins University Press, 1982.

Shellenberger, Michael, and Ted Nordhaus. *Break Through: From the Death of Environmentalism to the Politics of Possibility.* Boston: Houghton Mifflin, 2007.

Shklar, Judith N. *After Utopia: The Decline of Political Faith.* Princeton, NJ: Princeton University Press, 1957.

———. *The Faces of Injustice.* New Haven, CT: Yale University Press, 1990.

Short, Nicola. "The Role of NGOs in the Ottawa Process to Ban Landmines." *International Negotiation* 4 (1999): 481–500.

Siméant, Johanna. "What is Going Global? The Internationalization of French NGOs 'Without Borders.'" *Review of International Political Economy* 12 (2005): 851–83.

Skocpol, Theda. *Diminished Democracy: From Membership to Management in American Civic Life.* Norman: University of Oklahoma Press, 2003.

Stairs, Kevin, and Peter Taylor. "Non-Governmental Organizations and the Legal Protection of the Oceans: A Case Study." In *The International Politics of the Environment: Actors, Interests, and Institutions,* edited by Andrew Hurrell and Benedict Kingsbury, 110–41. Oxford: Oxford University Press, 1992.

Stoddard, Abby. "Humanitarian NGOs: Challenges and Trends." In *Humanitarian Action and the "Global War on Terror": A Review of Trends and Issues,* edited by Joanna Macrae and Adele Harmer, 1–4. HPG Report No. 14, July 2003.

Tamm, Ingrid J. "Dangerous Appetites: Human Rights Activism and Conflict Commodities." *Human Rights Quarterly* 26, no. 3 (2004): 687–704.

Tarrow, Sidney. *The New Transnational Activism.* Cambridge: Cambridge University Press, 2005.

Taylor, Charles. *Sources of the Self: The Making of the Modern Identity.* Cambridge, MA: Harvard University Press, 1989.
Terry, Fiona. "Feeding the Dictator." *Guardian,* August 6, 2001.
———. *The Paradox of Humanitarian Action: Condemned to Repeat?* Ithaca, NY: Cornell University Press, 2002.
Thompson, Simon. *The Political Theory of Recognition: A Critical Introduction.* Cambridge: Polity, 2006.
Tully, James. "Recognition and Dialogue: The Emergence of a New Field." *Critical Review of International Social and Political Philosophy* 7, no. 3 (2004): 84–106.
van den Anker, Christien. "Trafficking and Women's Rights: Beyond the Sex Industry to 'Other Industries'," in Rebecca Shah and Audrey Guichon, eds., "Women's Rights in Europe," Special Issue of *Journal of Global Ethics* 3, no. 1 (2006): 161–180.
van Deth, Jan W. "Interesting but Irrelevant: Social Capital and the Saliency of Politics in Western Europe." *European Journal of Political Research* 37 (2000): 115–47.
Vaubel, Roland. "Principal-Agent Problems in International Organizations." *Review of International Organizations* 1, no. 2 (2006): 125–38.
Wachman, Alan M. "Does the Diplomacy of Shame Promote Human Rights in China?" *Third World Quarterly* 22, no. 2 (2001): 257–81.
Walzer, Michael. "Political Action: The Problem of Dirty Hands." *Philosophy and Public Affairs* 2, no. 2 (1973): 160–80.
Wapner, Paul. *Environmental Activism and World Civic Politics.* Albany: State University of New York Press, 1996.
Ward, Barbara, and René Dubos. *Only One Earth: The Care and Maintenance of a Small Planet.* London: Norton, 1972.
Warkentin, Craig. *Reshaping World Politics: NGOs, the Internet, and Global Civil Society.* Lanham, MD: Rowman & Littlefield, 2001.
Weber, Max. *The Essential Weber: A Reader.* Edited by Sam Whimster. London and New York: Routledge, 2004.
Western, Jon. "Sources of Humanitarian Intervention: Beliefs, Information, and Advocacy in the U.S. Decisions on Somalia and Bosnia." *International Security* 26, no. 4 (2002): 112–42.
White, Lyman C. *The Structure of Private International Organizations.* Philadelphia: George S. Ferguson, 1933.
Zelko, Frank. *"Make It a Green Peace": The History of an International Environmental Organization.* PhD diss., Department of History, University of Kansas, 2003.

Index

affirmation of ordinary life, 44, 62
　See also Taylor, Charles
Afghanistan, 7, 134–36, 152, 164
　See also security rights
Agarwal, Anil, 86, 186n15
AIDS, 54, 98–99, 116, 127, 129, 157, 163
Alexander, Jeffrey, 17, 111, 161
aloofness from politics, 17–20, 25, 26, 73, 88
Alvares, Claude, 81–82
Amnesty International, 7, 18, 55, 71, 128–29, 140, 145, 164
Anderson, Benedict, 122, 123
Angola, 147
animals, 23, 24, 67, 73, 77–78, 115–18, 141, 146, 186n10
anti-Americanism, 155
Arendt, Hannah, 115, 171n32
Argentina, 95
Aron, Raymond, 45
Australia, 92, 95
Austria, 94
Axworthy, Lloyd, 3

"bad Samaritans," 54
Barnett, Michael, 56, 90
Belgium, 94, 127
biodiversity, 25, 55, 73, 75–76, 79–80, 81, 83

biopiracy, 79–82
biosafety, 91, 94–96, 101, 102, 108, 112, 143
biotechnology, 80, 83, 84, 85, 94, 95, 108, 120, 145
　See also genetically modified organisms (GMOs)
Blair, Tony, 49, 164
Bloodgood, Elizabeth, 141, 144
Booth, Ken, 33
Bosnia, 34, 104
Bourdieu, Pierre, 32
Bradol, Jean-Hervé, 104
Brazil, 103
Britain, 8, 18, 34, 46, 48, 49, 52, 65–66, 68–69, 74, 83, 109, 115, 146, 147, 151, 162, 164
Brody, Hugh, 78
Brower, David, 60
Brühl, Tanja, 143, 182n79
Bryant, Raymond, 16, 25, 187n23
Bull, Hedley, 8–9, 90, 161
Burma, 136, 190n79

Cambodia, 92, 132
Canada, 3, 24, 31, 51, 56, 72, 75, 76, 77, 78, 94, 95, 146, 156, 164
CARE International, 54, 55, 57, 130–32, 133–35
Carpenter, Charli, 118

Chandler, David, 49, 155
children
  and post-Malthusianism, 47
  and slavery, 67
  and sponsorship programs, 28, 30
  as symbols of innocence, 60, 98, 118, 164
  and war, 93, 106, 117–18, 148
  See also "kinderculture"
Chile, 95
China, 97, 108, 109, 110, 150, 172n42
civil society, 5–7, 16, 19, 33, 34, 55, 69, 89, 163
  in France, 35–36
  in Germany, 35–36
  in India, 85
  See also global civil society
climate change. *See* global warming
Clinton, Bill, 3
Cohen, Stanley, 45
Cold War, 18, 50, 70, 107, 113, 114, 147, 182n73
colonialism, 66, 75, 83, 84, 111, 124, 145
competition for funds, 34, 60, 163
complicity, 69, 74, 77, 86–88, 96, 101, 105, 110, 133, 147, 150, 151, 154, 158
  invention of the idea of, 68, 103
conflict diamonds, 142, 146–48, 148, 154, 157–58
Congo, 106, 147
conservation refugees, 76–77, 111
Cooley, Alexander, 34
corporations, multinational, 53, 86, 108, 119, 129, 137, 142
  emulated by NGOs, 2, 6, 119
  as potential allies of NGOs, 38
  targeted by NGOs, 73–74, 79–84, 116, 145–46, 147–48, 151, 160
crimes against humanity, 91, 92, 96, 104
Cuba, 152

Culture Wars, 49–50, 53, 61, 62, 86, 153–54

Dalton, Russell, 33
democracy
  not advanced by NGOs, 6, 18, 100, 151, 162, 165
  as a precondition for NGOs, 43, 61–62
denial, 44–45
Dewey, John, 160
dirty hands, problem of, 18
Doctors Without Borders (MSF), 2, 18, 47, 50, 59, 98, 100, 104, 126–29, 134, 135, 136, 163
donors, 22, 63, 83, 84, 123, 154, 163
  and the internationalization of NGOs, 53–59, 119, 121
  and control over NGOs, 61, 140, 152
Dunant, Henry, 125
Durkheim, Emile, 59, 70, 71, 72, 82, 180n25

emergency-oriented policies, 48, 124, 161–62
emotions/feelings, 14, 30, 31, 32, 44, 45, 47, 51, 58, 59, 67, 70, 122, 123, 142, 145–46, 148, 149, 157
  See also passions
Empire (Hardt and Negri), 7–8, 36–37, 41, 101, 168n20
English School, 8–10, 12, 36–37, 40
  See also harm conventions
environmentalism, 6, 12, 27, 28, 33–34, 71, 95, 97, 152
  and accumulative harm, 30, 96, 118
  in India, 47, 79–86, 109–10, 120–21, 186–87n15
  and indigenous rights, 78–79
  and misanthropy, 74–75, 79
  polarizing discourses of, 72–74
  as special interest, 154–55, 157
  in the United States, 50, 72–73, 110, 114, 120–21, 186n4

and the unity of humankind, 114
ethic
　of benevolence, 44, 48, 60, 93, 159
　of conviction, 155–57
　of discretion vs. speaking up, 128
　global, 33, 35
　of responsibility, 155–57
Ethiopia, 132–33, 152
Eurocentrism, 119
European Union, 54, 95, 108, 141
evil
　as harm, 44, 52, 73, 74, 114–15, 149
　narratives of good and, 69–88
　nonessentialist notions of, 70–71, 111, 160
　as value-driven, 161

Feinberg, Joel, 21, 27, 30
Ferguson, Niall, 7
Finland, 108
Finnemore, Martha, 56, 69, 90
force, use of, 99–100, 104, 106–7, 126, 134, 164
　by NGOs, 3, 105
Foucault, Michel, 32, 168n20
France, 36, 43, 47, 69, 104, 126–29
Frankfurt School, 10, 12, 21, 40, 171n26
Friends of the Earth, 60, 141, 146, 165
Happy Planet Index, 141
Fromm, Erich, 50

Gandhi, 46, 81
Geisler, Charles, 76
genetically modified organisms (GMOs), 2, 27, 91, 94–96, 108
Geneva Conventions, 26, 115, 125–26, 129, 137
Germany, 35–36, 45, 47, 94, 108, 109, 165
　German Democratic Republic, 109
global warming, 5, 18, 48, 49, 72, 87, 96–97, 109–10, 145

global civil society, 5–9, 32–36, 37, 40, 63, 101–2, 107–8, 109, 112, 119, 122–23, 159
globalization, 5, 36, 120
Gramsci, Antonio, 32
Greenpeace, 2, 18, 43, 50, 59, 72, 73–74, 75, 77–79, 87, 95, 97, 104, 109, 144, 145, 146, 165, 170n12, 191n22
Green Revolution, 81–83, 120
Gutmann, Amy, 165

harm
　done for good reasons, 100, 103, 110
　as injustice, 27–28, 114–16, 148–53
　measures of, 141
　and responsibility, 103, 105, 110–12
　sources of, 13, 94–102, 115–17
　three faces of, 29, 153
　types of, 30, 101–2
harm conventions, 12, 89–91, 94–102, 117, 126, 154
"helicopter organizations," 44
Henderson, Sarah, 163
Herring, Ronald, 121
Hobbes, Thomas, 29
Holocaust, 48, 84, 126, 161, 176n17
　"against the poor," 98
Honneth, Axel, 28–32, 40, 66, 111
　See also recognition
Horkheimer, Max, 21
human rights
　and AIDS, 97–98
　and interventionism, 7, 88, 104–7, 126–29
　as manifesto rights, 28, 31
　and sanctions, 100
　and secular theodicies, 47
　and truth-seeking, 23, 61, 91–93, 143, 155
　and the United Nations, 55, 57, 113–14, 118, 122, 143, 152
　interpretive conflicts over, 154, 160

humanitarian intervention, 31, 49, 104, 134
humanitarian organizations. *See* single organizations
Hunter, Bob, 50, 59
Hussein, Saddam, 152

Iceland, 156
ideal type, 17, 19, 25–26
Ignatieff, Michael, 52, 162
imperialism, 7–8, 36, 37, 69, 78, 168n23
  See also colonialism; Empire
India, 11, 46, 47, 51, 79–88, 99, 108, 110, 111–12, 119–21, 123, 137, 149, 156, 158
indifference, 47, 56, 61, 67, 125, 129, 135, 145
indigenous peoples, 22, 86, 99, 111, 156, 161, 163
  Inuit, 77–78, 97
  Maasai, 75
  Makah, 78
information
  asymmetrical flows of, 33–34
  collected by NGOs, 19, 38, 41, 141–44, 160, 191n14
  key to success of NGOs, 142–44
  provided by NGOs, 41, 57–58, 63, 71, 92, 107, 113, 141–44, 159
  and storytelling, 144
  "information politics," 68
injustice, 13, 24, 32, 45, 51, 65–66, 69, 70, 90, 105, 110, 112, 115, 137, 148, 149, 158, 159, 160, 165
  passive, 116, 128
intellectual property rights. *See* trade-related aspects of intellectual property rights (TRIPS)
"interface experts," 124
International Committee of the Red Cross (ICRC), 25, 26, 59, 93, 115–16, 124–26, 127, 128, 129, 130, 136, 137, 152, 189n74, 190n79

International Criminal Court (ICC), 55, 91–93, 96, 101, 102, 105–7, 109, 119, 120, 121, 122, 134
International Monetary Fund (IMF), 57, 157
international organizations
  as global rule-makers, 27, 56–57, 90–101
  as hybrid bureaucracies, 58–59, 63, 90
  lack of oversight, 6, 56
  pathologies of, 57, 101
  symbolic power of, 15–16, 40, 56, 153
  See also International Monetary Fund; United Nations; World Bank
intertemporal equity, 23, 32
Iraq, 100, 136, 152, 164
Ireland, 94
Israel, 108, 151, 161, 186n10
issue emergence, 116–18, 148–50

Japan, 22, 34, 156

Kaldor, Mary, 5, 33, 119
Kant, Immanuel, 153
Keane, John, 33
Kellow, Aynsley, 109
Kerouac, Jack, 50
"kinderculture," 146
Koestler, Arthur, 44
Kosovo, 18, 136
Kouchner, Bernard, 47, 126, 145
Kyoto Protocol, 91, 96–97, 101–2, 109–10, 190n1
  See also global warming

Laïdi, Zaki, 48, 161
landmines, 55, 57, 87, 91, 109, 112, 141, 144, 145, 146, 148, 149, 156
  Mine Ban Treaty (Ottawa Convention), 58, 93–94, 107–8
Liberia, 100
Libya, 152

Linklater, Andrew, 9, 89, 90, 94, 126
love, 12, 21, 28, 29, 31, 40, 67, 93, 148, 159–60
"brotherly love," 50
Lovejoy, Thomas, 72–73

Malthusianism, 46, 47, 55, 75, 176n13
managerialism, 59–60, 161, 163
Marcuse, Herbert, 50
Marx, Karl, 46
Marxism, 8, 37, 41, 46, 47, 53, 101, 165
Mead, Margaret, 129
media, 21, 123, 129, 133, 145, 150, 165
  campaigns, 14, 146
  clichés, 3
memory activism, 23, 103
Mexico, 94
Miller, David, 103
missionaries, 53, 124
"mendicant orders," 7, 22
modernization, 5, 33, 36, 37, 47, 51, 81–83, 111, 120
  modernization theory, 37, 46, 55, 62
Mooney, Pat, 79
Moore, Barrington, 155–56
moral geographies, 86–88
moral progress, 32, 111, 153, 154
mutant NGOs, 25–26, 34, 43, 58, 122

nanotechnologies, 148
national interests, 47, 49, 61, 62, 86, 105, 110
nationalism, 49, 121, 123
  in NGOs, 51, 82–84, 110, 111–12
needs, 4, 10, 28, 29, 30, 49, 67, 75, 78, 89, 93, 97, 101, 102, 110, 130, 185n122
Neier, Aryeh, 91
Netherlands, 109, 131

neutrality, 26, 106, 129–30, 135, 186n4, 186n5, 188n41
nongovernmentality, 54
nonterritoriality, 19–20
North Korea, 136, 151, 152, 156
Norway, 35, 94, 107, 150

oceans, 59, 72, 73, 74, 96, 141
orientalism in reverse, 84
other-regarding ethics
  and abolitionism, 66–67
  and foreign policy, 49–50, 107
  hallmark of NGOs, 18–21, 75, 79, 96, 116, 163, 170n18
  moral superiority of, 21, 171n26
  neglected in recognition theory, 31–32
  and the nouveaux riches, 152
  paradox of, 163–64
  and secular theodicies, 26, 47
Oxfam, 7, 54

Pace, William, 91
Pakistan, 108
paradoxes, 7, 12, 14, 18, 63, 74, 75, 84, 107, 133, 137, 142, 159–66
  See also dirty hands, problem of
parasites, organizational, 2, 37–40, 41, 56, 58, 63, 144, 159
passion, 20–22, 58, 59–61, 79, 88, 145–46
  See also emotions/feelings
perpetrators/evildoers, 68–70, 74, 83, 86–88, 148, 149, 150, 158
  victors as, 52, 62, 116
  See also complicity; victims
Philippines, 81, 94
Pierce, Bob, 59
Poland, 126
political romanticism, 50–51, 62
politicization/depoliticization, 114, 134, 135–36, 152, 186n4, 186n5
Polluter Pays Principle, 103
Portugal, 69
professionalization, 53, 59–61, 62

psychic numbing, 89
public, the
  influenced by NGOs, 17, 18, 36, 48, 58, 60, 68, 74, 81, 87–88, 94, 98, 116, 128–29, 140, 142–48, 151, 152, 158
  morally expropriated, 14, 165–66
  served by NGOs, 25, 75–76
  supportive of NGOs, 21, 40, 51–52, 62, 142, 165
  See also indifference; spectators

rainforests, 72, 73, 74, 154
recognition
  as opposed to denial, 29, 173n55
  diplomatic, 10, 26
  law-based and law-transcending forms of, 28, 93, 96–97, 159
  politics as a barrier to, 50, 52
  principles of, 29–31, 36, 67, 86, 160
  theory of, 28–32, 40, 66
  tripartite scheme of, 28–29, 40, 89, 111, 153, 159–60
responsibility
  avoidance of, 155
  causal, 103, 109, 154–5
  differentiated, 109
  indirect, 101, 116
  moral, 69, 103, 109, 110, 146, 147, 154–5
  remedial, 103–5, 146, 184n110
  See also complicity; ethic of responsibility
Revel, Jean-Francois, 127
"right to be cold," 97
"right to intervene," 127
Rohrschneider, Robert, 33
Ron, James, 34
Rufin, Jean-Christoph, 127
Russia, 23, 103, 108, 151
  See also Soviet Union
Rwanda, 57, 92, 104, 105, 190n79

Sahai, Suman, 84, 120
sanctions, 18, 34, 91, 99–101, 102, 112, 147, 164

secular theodicies, 44, 46, 47–48, 61, 62, 129, 142, 176n12
sects, 22, 44, 160, 180n25
security rights, 134–35
Serbia, 100
Serres, Michel, 38–39
shaming/shameability, 13, 58, 68, 87, 158
  limits of, 150–51
Shaw, Martin, 33
Shiva, Vandana, 82–83, 108, 120–21, 187n21
  See also orientalism in reverse
Shklar, Judith, 24, 50, 89, 161
Sierra Club, 59, 60
Sierra Leone, 92, 147
Skocpol, Theda, 162–63
slavery, 28, 48, 65–69, 81, 103, 110, 115, 116, 117, 148, 151, 179n1
  sexual, 92, 105, 118
small arms, 149, 158
social movements
  as distinct from NGOs, 17, 20–23, 26–27, 52, 119–21
  hijacked by NGOs, 84, 121, 187n21
  "quality of life," 72, 155
  as sources of inspiration, 48, 50, 65, 110, 115
  taming of, 101, 119–21
Somalia, 104, 134, 152
South Africa, 2, 16, 94, 98, 127, 162
South Korea, 156
Soviet Union, 23, 46, 113, 132, 145, 164, 165
  See also Russia
Spain, 69
spectators, 6, 45, 48, 51–52, 166
  blameworthy, 66, 110
  See also indifference; public
stag hunt, parable of (Rousseau), 130, 132, 136
state sovereignty
  backed by NGOs, 1, 104–5, 107, 110, 134, 154

challenged by NGOs, 91, 105, 127, 164
persistence of, 1, 3, 8, 36–37, 107–8, 137, 151–52, 159
taming of, 12, 101–12
success
  conditions of, 142–48
  desirability of, 13–14, 153–57
  limits of, 13, 148–53, 158
  meanings of, 139–42
  "success stories," 140
Sudan, 2, 57
Suganami, Hidemi, 9, 89, 94
Swaminathan, M. S., 81
Switzerland, 94, 109, 126–28, 152
symbolic labor, 72–74, 79, 82, 86

Taylor, Charles, 44, 46, 48, 62, 159, 179n3
Tarrow, Sydney, 26
terror, 18, 24, 87, 150, 161, 164
Thompson, Dennis, 165
tradition as pretext, 116
Transparency International, 71–72, 104
trade-related aspects of intellectual property rights (TRIPS), 80, 91, 97–99, 101, 102, 120
Truman, Harry, 114
Tully, James, 31, 40
Turkey, 145

Uganda, 106, 126
United Nations
  bypassed by NGOs, 89
  as classifying NGOs, 15–17, 27, 113, 153, 173n48
  as hosts for NGOs, 35, 38, 55–59, 113–14, 140
  as a "small world," 89
  See also hybrid bureaucracies
United States
  as "empire," 7
  cultural changes in, 23, 50, 153–54
  home of "Wilsonian" NGOs, 129–32

supportive of NGOs, 47, 55, 104, 178n40
targeted by NGOs, 34, 43, 77–79, 85, 86, 94, 100, 101, 141, 145, 150, 182n73, 186n10
Uruguay, 95

Venezuela, 92
victims
  dualism of perpetrators and, 12, 52, 62, 69, 96, 111, 116, 128, 148, 158, 160
  growing list of, 13, 117–18, 137
  hierarchy of, 19
  passive vs. active, 128–29
  recognition of, 24, 89, 159
  representation of, 21, 23–25, 60, 68, 87–88, 141, 148, 164
  and rescuers, 19, 24, 98, 125–26, 127, 152, 162
  Western obsession with, 162
  See also perpetrators/evildoers
Vietnam, 131, 132
Vonnegut, Kurt, 75

Walzer, Michael, 18
war crimes, 2, 91–93, 96, 118, 143
Watt-Cloutier, Sheila, 97
Weber, Max, 3, 4, 14, 20, 22, 155, 157, 158, 170n19, 180n25
Weld, Theodore Dwight, 67
Wilberforce, William, 115
wilderness, 72, 76
women's rights, 31, 105, 118, 142, 160–61
World Vision, 54, 55, 59–60, 132–33
World Trade Organization (WTO), 27, 56, 80, 85, 90, 98, 99, 104, 108, 122
World Wildlife Fund (WWF), 34, 72, 74–77, 79, 87, 97, 104, 146, 181n42

Yippies, 50

zealots, 21, 60, 108